THE JOHNS HOPKINS UNIVERSITY STUDIES IN HISTORICAL AND POLITICAL SCIENCE

SERIES LXXXV
(1967)

NUMBER 2

EIGHTY–FIFTH SERIES (1967)

1. Modern Yemen: 1918–1966
   BY MANFRED W. WENNER

2. Beloved Lady: A History of Jane Addams'
   Ideas on Reform and Peace
   BY JOHN C. FARRELL

BELOVED LADY:

A HISTORY OF JANE ADDAMS' IDEAS ON REFORM AND PEACE

Beloved Lady:
A History of Jane Addams'
Ideas on Reform and Peace

By

JOHN C. FARRELL

THE JOHNS HOPKINS PRESS

BALTIMORE, MARYLAND

FOREWORD

The typescript of *Beloved Lady*, almost ready for John Farrell to present as his doctoral dissertation at The Johns Hopkins University, was delivered to him on March 9, 1965. Although he was keeping his appointments that day, at the State University of North Carolina at Raleigh, where he taught American history, he said that he was not feeling well. He died the next morning, victim of a virus attack.

John Christopher Farrell lived not quite thirty-two years. After undergraduate study at Yale and graduate work at the University of Minnesota in American studies and at Johns Hopkins in history, he was as near to the doctorate of philosophy as the completed dissertation suggests. Johns Hopkins awarded a posthumous degree the following June. Meanwhile, thanks to the concern of a sizable group of graduate-school friends, any fears that practical difficulties would obstruct the publication of his book were quickly overcome. Two members of the group, young professors, undertook to do most of the work. This came to mean giving the manuscript an expert review, brushing up the text, and preparing the index. Except for some minor cuts and changes in phrasing, the manuscript was not altered. This is John Farrell's work. All concerned have wanted it published, as nearly as possible, the way it would have appeared had Farrell lived. The co-operating friends prefer to remain anonymous, lest any public credit given to them be misread to indicate that they have intruded on authorship.

Some parts of the book which follows will surely endure longer and stand on firmer ground than specialized histories usually do. The bibliography of Miss Addams' writings is wonderfully complete; it will be useful to other scholars and will be hard to improve on significantly. The whole work is made the more solid by that foundation, and by the strong support the author constructed between those materials and the superstructure of his own narrative and interpretation. Even so, there cannot help being a difference between the present text and the text the author would have sent to press, had he been allotted time to reconsider and rewrite in the usual way. Historical thought during the 1960s is

7

revising the interpretation of United States history by periods and themes, from first to last. It is transforming our views of the Progressive period—Miss Addams' own. It is concentrating on the history of philanthropy, education, urban life, cultural relations among nations, and of peace-making—the very areas on which Miss Addams concentrated her own effort. Naturally John Farrell enjoyed working in a field which was drawing the attention of numerous members of the history profession—his profession. He was stimulated, as were many of his seniors, by the coming of 1960, the centennial year of Jane Addams' birth. Yet I think that it was the similarity of her ideas to present-day liberal thought about race relations, and her convictions about world government and international peace, always on the side of humanity, which meant more to him than any other stimulation. The two overarching moral problems of his country, racial justice and keeping peace in the world, had uncommonly vivid life in the mind of the author of this book. He was personally involved, yet also judicious about them.

While he was doing his research and writing, moreover, he received ample suggestion that many scholars agreed with him, that Miss Addams still has relevance to social thought and social action. Books and articles appeared in number, some of them by eminent historians, others by young scholars. The following list represents the accumulation, as of early 1965: Merle E. Curti, an article on Miss Addams' ideas about human nature, which helps place her in intellectual history; Henry S. Commager, the foreword for a new edition of her classic of 1910, *Twenty Years at Hull House*; Ann Firor Scott, an edition, with scholarly introduction, of Miss Addams' prime discussion of public morality, *Democracy and Social Ethics*, which had come out first in 1902; Jill Conway, an article on Miss Addams as the first American woman of her time, a very special time in the history of her sex; Staughton Lynd, one on her role in American radicalism.[1] None of these writings, nor all of them together, accomplished what

1. Curti, "Jane Addams on Human Nature," *Journal of the History of Ideas*, 22: 240–53 (April–June, 1961); Commager, in Addams, *Twenty Years at Hull House* (1961 ed.), vii–xvi; Mrs. Scott, in Addams, *Democracy and Social Ethics* (1964 ed.), vii–lxxv; Miss Conway, "Jane Addams: An American Heroine," *Daedalus*, 93: 761–80 (Spring, 1964); Lynd, "Jane Addams and the Radical Impulse," *Commentary*, 32: 54–59 (July, 1961).

Farrell intended to accomplish, but they increased the pressures on him as a writer, simply by surrounding his work.

Since Farrell's death, *Beloved Lady* has become even more tightly surrounded by new scholarship. Two works which appeared in 1965, studies of phases of twentieth-century social thought, placed Miss Addams nearer center-stage and gave her a more important speaking role in the drama of American protest than general histories had ever before assigned her. Daniel Levine, in *Varieties of Reform Thought*, examined her reformist principles vis à vis those of Samuel Gompers, Senator Beveridge, Senator LaFollette, and other representatives of Progressivism. Christopher Lasch's *The New Radicalism in America, 1889–1963; The Intellectual as a Social Type* portrayed Miss Addams as practically the archetype of a mode of social protest which was new and pressing in the United States shortly before World War I. The Lasch and Levine books considered together, without regard for the differences between them, enhance the impression, which cumulates from earlier revisionist scholarship, that Miss Addams' writings were fully as important a part of her achievement as were her better recognized deeds of administering a famous settlement house and of organizing and leading international peace organizations. This impression is again enlarged by the lively anthology which Professor Lasch has assembled and edited, for the college reader mainly, *The Social Thought of Jane Addams* (1965).

More is at stake here, to the point of seeing what the present book signifies, than simply recognizing that John Farrell was moving into a field of history rich in human effort and aspiration but only recently submitted to detailed survey and estimation. Proceed from the books and articles which revise the history of Jane Addams, or from any other starting point, through the long list of recent books about the Progressive epoch, and the total picture of American life in the four decades during which Miss Addams was a public figure seems to have been more than just filled in. It seems to have been transformed. Only a short time ago the history of the Progressive period appeared, as history goes, to be almost unilinear: Progressivism was a stream which, after gathering from many tributaries, reached Washington about 1900, flooded and receded by stages, and went underground about 1920.

But today Progressivism seems thoroughly multilinear. Instead of a stream, Progressivism now looks like a delta that broadened out widely, both right and left, and carried on, in certain channels, well beyond the year 1920. Before John Farrell began his study, and while he was writing, scholars were being especially prolific in demonstrating that the right side of the delta—the channels which sustained conservation, government efficiency, business reforms, and the like—was important. They also were strong in saying that all the main channels were stable, and that none of the channels was so turbulent as to erode the contours of society. Concerning this conservative emphasis, Farrell blended a brief comment, from his respects and his disrespects, in his opening chapter. His own taste carried him to the left side of the delta.

Had John Farrell lived to revise his book, like a city dweller who after a summer looks out his window to find the view altered by new buildings and clearings, he would have needed to adjust himself freshly to his surroundings. He could hardly have avoided being gratified by the focal position *The New Radicalism in America* assigns Miss Addams; I cannot guess how fully he would have been persuaded by the sociological-mindedness of Professor Lasch and the comparative-mindedness of Professor Levine. What follows is an interior, intellectual biography of a person of splendid mind and uncommon integrity: William James believed it given to Jane Addams to " inhabit reality." Perhaps if Farrell had lived he would have composed new chapters which, extending his conception of the house of Jane Addams's mind, would have widened our vistas into the history of the moral intellect of the Progressive and later years.

On the other hand, a close correlation between the present book and much of the scholarship of the Progressive age might have proved impossible, even undesirable. Jane Addams believed, counter to public convictions which came to prevail among her countrymen before 1917, that the logic and values which underlay her work in philanthropy held equally in favor of world peace and world government, and against participation in World War I. John Farrell believed her to have been right, and he describes her course as having been consistent and honorable—even heroic— as she maintained her ideas against war. Not many historians agree, or at any rate their conviction is not deep enough to let that same judgment affect their own treatment of United States history.

Whatever his own conclusions might have been, John Farrell's work opens such considerations, with poignancy. " The one thing I remember most clearly about John," remarked a man who knew him well and whose opinion I share, " was his great fund of sympathy and understanding. He loved and understood people. He was good at demonstrating for Negro rights, which he did frequently, or comforting a distraught roommate." On that account, as well as for reasons of scholarship, this book finds its way into the world.

CHARLES A. BARKER

The Johns Hopkins University
16 January 1967

CONTENTS

BELOVED LADY:

A HISTORY OF JANE ADDAMS' IDEAS ON REFORM AND PEACE

CHAPTER I

INTRODUCTION

After a short introduction, Jane Addams rose and spoke with her usual vigor. Although the year was 1917, she expressed her conviction that war and its destruction of human life were always wrong. Many of those at this Sunday-evening meeting at the Evanston Congregational Church had known Miss Addams during the twenty-eight years since Hull House had been founded; many had been long-time financial supporters of Hull House. These old friends and admirers knew the insight and determination that Jane Addams brought to a discussion of public affairs.

Miss Addams' rejection of war was cogent and thorough. Ever since America's involvement in Cuba and the Philippines, she had been an outspoken opponent of war and preparations for war. Instead of solving problems, she believed, armed conflict created new problems and made the solution of the old ones more difficult. War was the very antithesis of that justice and righteousness which formed the only sure foundation for international order. Americans should not expect this war to contradict all our previous experience, she said sharply, just because America had entered it, or even because Americans were convinced of the purity of their motives for entering it. Pacifists in wartime, she was willing to agree, had to abandon the perfectly legitimate propaganda which they conducted before war was declared. But wartimes demanded the continuing discussion of the conduct of the war, of war aims, of the failures of statesmanship, and of the moral failures of the country. Pacifists had a right to " insist on a more humane prose-cution of the war at least so far as civilian populations are con-cerned, a more merciful administration of the lands occupied, and distribution of foodstuffs to all conquered peoples." [1] American

1. For the complete text of Miss Addams' speech see " Patriotism and Pacifists in Wartime," *City Club [of Chicago] Bulletin*, X (June 16, 1917), 184–90.

17

involvement in the war, in short, did not relieve the nation or its citizens from moral accountability.

Jane Addams believed that each human life was sacred. This was the lesson of twenty-eight years of pacific humanitarian service among her neighbors of twenty different nationalities. Exactly because of her experiences at Hull House, Jane Addams believed that human compassion and pity and the opportunity for neighborly kindness could break down differences of nationality, religious tradition, or race. In immigrant neighborhoods, Jane Addams reminded her suburban audience, America possessed the beginnings of both a method and the desire to rid the world of war. That America had failed to use its best resources called not for praise, nor for silence, but continuing public review and criticism.

Among the friendly admirers of Jane Addams that evening was Orrin Carter, Judge of the Illinois Supreme Court. Judge Carter had worked closely with Miss Addams to establish the first juvenile court in the United States, and later to provide psychiatric examination as part of the juvenile court. He could be counted on at Hull House for sympathy, money, and enthusiasm.

"I have always been a friend of Miss Addams," Judge Carter said when questions were called for, "but . . . ."

"The 'but,'" Jane Addams broke in lightly, "sounds as if you were going to break with me."

"I am going to break with you. Anything which tends to cast doubt on the justice of our cause in the present war is very unfortunate. No pacifist measures should be taken until the war is over," Judge Carter said almost angrily.

"Perhaps my subject was an unfortunate one to be discussed at this time," replied Miss Addams slowly, "but surely that should be referred to the committee which invited me to speak."[2]

The meeting ended quickly in an embarrassing silence.

Newspaper publicity about this Evanston meeting started a long series of public attacks on Miss Addams in the press, in pulpits, and in scurrilous personal letters to her. As a result of

2. For the dialogue see James Weber Linn, *Jane Addams, a Biography* (New York & London, 1937), pp. 331–32; see also Chicago *Examiner*, Chicago *Herald*, and Chicago *Tribune* articles of June 11, 1917.

these attacks Miss Addams felt completely alone and isolated, a feeling that shook her deep confidence in the ways of democracy. She wrote later how the force of the majority against her seemed overwhelming. Even if one were right a thousand times over in conviction, she asked herself, was there the right in a modern democracy to oppose an overwhelming popular consensus and instinctive mass enthusiasm? During this period of doubt Jane Addams found her every public utterance misconstrued, sometimes willfully misunderstood by the same reformers who had helped her to "moralize public opinion" for reform goals before the war. In this crisis she came to reaffirm categorically that man's primary allegiance must be to his own individual vision of the truth. This assertion represented a break from much of the style and method of progressive reform. The feeling of isolation during and after the war sapped a vitality that had depended greatly on the reassurance and fellowship of public confidence, approval, and support.[3]

Jane Addams was one of a handful of urban progressives who opposed American participation in the war. She believed that all her work for reform before the war was a natural and logical preface to her pacifism. Although public opposition, deep personal doubts, and illness filled the war years, Miss Addams could never persuade herself to embrace military goals or methods. She believed that American entry into the war would put an end to the attempts to establish more just and democratic social relations. These were the goals to which she was most deeply committed. Thus she withstood the temptation to join many of her colleagues and friends in supporting the war, even a war to end war.

The story of Jane Addams' lonely experience during and after the conflict illuminates how the war tested progressive ideals and accomplishments. The story of her response to war can help answer the difficult question of what happened to the Progressives in the 1920's.[4] The crisis of pacifism during World War I drove Miss Addams to seek new ideas and instrumentalities for promoting peace. She insisted that the humanitarian and democratic goals for which she and other Progressives had labored were the

---

3. Jane Addams, *Peace and Bread in Time of War* (New York, 1922), especially Chap. VII.
4. See Arthur S. Link, "What Happened to the Progressive Movement in the 1920's?," *American Historical Review*, LXIV (1959), 833–51.

only sure bases of peace. In the war years and the years of post-war reaction she demanded reform, not in the name of social justice for Americans but in the name of that justice essential to international peace.

This book is an *intellectual* biography of Jane Addams. The personal details that constitute a large portion of the usual biography are included in the present work only when they elucidate Miss Addams' beliefs and commitments. The more personal story has been told in an appreciative—if sometimes uncritical—biography by Jane Addams' nephew. In writing his authorized biography while his aunt was still alive, Weber Linn had access to more family lore and anecdotal material than is now available to the scholar.[5] An intellectual biography written from the viewpoint of the current generation and dealing with the contribution of Jane Addams to the social and political ferment of her time is greatly needed. Historians have been re-examining the Progressive movement intensively in recent years, and many rich insights have emerged from their research. Jane Addams has not been neglected by these scholars, but as yet there has been no full-scale effort to analyze the role of this woman who was a central figure in so many facets of Progressivism. This study, which is based on a thorough examination of all available published and unpublished writings of Jane Addams, is an attempt to fill the need for an understanding of her ideas and convictions.

The *New Republic* obituary of Miss Addams noted that " justice has scarcely been done to her keen, precise, critical mind, or to the effective quality of her public speech and writing, which persuaded not only because of simplicity, honesty and utter disinterestedness, but because she knew the facts." Weber Linn concurred in this opinion and closed his biography by predicting that if his aunt were " long remembered, it will be for the quality of her thinking." Yet historians have been slow in taking up the task of assessing her thought. In 1961 Professor Merle Curti reflected that " if justice has been done her heart and her social vision, it has not been done her mind. Her ideas illuminate in

5. Linn, a professor of English at the University of Chicago, was close to his aunt and to Hull House activities. He was made Miss Addams' literary executor in order to write the biography. " My aunt read over and annotated the first draft of the first eight chapters . . . talked over the next three, and agreed upon the proportion of the remainder." Linn, *Jane Addams*, pp. vii–viii.

sensitive and often keen ways major movements of thought in her time." [6]

In writing about William Morris, G. D. H. Cole declared that at no anniversary was it more difficult to write about a man's life than at the centenary of his birth. "He is at once too near and too remote. There are many still alive who remember him, . . . and can tell how they met him and talked with him, and how he behaved . . . . But all too often our elders are to us in such circumstances but as ghosts talking to ghosts. What should make the dead come alive often serves only to remind us how very dead even the living can be." Professor Cole's experience with Morris was different from what mine has been with this study of Jane Addams. The men and women who have allowed me to talk with them have a vitality and interest in contemporary events which is remarkable. And much of Miss Addams' writing, unlike William Morris', needs only to be attentively read to come alive. As Professor Curti notes, "at its best, the writing in which her ideas are expressed rises to a level of literary distinction." [7]

This is perhaps an unfortunate time to be writing about a leading Progressive reformer. Reformers have had rough treatment of late. Arthur Schlesinger, Sr., has generalized that

The [American] reformer is apt to be self-righteous, untidy in dress, truculent, humorless, with a single-track mind and an almost ostentatious liking for the hair shirt and martyrdom; he makes virtue repulsive. Besides, he is frequently so indiscriminate in his choice of causes, taking on all comers, that the underdog appears to have him on a leash. In addition, he is often a failure at his own business, and though a strident lover of mankind, may neglect his family and shirk his neighborhood obligations. . . . Unfortunately, history never succeeds in making clear to posterity that the shock

6. "Jane Addams," *New Republic*, LXXXIII (June 5, 1935), 91; Linn, *Jane Addams*, p. 439; Merle Curti, "Jane Addams on Human Nature," *Journal of the History of Ideas*, XXII (April–June, 1961), 241.

7. G. D. H. Cole, *Persons and Periods, Studies* (London, 1938), p. 284; Curti, "Jane Addams on Human Nature," p. 241. I have benefited from interviews and correspondence with the following people: Jessie F. Binford, Alice Hamilton, Lea D. Taylor, Mr. and Mrs. Bernard Schaar, Mrs. Elizabeth Linn Allen, Albert J. Kennedy, Jordan Cavan, Mary Gleason, Mrs. William McC. Blair, Henry P. Chandler, Mrs. Kenneth P. Rich, and Charles P. Schwartz.

troops of reform are almost necessarily captained by the headlong and the ungenteel—men of explosive temperament and rude manners.

The example of Jane Addams, with a sensitive mind, a ready appreciation of public approbation, hardly a shirker of neighborhood duties, and neither headlong nor ungenteel, casts doubt on Schlesinger's generalizations.[8]

Added to the burden of being a reformer, Jane Addams was a Progressive, another much patronized group at this moment. American historians of Progressivism have emphasized some highly unattractive elements. They have pointed out the existence of a blatant individualism and " almost compulsive desire for power " in Progressivism and stressed the movement's nativism, racism, and preoccupation with domestic matters.[9] But Jane Addams' earliest purpose at Hull House was " to add the social function to democracy "; she was little interested in power. She was publicly concerned about the Negroes' plight as early as 1892 and was one of the founders of the National Association for the Advancement of Colored People. She opposed the agitation for restriction of immigration. After 1914 her major interest was in the field of international co-operation and understanding. Perhaps one may demur at some of the current generalizations about Progressive reformers when they fail accurately to describe as famous a Progressive reformer as Jane Addams.

It is fashionable to dismiss Progressivism and prewar reform as nostalgic, complacent, moralistic, and rhetorical rather than concrete and realistic. " The Progressive Era may be defined,"

8. Arthur M. Schlesinger, *The American as Reformer* (Cambridge, Mass., 1950), p. 67. Miss Addams' dress was not always impeccable. Francis Hackett wrote " there have been times at Hull House when the disgracefulness of Miss Addams' hat has led to protest. . . ."; see his " Hull House—a Souvenir," *Survey*, LIV (June 1, 1925), 279. Louise DeKoven Bowen, *Open Windows, Stories of People and Places* (Chicago, 1946), p. 222: Jane Addams " really liked to be well dressed, but never wanted to be bothered with clothes, and if she were in a hurry, she did the easiest thing."

9. George E. Mowry, *Era of Theodore Roosevelt, 1900–1912* (" New American Nation Series "; New York, 1958), p. 88; C. Vann Woodward, *Origins of the New South, 1877–1913*, Vol. IX of *A History of the South*, eds. Wendell Holmes Stephenson and E. Merton Coulter (10 vols.; Balton Rouge, 1947—), p. 373; Henry F. May, *The End of American Innocence, a Study of the First Years of Our Times, 1912–1917* (New York, 1959), pp. 26–7.

writes Henry F. May, " as the time when people wanted to make a number of sharp changes because they were so confident in the basic rightness of things as they were." It is true that most of the Progressives fit an Englishwoman's description of Jane Addams: "Jane was not revolutionary." [10] Some Progressive thought and action was clearly characterized by a backward-looking attempt to restore the past. But this should not be confused with the use of the past to illuminate demands of justice and righteousness. Following the lead of Professor Richard Hofstadter, unsympathetic historians have exaggerated the substitution of rhetoric for action and the Progressives' failure to act realistically.[11] The accomplishments of the Progressives in legislation and in the social consensus that underlay this legislation need not be rehearsed. There were among the Progressives consummate politicians—those who engineered legislation and those who, like Jane Addams, worked to create the sharpened compassion that moved Americans to look at social and political relations in a new way. She had a passionate concern to end injustice and thereby bring a better order to international relations. If realism means dealing with actual social and political relationships effectively, Jane Addams and many Progressives must be counted as realists. " No other reform wave in American history matches it [Progressivism] in longevity," Charles Forcey writes, "and few exceed it in accomplishment." [12]

Some historians of American immigration have criticized the settlements' failure to help the immigrant adjust himself to American life. Oscar Handlin's analysis stresses the social worker's disregard of immigrant sentiment as well as their social and personal superiority worn as a badge of superior, but superficial, standards. The idea of " immigrant gifts " which many settlements adopted is labeled insignificant and a survival of a genteel tradition by John Higham. Mrs. Barbara Solomon has described the anxieties that led Robert A. Woods of Andover House, Boston, a leader in the settlement movement, into general disillusionment

10. May, *The End of American Innocence*, p. 29; Helena M. Swanwick, *I Have Been Young* (London, 1935), p. 452.

11. Richard Hofstadter, *The Age of Reform, from Bryan to F. D. R.* (New York, 1955), pp. 210–2.

12. Charles Forcey, *Crossroads of Liberalism, Croly, Weyl, Lippmann, and the Progressive Era 1900–1925* (New York, 1961), p. xviii.

with the possibility of making Americans out of immigrants and into active leadership in the Immigration Restriction League.[13]

The activities and services of Hull House contravene parts of Handlin's description of the relationship between immigrant and settlement. Finding ways of giving stability to the immigrant family was the earliest and one of the most lasting Hull House goals. The nursery and kindergarten, and the clubs for boys and girls, freed mothers who had to work outside the home. Much of the formal entertainment was an attempt to reconcile immigrant children to their parents by showing American appreciation of old-world culture and customs. The intention was to show immigrant parents to their children in a role other than that of money-maker and money-spender.

The settlement admiration for folk art, handicrafts, and folk dancing seems genteel today. The mass electronic media have sapped the tradition of folk art. Some of the Hull House arts and crafts activities, however, may have given the immigrant a sense of tradition, of recognition of his various skills, a feeling of social stability. Higham's description of the settlement as genteel is not altogether fair. We now use the word genteel only to mock or patronize. Standards of gentility and respectability have changed considerably since the 1890's. A person without " at least one strand of respectability " was " very poor, indeed," Jane Addams said in 1897. The personal relationships between the settlement workers were certainly formal; the correspondence of these women was most formal and polite. Lillian Wald always greeted Jane Addams as " Beloved Lady " in her letters. But these genteel ladies dealt with sewage and prostitution, delinquency and corruption of many kinds. They " educated a whole generation " to feel responsibility for these unladylike circumstances.[14]

13. Oscar Handlin, *The Uprooted, the Epic Story of the Great Migrations that Made the American People* (New York, 1951), p. 283; John Higham, *Strangers in the Land, Patterns of American Nativism, 1860–1925* (New Brunswick, 1955), p. 254; Barbara Miller Solomon, *Ancestors and Immigrants, a Changing New England Tradition* (Cambridge, Mass., 1956), pp. 142–3.

14. Jane Addams, " Social Settlements," in National Conference of Charities and Correction, *Proceedings* (1897), p. 340. Richard Hofstader characterizes the Progressive as essentially " genteel, proper, and safe " in his *Age of Reform*, p. 184, and see also p. 216. Weber Linn despairingly asked Ellen Gates Starr how he could " get at and properly set forth, without exaggeration her [Jane Addams']

Jane Addams emphasized the ideas of culture and civilization. Culture was something to be prized not shunned; it was " knowledge of those things which have been long cherished by men, the things which men have loved because through generations they have softened and interpreted life, and have endowed it with value and meaning." Culture was not the consumption which took place during leisure-time activities, but was " an understanding of the long-established occupations and thoughts of men, of the arts with which they have solaced their toil." [15]

These conceptions of culture and civilization were most important for Jane Addams. At the heart of her commitment to social reform and pacifism one finds the idea of culture. She used the words culture and civilization to refer to the highest ideals men had discovered and the best things men had invented. For twenty-five years at Hull House she advocated measures to ensure a civilized standard of life for every one of her neighbors. She opposed the war because she was convinced that war destroyed civilization itself. After 1918, Miss Addams worked for peace which, she insisted, was impossible without the realization of civilized standards on an international scale.

Joined to this idea of culture was Jane Addams' belief in democracy. " Although [Hull House's] influence cannot be measured," wrote Charles and Mary Beard, " the guess may be hazarded that no other single institution . . . did as much to counteract the dogma of individualism and restore the social principle to thought about civilization." [16] Hull House stood first of all for social democracy. Jane Addams' experiences at Hull House persuaded her of the necessity for progressive social legislation in the name of democracy. And her belief in democracy and progressive reform sus-

---

impersonality. It makes her so mad when I speak of it to her—she denies it almost with oaths! " Linn to Miss Starr, May 4, 1935, Starr Papers, Sophia Smith Collection, Smith College Library; hereafter cited as Starr Papers. Letters between Lillian Wald and Jane Addams are in the Wald Papers, Manuscript Division, New York Public Library. Arthur M. Schlesinger, Jr., *The Age of Roosevelt*, Vol. I: *The Crisis of the Old Order, 1919–1933* (Boston, 1957), p. 25.

15. Jane Addams, " The Public School and the Immigrant Child," in National Education Association, *Journal of the Proceedings and Addresses* (1908), pp. 99–100; Addams, *Twenty Years at Hull-House with Autobiographical Notes* (New York, 1910), p. 242.

16. Charles A. and Mary R. Beard, *The American Spirit, a Study of the Idea of Civilization in the United States* (New York, 1942), p. 478.

tained her opposition to the war; for, she said, war methods were always undemocratic and resort to war enfeebled democracy.

Jane Addams justified her Progressive activities and her pacifism by her ideals of culture and democracy. In the most serious crisis of her life, when her integrity and beliefs were sorely tested by war, these two ideals sustained her. The twin themes of culture and democracy form the center and nexus of Jane Addams' thought.

Chapter II

ROCKFORD FEMALE SEMINARY—AND AFTER

*Jane Addams who is . . . albeit matured, still so much a fresh
young intellectual of the 'eighties.*
                                    HERBERT M. DAVIDSON, 1928

By 1860, the year of Jane Addams' birth, the northernmost tier
of counties in Illinois had passed through the pioneer stage and
had reached the beginning of economic maturity. The original
settlers—called " old settlers " by 1860—were no longer primarily
concerned with planting and harvesting crops but were increasingly absorbed in commerce and manufacturing and in the building
of railroads, colleges, and libraries. " The crudity and harshness
of the pioneers had been subdued to a graciousness and idealism
that found a shining example in the later Lincoln. This finer
heritage of the pioneer came to Jane Addams, a spirit of mutual
aid, of cooperation, of sharing experience, and of experiment for
the common good." [1]

Although he was a man with no more than a common-school
education, John Huy Addams transmitted this fine pioneer heritage
to his daughter Laura Jane. John Addams was a successful miller,
a large landholder, and a leader in the public affairs of the region.
He used part of his wealth to equip the community with cultural
facilities. He labored long to make sure that the Chicago and
Galena Railroad was not constructed south of the nearby commercial center of Freeport. In 1854 when the Republican party
was organized, he ran as a Republican for the state senate, was
elected, and served continuously from 1854 to 1870. During the
Civil War he helped found, and became president of, a bank in
Freeport. John Addams was not simply a man on the make. His
political career and his bank career were based on the community's
faith in his probity and rectitude. Widowed when Jane was two,

---

1. " Jane Addams," *New Republic*, LXXXIII (June 5, 1935), 91.

John Addams' deep and frequently stern affection inspired in his children his own devotion to truth and individual conscience.[2]

John Addams' remarriage in 1867 when young Jennie was seven brought a spirited disciplinarian into the Addams household for the first time. Anna Haldeman brought high style and cultural accomplishment—along with two boys, the younger just Jennie's age—to the house at Cedar Creek Mills. Anna H. Addams knew the life of eastern cities. In her high-spirited way, she equipped John Addams' simple home with appurtenances suitable to what she felt was his social position. Mrs. Addams was widely read, and she was what was described in those years as "musically accomplished." She enjoyed fine clothes; she had traveled, and expected her children to enjoy the same advantages. Anna Addams also "could not always control her temper," but her temper alternated with a sweeping tenderness and deep understanding. Young Jennie, accustomed to the unfailing serenity and indulgent love of her father and older sister Mary, must have resented the new discipline.[3]

In 1847 John Addams helped start the first subscription library in the county. The books were located at the Addams household. While not a large library, nor one that contained the scientific exhibits and apparatus usually connected with libraries in more settled parts of the country, the Union Library Company at Cedar Creek Mills gave its members access to a wide range of information. American history and biography predominated. There were books on scattered scientific, religious and ethical, and economic subjects. The library also contained a surprising number of books of special interest to women. Included were Catherine E. Beecher, *Treatise on Domestic Economy*, Miss Margaret Coxe, *Claims of the Country on American Females*, Hannah More's *Works*, Mrs. Sarah Stickney Ellis, *Daughters of England* and *Wives of England*,

2. John Addams was a friend of Lincoln's in the Illinois legislature; there were letters from Lincoln which made personal what has been called the Lincoln ideal. See Ray Ginger, *Altgeld's America, the Lincoln Ideal Versus Changing Realities* (New York, 1958). Although John Addams' bank was agent for Jay Cooke's Northern Pacific bonds, "we think no one invested in those securities on his advice, so careful and conscientious was he in all business matters." Unidentified newspaper obituary, August 18 [1881], in "Miss Sill's Scrapbook," Rockford College Archives.

3. Marcet Haldeman-Julius, "Jane Addams as I Knew Her," *Reviewer's Library*, VII (1936), 4.

and a *Guide to Social Happiness*. Young Jane Addams had easy access to this library and to the large personal collection of her father. John Addams was devoted to books. By offering his children five cents for each of Plutarch's *Lives* they could report to him, he tried to pass on his cosmopolitan reading tastes. Mrs. Anna Addams recalled later how the family used to enjoy reading modern fiction together.[4]

These resources multiplied many times Jane's formal academic training which the village school in Cedarville provided. There was never any doubt that she would go on to college. John Addams was a trustee of Rockford Female Seminary, which had been chartered in 1847, a year after its brother institution, Beloit College, to serve northern Illinois and southern Wisconsin. The seminary and college were founded by Congregational and Presbyterian clergymen who decreed that " moral and religious influence " was to be of prime importance in the schools. In addition, " the standard of mental culture was to be . . . set and maintained at the highest practicable point." [5] Jane's older sisters had the benefit of the seminary's mental culture, and then finished their education by travel in Europe. Her aspirations for schooling in the East at the new Smith College were not strong enough to break this pattern. In the fall of 1877, Jane Addams entered the seminary with some feelings of condescension about its limitations and provinciality. Instead of New England, here she was at the " Mount Holyoke of the West."

As in the case of its eastern namesake, an intense religious spirit embodied in a strong-willed woman dominated the seminary. Anna Peck Sill—like Mary Lyon—always considered herself a missionary, and regarded her educational tasks as the equivalent of service among foreign heathen.[6] Miss Sill was a Connecticut

4. Printed catalogue for library, Stephenson County Historical Museum; for Plutarch see Addams, *Twenty Years at Hull-House*, p. 47; Mrs. Addams was interviewed in " The Girl of Cedar Cliff," Chicago *Record*, June 17, 1915.

5. Cited by Sally Lou Coburn, " Anna Peck Sill, 1852–1884," in [Rockford College, Rockford, Ill.,] *Profiles of the Principals of Rockford Seminary and Presidents of Rockford College, 1847–1947* (Rockford, 1947).

6. Anna Peck Sill and Mary Lyon are more directly connected through a shared friendship with Zilpah Grant Bannister, Miss Lyon's earliest teaching partner. Mrs. Bannister made large, and crucial, gifts to Rockford during the seminary's first decade, and organized large support by founding the Board of National Popular Education. See Arthur C. Cole, *A Hundred Years of Mount Holyoke College, the Evolution of an Educational Ideal* (New Haven, 1940), p. 123.

Yankee by way of western New York. At the age of fifteen she found her salvation and dedicated her life to the evangelization of the American West. Hearing that a charter had been granted for a school, Miss Sill journeyed to Rockford. She immediately advertised her willingness to teach college preparatory lessons. An entry in her diary for November, 1849, just after she had arrived in Rockford, says, " my desire for usefulness is an unsatiable thirst which increases as the field widens before me." [7]

Miss Sill patterned the routine at her seminary on the more famous Mount Holyoke. Students performed most of the domestic chores. Expenses were kept low by having each girl furnish all her own linen and her own table service; food was not lavish and was prepared and served by the students. Board and tuition charges at Rockford were $175 a year, for a clergyman's daughter $115; fuel, lights, lecture and library fees added $45 to these charges. The catalogue discouraged parents from sending jewelry or expensive clothing with their daughters. These sumptuary restrictions, however, were honored most in the breach. [8]

As at Mount Holyoke, the distinguishing feature at Rockford was the religious and moral emphasis. Young ladies at Rockford attended daily chapel, weekly prayer meeting, and Sunday morning worship. Bible recitation was the first recitation of each week. There were regular monthly fast days, an annual prayer week in January (which developed into a revival in 1881), informal evening devotions during the half hour which separated the two evening study periods, and frequent missionary and temperance society meetings. At graduation the baccalaureate sermon was followed, the next evening, by the annual missionary address.

Usefulness is the key word that explains the purpose of this religious activity. Miss Sill defined usefulness as " Christian Mothers and Missionaries for the evangelization of the world."

7. On Miss Sill see Coburn, " Anna Peck Sill, 1852–1884," in *Profiles of the Principals and Presidents of Rockford College*, pp. 5–8, and *Memorials of Anna Peck Sill, First Principal of Rockford Female Seminary, 1849–1889* (Rockford, Ill., 1889). For diary see *ibid.*, p. 16.

8. Rockford Seminary catalogue, 1878–9. As at Mount Holyoke, an hour's labor was expected from each girl at domestic tasks; those who did not wish to perform these chores were assessed an additional $30 a year. Jane Addams' expense book for 1879–80, in Rockford College Archives, lists expenditures above the basic $175 of about $100 for books, stationery, travel, elocution lessons, notions, taxidermy instruments and equipment, and missionary and church contributions.

Her zealous interpretation of this creed through her fundamentalist theology explained the constant pressure on unconverted girls. Christian usefulness, "this primitive spiritual purpose," Jane Addams said at Miss Sill's funeral, was her "life-motive." [9]

For Miss Sill, revealed religion was the basis of true moral culture and the Bible the only true test of practical morality. She worked endlessly to inspire a missionary spirit of self-denying benevolence toward all, but especially toward the ignorant and sinful. The great Christian lesson—the purpose of life—Miss Sill held, was to give oneself fully and worthily for the good of others. During Jane Addams' years at Rockford, the special emphasis was on foreign missionary service.[10] But at all times it meant that each girl should "do what she could." As the class of 1881 heard the doctrine, "To the cows that gave us milk, to the hens that laid us eggs, we turn in speechless gratitude. To each of you it may be said, ' she hath done what she could.' " [11]

Miss Sill's rigidity and bluntness sometimes limited her success. Some of the high-spirited girls at Rockford, while conforming outwardly to the religious regimen, felt confined and stultified in this atmosphere. In the chain letter that the class of 1881 circulated after graduation, one of Jane Addams' classmates wondered how much longer the old cow could last; another described Miss Sill as "that fraud." [12] Jane Addams chafed under the confinement and rigid sense of piety that Miss Sill and her teachers imposed on the life at Rockford. The *Rockford Seminary Magazine*, the only student publication, assumed a more critical tone during the year that Jane Addams was editor-in-chief. An editorial

9. Jane Addams, "Rockford Seminary Endowment," in *Memorials of Anna P. Sill*, p. 73.

10. Of the 282 seminary graduates in 1882, 37 were missionaries and 8 had served with the Freedmen's Bureau; these totals do not reflect graduates who had married missionaries. See Anna P. Sill, *A Letter to Our Old Girls and to Them Only* (Chicago, 1882), in "Miss Sill's Scrapbook," Rockford College Archives. Jane Addams recalled in 1910 how Turkey had been pointed out to her as a promising field for missionary service, see *Twenty Years at Hull-House*, p. 50.

11. *Rockford Seminary Magazine*, IX (July, 1881), 210; for a more serious invocation of this slogan see Mrs. G. Clinton Smith, comp., "The Progress of Foreign Missions and the Reflex Influence upon Women," *ibid.*, VIII (January, 1880), 10.

12. The letters from classmates are with Mattie Thomas to Jane Addams, April 27, 1882, Jane Addams Papers, Swarthmore College Peace Collection; hereafter cited as SCPC.

complained that "our life in Rockford has been rather isolated and unsocial—[so] that the Rockford people have been strangers to us. . . ." [13] Complaints and suggestions were less guarded, the tone of the magazine fresher, after Miss Addams became editor.[14] Her pleas for additional social opportunities must have appealed to her classmates. She was elected president of her class, president of both her literary society and of the union, and she represented the seminary in regional debating. Miss Addams was also valedictorian of her class.

This scholastic attainment gains stature because the curriculum at Rockford was good, according to Professor Thomas Woody, "distinctly better than most seminaries." [15] The aim of the curriculum had always been collegiate, Miss Sill told an alumnae reunion in 1879. The seminary's 1847 charter had empowered the board of trustees to grant the bachelor of arts degree. But Miss Sill opposed adopting the title "college," since "the best ideal then existing of the liberal education of young women" excluded conferring degrees on young ladies. The granting of degrees, she said, "would not be approved by any college president or professor." Miss Sill maintained that young women deserved equal educational advantages with their brothers since they were equally capable of benefiting from a liberal education. "It was not thought, however, that they should have the same curriculum of study, but that which was equal in culture, and it should be adapted to their special responsibilities in life." [16]

Yet Jane Addams was determined to be a college graduate, with a bachelor's degree, not just a seminary certificate. In 1876 the seminary had instituted a strong collegiate course which made available the mathematics and Greek equal to the qualifications for a B.A. at Beloit. During her four years, Jane Addams fulfilled the necessary requirements for a bachelor's degree. Her studies included four years of German, Latin through Virgil, Cicero, and Tacitus, two years of Greek, history and literature—standard

13. *Rockford Seminary Magazine*, VII (July, 1879), 204.

14. During her junior year Miss Addams handled magazine exchanges. These exchanges provided her with many new ideas for school activities. Innovations sparked by the class of 1881 were a Junior Exhibition, new class parlor regulation like those at Vassar, and ceremonies which duplicated the Vassar "Trig Day."

15. Thomas Woody, *A History of Women's Education in the United States* (New York, and Lancaster, Penn., 1929), II, 171.

16. In "Report of the Sixth Chicago Reunion," *Rockford Seminary Magazine*, VII (April, 1879), 76.

English authors, Chaucer to Tennyson, and at least one semester of American Literature.[17] She also took algebra, plane and solid geometry and trigonometry, geology, chemistry, mineralogy, and astronomy. Her transcript also records a year of music, great chunks of Bible history, and the senior-year mental and moral philosophy class taught by Miss Sill.[18]

An unusual and famous feature of the seminary that helps to explain how the students thought about themselves and about the role of women was the emphasis on physical education, health, and hygiene. The " Rockford Student Manual "—like the " Mount Holyoke Book of Duties "—provided for an hour of exercise daily. At Rockford there were lectures in hygiene and physiology. After Miss Addams graduated, the seminary used part of its " scanty means " to " put up a gymnasium, elaborate, out of proportion to our other equipment. . . ."[19] The historian of physical education for women noted that the various systems of exercises, calisthenics, and gymnastics appeared at Rockford at the same time, or earlier, than at Mount Holyoke, Vassar, or Smith.[20] Doubtless the gymnastic exercises were conducted in a most decorous manner, since the woolen gym suit was quite cumbersome. And probably the lectures on hygiene and physiology were prim and proper. But the emphasis on physical health, on knowledge about the body, was strong; and at least one writer has found the basis of modern feminism in " a new view of the body, its functions, its needs, its claim upon the world. . . ."[21]

17. Course offerings with texts are in seminary catalogues.
18. Transcript in Rockford College Archives. Miss Sill was anxious that this amount of work should be recognized with the college degree. Jane Addams and a classmate, Helen Harrington, were the first to qualify themselves. Jane Addams wrote her stepbrother, a student at Beloit, that Miss Sill had offered her the degree. Coyly she wrote that Miss Sill " thinks I have refused, but will undoubtedly renew the subject." Jane Addams to George Haldeman, May 8, 1881, Stephenson County Historical Museum. Whether the board of trustees refused Miss Sill's request that they exercise their full powers or whether Miss Addams' coyness discouraged Miss Sill is impossible to determine. At the 1882 graduation, two girls from the class of 1882 received the B.A. degree, then the Misses Addams and Harrington were awarded the degrees for which they had qualified a year earlier.
19. Jane Addams, " Rockford Seminary Endowment," p. 75.
20. Dorothy S. Ainsworth, *The History of Physical Education in Colleges for Women, as Illustrated by Barnard, Bryn Mawr, Elmira, Goucher, Mills, Mount Holyoke, Radcliffe, Rockford, Smith, Vassar, Wellesley, and Wells* (New York, 1930).
21. Floyd Dell, *Women As World Builders, Studies in Modern Feminism* (Chicago, 1913), p. 44. Not all the girls at Rockford were feminists, of course.

Miss Sill's conception of women's role was a conservative one. It was not thought scriptural, she reminisced in 1879 at a Rockford reunion, to let young ladies speak in public. The first year that essays by students were featured at the seminary commencement, Miss Sill appointed a young gentleman to read them. She recalled the protests of the graduating seniors: " Can you loyal ones before me believe that one of the class should so far forget herself as to say ' Well Miss Sill, you and the gentleman may have the anniversary all to yourselves, and send us our diplomas with our dinners in our rooms.' " A description of Mary Lyon's feminism fits Miss Sill's feminism as well. She " never talked much of woman's rights; she said very little, if anything of woman's sphere. But she believed in, and loved to dwell on, the great work a woman may do in the world." In Miss Sill's own words, the " chief glory of the Seminary lies in its Christian ideal. . . ." Its aim is to develop a moral and religious character in accordance with right principles, and to send out cultivated Christian women to the various fields of usefulness. No education can be of great value which does not prepare for the practical duties of home and social life, and is in consonance with the demands of the age in the progress of the evangelization of the world." [22] Thus, concern for woman's duty was interwoven with the religious enthusiasm and training at the seminary. Miss Sill's conservative religious ideas supported her conventional ideas about women's social role.

Miss Sill's certainly about religious matters eluded Jane Addams. In *Twenty Years at Hull-House* she recalled her singular unresponsiveness to the emotional appeal of religious evangelism and her embarrassment at her teachers' attempts to convert her.[23] She expressed her religious uncertainties in a long series of letters to Ellen Gates Starr, who had been at the seminary for the year

In her commencement paper Miss Kate Louise Turner (1881) scorned the woman who ignored her home and strove for " more avenues to power, more opportunities for employment." A woman who neglected her home in order to reform the world was simply " no more a lady." Kate Turner in unidentified newspaper clipping, " Miss Sill's Scrapbook," Rockford College Archives.

22. In " Report of the Sixth Chicago Reunion," p. 76. In defense of Miss Sill, even at advanced Oberlin it was not considered proper for a woman to address a mixed audience, see Ernest R. Groves, *The American Woman, the Feminine Side of a Masculine Civilization* (New York, 1937), p. 314. On Miss Lyon see Mary Caroline Crawford, *The College Girl in America* (Boston, 1904), p. 71; Miss Sill's speech quoted in " Report of the Sixth Chicago Reunion," p. 76.

23. Jane Addams, *Twenty Years at Hull-House*, pp. 49, 56.

1877–8. In one letter she wrote of trying to get back of all systems of religion, ". . . back of all of it [religion]—superior to it I almost feel. Back to a great Primal cause—not nature, exactly, but a fostering Mother, a necessity, brooding and watching over all things, above every human passion. . . ." While she searched, she took as her motto " ever be sincere and don't fuss." Several months later after a talk with her favorite teacher, Jane Addams was convinced that the success of one's work depended largely on the resolution of one's religious beliefs. She could never, she wrote Ellen Starr, go ahead and use her best powers until she had decided what her religion was. Until that decision was made, she wrote, I " go ahead building my religion wherever I can find it, from the Bible and observation, from books and people, and in no small degree from Carlyle."

This last letter must have been accompanied with a resolution; for three months later she wrote " I have been trying an experiment[.] I didn't pray, at least formally, for almost three months, and was shocked to find that I feel no worse for it, I can think about a great many other things that are noble and beautiful, and I feel happy and unconcerned and not in the least morbid. . . . I only feel," she continued revealingly, " that I need religion in a practical sense, that if I could fix myself with my relations to God and the universe, and so be in perfect harmony with nature and deity, I could use my faculties and energy so much better, and could do almost anything." These letters illustrate the rational and practical Jane Addams. A decision about her relations to God and the universe would make her personal life efficient. Such a decision about nature and deity would help discover where her special duty lay.[24]

Whatever hesitations Jane Addams had about religion, she championed the idea of special work for women. Mrs. Anna H. Addams, interviewed in 1915, recalled these early ambitions of her stepdaughter: " Even as a little child she seemed inclined toward special work of some sort. In fact," Mrs. Addams noted without enthusiasm, " she was anxious for a career. . . ."[25] As a student at Rockford, Jane Addams expressed a strong and earnest desire

24. Quotations are from Jane Addams to Ellen Starr, letters dated August 11, 1879, *ibid.*, November 22, 1879, January 29, 1880, respectively, in Starr Papers.
25. " The Girl of Cedar Cliff," Chicago *Record*, June 17, 1915.

to do something important with her life. She optimistically noted
that "woman has gained a new confidence in her possibilities,
and a fresher hope in her steady progress . . . as young women of
the nineteenth century, we gladly claim these privileges [sic], and
proudly assert our independence . . . on the other hand we still
retain the old idea of womanhood. . . ." Her "intense desire to
make something of life" was not rooted in religious ideas as much
as in the idea of a special duty and work for women.[26]

The class prophet at Class Day for the class of 1881 reported
on some of Jane Addams' other intellectual concerns. She said
that Miss Addams had "rebounded at the age of fifteen in
Emerson's essays; here she delved and lingered long, and after
passing through a scientific infection came to Byron, DeQuincy
and Carlyle."[27] Emerson appealed to Jane Addams perhaps because he applauded the demise of religious dogma; he rejoiced
that religion had finally become morals. She must have found this
sentiment congenial. It agreed with her father's example, for
his religion was ethical rather than dogmatic, like his hero Mazzini's. And it agreed with her own belief.[28]

Miss Addams' infection with science is easier to describe.
Several members of her family were interested in scientific speculation, especially George Haldeman who took graduate work at
the new Johns Hopkins University in the 1880's. While still in
his teens George, along with Jane and his mother Mrs. Anna
Addams, founded a family phrenological society. The earnest,
amusing minutes of the society, dated 1876 and 1877, survive.[29]
Perhaps from this early taste of science young Jennie Addams
caught the "central message of phrenology, . . . that man himself

26. Jane Addams, "Bread-Givers," Rockford *Daily Register*, April 21, 1880;
Dr. Alice Hamilton in an interview in May, 1961, characterized Miss Addams
as getting at Rockford her "intense desire to make something of life."

27. [Annie Sidwell], "Sage and Sibyl," *Rockford Seminary Magazine*, IX
(July, 1881), 193–4.

28. John Addams contributed to all four protestant churches in Cedarville and
identified most closely with the Quaker meeting. On Mazzini, see Jane Addams,
Twenty Years at Hull-House, p. 21. Jane Addams called her father a Unitarian
in 1912. I have been unable to verify the reference, which appeared in "Woman
in Politics," *Progress*, I (November, 1912), 37–40.

29. Records of the Capenic Phrenological Society, Minutes dated August 21,
1876 to June 11, 1877, in Stephenson County Historical Museum. Article II of
the constitution of this family project provided that each member had the privilege
of examining any other member's head.

could be brought within the purview of science and mental phenomena could be studied and explained by natural causes. . . ." [30]

In their freshman year at Rockford, Jane Addams and Ellen Starr helped found a scientific society. It sponsored lectures and solicited artifacts and equipment for use at the seminary. The scientific society did not prosper, however. In 1880 it transformed itself into a " club, the sole object of its members being self-improvement. They used mainly as their text-book ' The Popular Science Monthly.' . . ." [31] With her step-brother as her tutor, Jane Addams devoted the summer of her sophomore year to serious study of comparative anatomy. As a junior at the seminary, she took taxidermy lessons and proved her mettle by dealing with a live hawk sent by her father. The six months Jane Addams spent in Philadelphia studying medicine in the winter of 1881–2 also reflected her early interest in science. And in 1882, she gave the seminary one thousand dollars of her inheritance to buy scientific books for the library.[32]

Miss Addams' interest soon turned away from science. Her medical studies, even with experience in taxidermy and preparation in anatomy, were not at all successful. In a letter written late in 1884 to George Haldeman—her one-time tutor in scientific study—she admitted that she was impressed by the dazzling scientific displays she and Mrs. Addams had visited in Philadelphia but declared that she thought " modern science is a trifle esoteric and exoteric in its relation to the world." [33] Her lasting enthusiasm was for the literary rather than the scientific part of

30. John D. Davies, *Phrenology, Fad and Science, a Nineteenth Century American Crusade* (New Haven, 1955), p. 171.

31. *Rockford Seminary Magazine*, VI (April, 1878), 81–2, and VIII (December, 1880), pp. 266, 286–8.

32. On taxidermy, see *Rockford Seminary Magazine*, VIII (March, 1880), p. 57; on anatomy study see Jane Addams to Ellen Gates Starr, August 11, 1879, Starr Papers. At the class day for Miss Addams' class of 1881, the seminary library was described as having two thousand volumes: 1,999 patent office reports and a volume of intelligence of missionary enterprise, see *Rockford Seminary Magazine*, IX (July, 1881), p. 210.

33. Jane Addams to George Haldeman, December 19, 1884, SCPC. Some writers have stressed positivism as an influence on Miss Addams' thought—see Merle Curti, " Jane Addams on Human Nature," *Journal of the History of Ideas*, XXII (April–June, 1961), 243–4, and Linn, *Jane Addams*, pp. 77, 88–9. It is true that Jane Addams rejected the metaphysical, that she was interested in science, and that she held a practical ideal of knowledge. These similarities with positivism were coincidental rather than systematic.

her education at Rockford. The ideals and interpretations of life that she found in imaginative literature formed the lasting and influential part of her formal education. Carlyle, Ruskin, and Arnold especially expressed the ideals Miss Addams learned at the seminary. Thus even while enjoying the summer's study of anatomy she wrote Ellen Starr with obvious satisfaction, " there is something in Carlyle that suits me as no one else does." [34]

Carlyle's emphasis on duty must have struck a response chord in Jane Addams. Carlyle tried to expose what he considered the great social crime: neglect of duty by the natural leaders of England. Society was helpless, he was sure, unless the natural leaders returned to their duties of leading. Only through each individual performing his responsibilities could society function in the proper way. Doing one's duty was, according to Carlyle, the first and most important social responsibility.

Miss Addams also read a great deal of Ruskin, " and liked the most abstruse parts the best." [35] Perhaps she found Ruskin's moralization of social life attractive. Ruskin's whole critique of the ' dismal science ' of political economy came down to his assertion that human welfare, justice, is the life of the state. He eloquently indicted the misery and social injustice caused by poverty and the corrupting influence of wealth. Ruskin's protest insisted on the right of each man to enjoyment in his work, and to ennobling participation in the graces and joys of life. This democracy of " the manifold gifts of life " was balanced, of course, by Ruskin's constant emphasis on order, subordination, stability, and authority. [36]

Ruskin also put his faith in the individual doing his duty. He saw no hope for England unless the existing aristocracy would voluntarily reform itself and perform its duty of leading the masses. Ruskin equated modern anarchism and the effects of laissez-faire competition. No one was his brother's keeper; poverty, social disorganization, and ugliness were the result.

Jane Addams' resolution not to fuss was an excellent summary

34. Jane Addams to Ellen Gates Starr, August 11, 1879, Starr Papers.
35. Jane Addams, *Twenty Years at Hull-House*, p. 47.
36. The citation is from Vida D. Scudder, *Social Ideals in English Letters* (New York & Boston, [1896] 1910), pp. 175–6. I have used Miss Scudder because she was one of the group who started a college settlement in the East, independently from the Misses Addams and Starr.

of Matthew Arnold's position. She rejected, like Arnold, both literal inspiration and metaphysical knowledge, and firmly grounded her religion in humanistic ethics. Like Arnold, she conceived of God in terms of man's moral experience.[37] Arnold on democracy and culture is almost prophetic of Hull House. He wrote that culture " seeks to do away with classes; to make the best that has been thought and known in the world current everywhere; to make all men live in an atmosphere of sweetness and light, where they may use ideas, as it [culture] uses them itself, freely,— nourished and not bound by them. This is the *social idea*; and the men of culture are the true apostles of equality." [38] These English authors whose social idealism Jane Addams absorbed at Rockford were a most important part of her formal intellectual training.

For Jane Addams the period after graduation, from 1881 to 1889, was one of unhappiness, nervous crisis and depression, and of European travel " in search of a good time and this general idea of culture which [in] some way never commanded my full respect." [39] These years were filled with repeated attempts to define a purpose for her life. The imperatives learned at Rockford of woman's duty and of usefulness shadowed these eight years.

John Addams' death in August, 1881, deeply depressed his daughter. She wrote to Ellen Gates Starr in September, 1881, that her father's death was " the greatest sorrow that can ever come to me." His death had utterly confused her " moral purposes "; it had rendered her " purposeless and without ambition." [40] After a start at medical study in Philadelphia in the winter of 1881–2, she returned to Cedarville. No records exist for the next half year which she spent bedridden after an operation by her doctor brother-in-law, Dr. Harry Haldeman. (Jane Addams' sister, Alice, had married her stepbrother.) Dr. Haldeman performed an operation to correct a slight curvature of the spine, the

37. See William Robbins, *The Ethical Idealism of Matthew Arnold, a Study of the Nature and Sources of His Moral and Religious Ideas* (London, 1959).

38. Miss Scudder quoted these sentences from Arnold's *Anarchy and Culture* in her *Social Ideals in English Letters*, p. 256. Jane Addams was increasingly interested in Arnold after seminary. She devoted the first half of her memorial address for Miss Sill in 1889 to the inspiring example of Arnold at Eton and at Christ Church, and traced the results in the founding of Toynbee Hall. See her " Rockford Seminary Endowment," pp. 70–72.

39. Jane Addams to Ellen Gates Starr, August 12, 1883, Starr Papers.

40. Jane Addams to Ellen Gates Starr, September 3, 1881, Starr Papers.

result of a childhood case of spinal tuberculosis. Jane Addams always talked of this period as involving mental recovery, as well as physical recovery from an extremely painful operation. She was ashamed, she apologized to Ellen Starr, " to show even to my good friends against what lassitude, melancholy and general crookedness I was struggling." She had emerged from her six-month seclusion, so she hoped, with a fresh hold on life and endeavor.[41]

The following months seemed to produce no real improvement. As her sense of isolation and uncertainty deepened and as the months of nervous depression continued, Jane Addams returned to religious speculation. Perhaps Ellen Starr's example was also influential in this new interest in religion. Miss Starr's decision to join the Episcopal church in July, 1883, was the occasion for Jane Addams to ask how she might also come to join the church. " My experiences of late have shown me the absolute necessity of the protection and dependence on Christ, his method and secret, as Matthew Arnold put it. . . . The good men and books I used to depend on will no longer answer." [42]

The same letter gave Ellen Starr the information that " it seems quite essential for the establishment of my health and temper [?] that I have a radical change and so I have accepted the advice given to every exhausted American, ' go abroad.' " The next twenty-seven months, spent in European travel with her step-mother, were passed in quite ordinary ways. Mrs. Addams and her daughter lived in pensions, took language lessons, toured galleries, and attended concerts and operas. The tour was leisurely, for, as Jane Addams wrote home, " I do not approve of doing any one thing to such an extent that no time or spirit remains for the gentler offices of life. . . ." These months with her stepmother failed to solve any of her problems and doubts. From Paris in June, 1884, she wrote to Ellen Starr—who had just been con-

41. Jane Addams to Ellen Gates Starr, January 7, 1883, Starr Papers. The operation, named *Baunscheidtmus*, after its German inventor, involved injecting irritant into the tissue with needle punctures. The scarred tissue then contracted to pull the spine straight. Interview, Dr. Alice Hamilton, 1961. A. L. Bowen, " The World Is Better That This Woman Lives," *New Age Illustrated*, XI (November, 1927), 27, quotes Miss Addams as saying " during my first year in medical school [1881–2], however, I was stricken with a nervous affliction which compelled me to abandon my studies."

42. Jane Addams to Ellen Gates Starr, July 11, 1883, Starr Papers.

firmed in the Episcopal church—" I am afraid that I was almost as unsettled and perplexed [on the Sunday you were confirmed] as in the days when we were ' estimable young ladies.' " On Palm Sunday, 1885, when again in Paris, she wrote, " I believe more and more in keeping the events, *the facts* of Christ's life before us and letting the philosophy go." This trip to Europe seemed to have solved none of Jane Addams' confusions and uncertainties.[43]

The winters of 1885–6 and 1886–7 were spent in Baltimore where Jane and Mrs. Addams visited George Haldeman, who was doing graduate work at The Johns Hopkins University. These winters were apparently extremely trying for Miss Addams. Mrs. Addams was promoting marriage between her son and Jane. In addition, her stepmother attempted to " launch " her in Baltimore society, an effort which Jane found very distasteful. She wrote her sister from Baltimore that she used to believe that adapting yourself to another person was simply a matter of the will, but she was beginning to find that there were persons to whom she could not adapt herself. The attempt was making her more and more nervous. Letters from these two winters confirm Miss Addams' later recollection that in Baltimore she reached " the nadir of my nervous depression and sense of maladjustment." [44]

The only thing that aroused her enthusiasm was her participation in city charities. Baltimore had an unusually up-to-date charity organization in the 1880's. Students and faculty from the new university participated in it and Miss Addams might have been introduced quite naturally to various city charities through her Hopkins friendships. She wrote her sister of spending Christmas afternoon at a " little colored orphan asylum [Johns Hopkins Colored Orphan Asylum, 519 West Biddle Street] I have grown quite interested in. They take little colored girls and help them until they are 15, training them to be *good servants*, the children themselves expecting to be that. . . . I heartily approve of the scheme." She also frequently visited a sewing school in East Baltimore and an industrial arts school. These gentle philanthropic errands did not burden her, nor did her nervous distraction prevent her from taking a keen interest in various charitable activi-

43. Jane Addams to Ellen Gates Starr, July 11, 1883, March 9, 1884, June 22, 1884, March 30, Palm Sunday, 1885, Starr Papers.
44. Jane Addams to Alice Addams Haldeman. [January, 1887?], Deloach Deposit, SCPC; Jane Addams, *Twenty Years at Hull-House*, p. 77.

ties. " I have been investigating city charities this winter," she
wrote enigmatically to her sister, " and have come to some rather
curious conclusions." [45] She did not find any clear idea of duty
while she and Mrs. Addams were in Baltimore.

Between these trying winters, Jane Addams was baptized and
joined the Cedarville Presbyterian Church. Six months before,
she had written to Ellen Starr, " I am always floundering when I
deal with religious nomenclature or sensations simply because my
religious life has been so small:—for many years it was my
ambition to reach my father's moral requirements, and now when
I am needing something more, I find myself approaching a
crisis. . . ." [46] It was the crisis of duty undefined. Her search for
a satisfying intellectual and emotional basis for vocational duty
was not fulfilled by random study and occasional charitable
activity. Rockford canons of duty and usefulness, even stripped
of their evangelicalism, demanded a positive contribution to the
world. These demands were all the more imperative for a well-
bred young lady without a family and home to serve. Perhaps
involvement in charity work sharpened these questions. As in a
previous crisis Jane Addams turned to religion. She recalled in
1910 that joining the church involved " little assent to dogma or
miracle," but simply affirmed her belief in humanitarian and
cosmopolitan solidarity, in the unity of society. [47] She hoped that
membership in the church might illuminate her desire to make
something of life.

She was able to define her purpose during a second European
trip in 1887-8. This time she was accompanied not by Mrs.
Addams but by school friends, among them Ellen Starr. The
purpose of the trip was partly therapeutic and recreational, to
escape the pressures of Cedarville and Baltimore, and partly

45. Jane Addams to Alice Addams Haldeman, December 28, 1886, January 22,
1887, Deloach Deposit, SCPC. One can only speculate about these conclusions,
and whether or not Jane Addams attended the Baltimore Conference on Charities,
April 15–16, 1887. There Professor Herbert Baxter Adams described and praised
the latest English attempts at charity, including Toynbee Hall. See p. 19, Appendix,
*Report of a Conference on Charities and on Other Subjects Pertaining to the
Prevention of Suffering, Pauperism and Other Crime* (Baltimore, 1887).

46. Jane Addams to Ellen Gates Starr, December 6, 1885, Starr Papers. Jane
Addams had attended the Unitarian church in Baltimore because, she said, the
Unitarian minister was the city's best, and " the sermon is more to me than the
service." See Jane Addams to Ellen Gates Starr, February 7, 1886, Starr Papers.

47. Jane Addams, *Twenty Years at Hull-House*, pp. 78, 79.

academic—to collect reproductions for the art collections at Rockford Seminary and at the art school in Chicago where Miss Starr taught. Perhaps a third purpose was for Jane Addams to continue her study of urban philanthropies, since she equipped herself with an introduction to a London clergyman who was active in that city's charities and was a member of the Toynbee Hall Circle.[48] During this trip Jane Addams saw the vocational opening for which she had searched so long. The basic idea was rooted in an old family story. When she was six, riding with her father through a poorer section of Freeport which had many small houses, Jane had said that when she was big she would live in a big house among such small houses. This childish fantasy was one of John Addams' favorite jests. He delighted in regaling visitors to the Addams home with her plans. It was an often repeated family joke at her expense.[49] But it came to have new meaning and relevance during this second tour of Europe.

While they were in Spain, the young ladies attended a bull fight. Disgusted by the brutality, Jane Addams' companions left early. But Miss Addams remained, held by a sense of " vivid associations of an historic survival " in the stylized spectacle before her. She had, she later recalled, the feeling " that this was the last survival of all the glories of the amphitheatre, . . . [or medieval] knights of a tournament, or . . . a slightly armed gladiator facing his martyrdom. . . ." Confronted with the disapproval of her companions, Jane Addams agreed that her behavior was shameful. Her indifference, upon reflection, revealed selfish indulgence; she had excused idleness in travel and study as preparation for no concrete end. She was postponing and, therefore, deserting her duty. To assuage these feelings of guilt, she asked Ellen Starr to join her in settling in a less-favored neighborhood of a city.[50] Her plan was probably little more at this first telling in 1888 than a desire to live among less-favored people where she might perform useful services for her neighbors.

48. Robert A. Woods and Albert J. Kennedy, *The Settlement Horizon, a National Estimate* (New York, 1922), p. 46, assert that Jane Addams happened on an account of Toynbee Hall in the back pages of a magazine, and noted its address. The references may be to R. R. Bowker, " Toynbee Hall, London," *Century*, XXIV (May, 1887), 158–9.

49. Letter from E. A. Berry to Kansas City *Star*, 1935, SCPC, tells how he, as a guest in the Addams household in the late 1870's, heard John Addams tell this story about his daughter's future plans.

50. Jane Addams, *Twenty Years at Hull-House*, pp. 85–6.

With Ellen Starr's tentative agreement, Jane Addams left the rest of the party and went to London. For six weeks she studied philanthropic efforts in the London slums, especially the first settlement, Toynbee Hall. We have the word of the wife of the warden of Toynbee Hall that Miss Addams was recognized as a " great soul." Perhaps for that reason, Canon and Mrs. Samuel A. Barnett " took pains to show her much and tell her more." [51] In addition to Toynbee Hall, Jane Addams studied the " People's Palace," and efforts at adult education like the University Extension Lectures and the Workingman's College.

Toynbee Hall reflected the personality of Samuel A. Barnett. Canon Barnett did not originate the idea of university men living in poor districts, but he provided the encouragement and setting which endowed the idea with permanence. In 1872 Barnett had been appointed vicar of St. Jude's parish in Whitechapel, a section of London's East End. With his wife Henrietta, he undertook striking innovations in his parish ministry. Canon Barnett early concluded that almsgiving destroyed the character of the poor. " He saw, without a shade of reservation from pity, that a man's soul was more important than a man's suffering. . . . It was spiritual murder so to act as to nullify for [a man] . . . the results of his own actions." [52] He coveted for every Englishman more nearly equal opportunity, an equal chance for a healthy life, and the enjoyment of the best gifts of the age.[53] The Barnetts turned the St. Jude's vicarage into a center not for the distribution of alms, but for the restored parish library, for flower shows and art exhibits, concerts, classes, and for a social life which introduced the men and women of Whitechapel to Londoners of all social classes.

Canon Barnett's experience in London's East End showed him the large needs and opportunities for social and political leadership in a working-class neighborhood. Aristocratic responsibility to provide this leadership was the theme of men like Ruskin and Arnold, whom Jane Addams had read at Rockford, and who had

51. [Dame Henrietta Octavia Barnett], *Canon Barnett: His Life, Work, and Friends by His Wife* (London, [1918] 1921), p. 422. Dame Henrietta was a regal lady who demanded a good deal of attention and flattery from her friends. She was known in America as " the wife of Toynbee Hall."

52. *Ibid.*, p. 622.

53. Barnett to Mrs. Dawson, cited in *ibid.*, p. 614.

been associated with Oxford University.[54] It is not altogether surprising, therefore, that the example of St. Jude's in London caught the attention of men at Oxford. Arnold Toynbee, a lecturer at Balliol, made the direct connection between Oxford undergraduates and Canon Barnett.[55] Toynbee's enthusiasm in Ruskin's famous road-building project—an attempt to show the Oxford undergraduate the dignity of the hardest kind of manual labor—brought him Ruskin's close friendship. Toynbee attempted to live on the same scale as a workingman in Whitechapel during the long vacation in 1875. At that time he joined workingman's clubs, visited the schools, studied the local organization of charities, and in general co-operated with Barnett.

Just before his death in March, 1884, Toynbee gave a series of lectures on the industrial revolution and on Henry George's ideas. His soul, Jane Addams wrote later, "was perplexed over the masses of inarticulate workmen who came so heavily to hear him . . . they were not organized socially. . . . Their ideas of mutual responsibility and need of association were . . . unformed and simple. . . . Men of ability and refinement, of social power, of university education, stayed away from them." [56] Toynbee's lecture fragments are the best formulation of his ideals of social duty and responsibility which were based directly on religious conviction. Toynbee was an idealist, almost a transcendentalist in his faith. But idealism such as his, so one of his biographers reported, "could only justify its existence by energetic devotion to the good of mankind. . . . He would not be behind the Positivists in the service of men, because he embraced that service for the love of God." [57] Like Canon Barnett, Toynbee saw how the absence of leadership in the poorer districts had allowed local government to fall into disrepair until the low and vicious set the tone of community life. Guilt at the desertion of duty by those who had been trained to lead—just what Jane Addams felt in 1888—impelled Toynbee to take up his residence in Whitechapel. His last speech is a good example of this guilt.

54. Arnold was professor of poetry from 1857 to 1867. Ruskin was professor of fine arts from 1870 to 1878 and for the year 1883–4.
55. For a description of the lasting effects of Toynbee's personal example see G. N. Clark, *The Idea of the Industrial Revolution* (Glasgow, 1953), Chap. I.
56. Jane Addams, "Outgrowths of Toynbee Hall," typescript of address to Chicago Woman's Club, 1890, p. 3, SCPC.
57. Alfred Milner, *Arnold Toynbee, a Reminisence* (London, 1895), p. 37.

We—the middle-class, I mean, not merely the very rich—
we have neglected you [the workingman]; instead of justice
we have offered you charity, and instead of sympathy we have
offered you hard and unreal advice; but I think we are
changing. If you would only believe it and trust us, I think
that many of us would spend our lives in your service. You
have—I say it clearly and advisedly—you have to forgive us,
for we have wronged you; we have sinned against you griev-
ously . . . [but] whether you will forgive us or not—we
will serve you, we will devote our lives to your service, and
we cannot do more. . . . We are willing to give up something much dearer than fame and social position. We are
willing to give up the life we care for, the life with books
and with those we love.[58]

Toynbee Hall embodied similar motives. As first projected,
Jane Addams wrote later, Toynbee Hall provided " an aid and
outlet to educated young men. The benefit to East Londoners was
then regarded as almost secondary." [59] The main difficulty in poor
neighborhoods, the founders of Toynbee Hall believed, was that
the people there " have few friends and helpers who can study
and relieve their difficulties, few points of contact with the best
thoughts and aspirations of their age, few educated, public-spirited
residents, such as elsewhere in England uphold the tone of Local
Life and enforce the efficiency of Local Self-Government." [60] In
1888, the year Jane Addams visited Toynbee Hall, the fifteen
residents—all university graduates—were involved in various local
activities. Six were managers in elementary schools; six conducted
evening classes. Four men served on committees of the local
Charity Organization Society. One was a Guardian of the Poor,
an elective office. Nine residents were members of various East
London clubs. Two were almoners for the Society for the Relief
of Distress. Five residents were working with the Children's
County Holiday Fund, a special interest of Mrs. Barnett. As
this enumeration makes clear, participation in local government

58. Cited in Werner Picht, *Toynbee Hall and the English Settlement Movement*
(London, 1914), p. 22.
59. Jane Addams, " Outgrowths of Toynbee Hall," p. 7, SCPC.
60. Cited in F. C. Montague, *Arnold Toynbee* (" Johns Hopkins University
Studies in Historical and Political Science," Vol. VII; Baltimore, 1889), p. 59.

and in clubs and classes was the major activity of Toynbee Hall residents.[61]

The strongest motive for residing at Toynbee Hall was religious. Of the original fourteen men at the hall, five went into the church or were already clergymen. The historian of Toynbee Hall wrote that " Christian Socialism was in one form or another, the most actively expressed philosophy." There were daily morning prayers at Toynbee Hall for those who cared to attend. Canon Barnett believed that religion was the only support the settlement needed; religion was " the one force which can turn the various and often antagonistic classes into fellow workers, making our great cities good for the habitation of both rich and poor." Barnett summed up his social philosophy when he wrote that " the problem of society seems to be at root a religious problem." [62] Yet Toynbee Hall was not an Episcopalian mission. Barnett never confused his job as vicar at St. Jude's with his position as warden of Toynbee Hall. The settlement offered no public religious exercise nor religious instruction. Canon Barnett insisted that the settlement must not compete with the functions and duties of the church. And although most of the residents identified themselves with the church, there was no corporate identification. Jane Addams must have noticed this absence of dogmatic or sectarian identification combined with deep religious concern, for these were the reasons she had joined the church months earlier.[63]

"A Settlement's distinguishing feature," Barnett wrote twenty-five years after Toynbee Hall opened, " is the absence of programme, and the presence of men and women who recognize the

61. [Barnett], *Canon Barnett*, p. 484. Later political office replaced participation in settlement activities which were turned over to nonresidents. Picht, *Toynbee Hall*, p. 96, said that residency at Toynbee Hall became an easy and convenient way for university men to prepare themselves for civil service careers without much emphasis on neighborhood service.

62. J. A. R. Pimlott, *Toynbee Hall: Fifty Years of Social Progress, 1884–1934* (London, 1935), p. 4; [Barnett], *Canon Barnett*, p. 496; Canon and Mrs. Samuel A. Barnett, *Towards Social Reform* (London, 1909), p. 32.

63. The lack of corporate religious identifications for Toynbee Hall was unusual among English settlements and brought accusation of irreligion. Edward Cummings, " University Settlements," *Quarterly Journal of Economics*, VI (April, 1892), 257–79, rehearses how a rival settlement, Oxford House, was founded for the Oxford students who felt Toynbee irreligious. Octavia Hill broke with the Barnetts over Toynbee Hall's lack of religion; for the Barnett's side, see [Barnett], *Canon Barnett*, p. 421. See also " ' Settlements ' or ' Missions,' " in Barnett *Towards Social Reform*, pp. 274–87.

obligations of citizenship." The insistence upon no program reflects the fear of institutions that characterized much settlement thought. Barnett maintained that the central principle of the work at Toynbee Hall should be " One by One." He believed that only friendship between man and man could have any lasting effect. Residents expended much worry to keep the atmosphere and activities at the hall simple and personal so that no organization should come between resident and neighbor. The settlement, according to the Barnetts, was a " protest against . . . the substitution of philanthropic machinery for human hands and personal knowledge "; " institutions are prejudicial to strength of character. Progress, everyone knows, depends on individual effort. . . ." [64] Similar statements by English settlement pioneers could be multiplied many times.

This " absence of programme " should not obscure certain specific aims that underlay the multiform activities of Toynbee Hall. " The establishment of the settlement," Barnett wrote, " is the work of those who believe that the gifts of modern times are good; that culture is gain, not loss; that cleanliness is better than dirt, beauty better than ugliness, knowledge better than ignorance. . . ." Barnett asserted that those in the settlement would " lay open the way to the enjoyment of beauty, of art, of travel. We would nationalize luxury." [65]

Jane Addams was particularly attracted by this emphasis on culture and art, and on the need for the extension of such culture. She later singled out this feature of the Toynbee Hall program to explain the motives behind settlements. The Toynbee settlement, she said, " disregards none of the results of civilization, casts aside nothing that the modern man considers beautiful or goodly. It rather stands for the fittings of a cultivated, well-ordered life, and the surroundings which are suggestive of participation in the best of the past." She was also attracted by the wide definition given to culture at Toynbee Hall. Perhaps recalling the Rockford emphasis on physical education she told a Chicago audience that " it would be unfair to Englishmen to omit [from her description] the cricketing clubs, the tennis clubs, the athletic life of all kinds which centers about Toynbee Hall." [66]

64. [Barnett], *Canon Barnett*, p. 184; Barnett, *Towards Social Reform*, pp. 286, 260, 118.
65. Barnett, *Towards Social Reform*, pp. 259, 12.
66. Jane Addams, " Outgrowths of Toynbee Hall," pp. 11, 10, SCPC.

Canon Barnett told all visitors about his educational hopes for Toynbee Hall. Jane Addams must have heard him describe how the hall might become the nucleus of a great people's university. Barnett envisioned the Toynbee Hall quadrangle surrounded by colleges committed to the education of the workingman. After all, he said, had not Oxford and Cambridge originated in the Middle Ages in this way? His vision was sustained by a broad conception of the function and purpose of education. For Canon Barnett, education was not merely academic or utilitarian; it was "the cultivation of personality through contact with what is excellent in human achievement." Jane Addams told later how impressed she was with the "tact and training, [and] love of learning" of the settlement's educational program. She had marveled at the liberation and "deliverance" such education brought to those who had "been allowed to remain undeveloped and whose faculties are inert and sterile." [67]

Jane Addams understood how the social activities at Toynbee Hall expressed these educational ideals. The settlement emphasized "the social side of teaching, not only for the pleasure it gives, but that it may make learning possible. Intellectual life requires for its expansion and manifestation, the influence and assimilation of the interests and affections. . . ." Learning, Miss Addams said following Canon Barnett, "has to be diffused in a social atmosphere." There were classes at Toynbee Hall on literally hundreds of subjects—usually taught by nonresidents, paid or volunteer. There were clubs and societies without any formal academic purpose, and there were the athletic clubs. In addition, concerts, special lectures, exhibits, and art displays filled the Toynbee calendar. There were also frequent entertainments, which attempted to introduce East and West London people to each other. The intention was "to provide a meeting place where, simply and naturally, without conventional restraint and wearying etiquette, people may come to know each other's characters, thoughts, and beliefs." But far from the anticipated simplicity and naturalness, many Toynbee Hall social affairs were characterized by the most painful artificiality and restraint. The sudden

67. A projection of the university is in Toynbee Journal for 1886, cited by Picht, *Toynbee Hall*, p. 50. Jane Addams, "Outgrowths of Toynbee Hall," p. 9, SCPC. Barnett's ideas of education were described by R. H. Tawney, once a Toynbee Hall resident, cited in [Barnett], *Canon Barnett*, pp. 495–8.

breaking down of class barriers bred snobbery rather than cor-
recting it. One irreverent resident labeled these social efforts
" tea-cum-service-cum-politico-economic-religious punch and judy
shows." Toynbee Hall became the scene for a lot of " slumming
without tears "; visiting and partying with the poor became
modish and fashionable.[68]

Character, not social activities or social reform, was the highest
aim of Toynbee Hall. The moral qualities of character concerned
Canon Barnett most, and the activities at the settlement were
shaped to emphasize and cultivate moral qualities. Color-blind
himself, Canon Barnett delighted in lecturing and " explaining "
the pictures to crowds at the annual Whitechapel art exhibit.
" Secretly he regretted," wrote a resident who became director
of the Tate Gallery, " that all pictures could not be ethical
allegories. . . ." [69] Jane Addams appreciated the Canon's concern
for character and understood how he used the art displays for
this purpose. She explained to an audience in Chicago two years
later that settlements would " at least, keep fine pictures with a
didactic value from being shut up in rich men's houses, and put
them into popular galleries, as Toynbee Hall and the People's
Palace had done." [70]

The " People's Palace " was a large philanthropic institute in
East London. The philanthropic trust that constructed and operated the buildings had its offices in Toynbee Hall. The buildings
were opened in October, 1887. Facilities included a large library,
a gymnasium and pool, industrial workshops, club rooms, and a
large meeting hall. Fees were charged for classes and for some
exhibits and concerts. In its first year, more than one and a half
million people used the buildings, the majority of whom were

68. Jane Addams, " Outgrowths of Toynbee Hall," p. 9, SCPC; Pimlott, *Toynbee
Hall*, pp. 73, 75; [Barnett], *Canon Barnett*, p. 157.
69. Cited in [Barnett], *Canon Barnett*, p. 570.
70. Jane Addams, " Outgrowths of Toynbee Hall," p. 11, SCPC. Barnett's stress
on moralism prevented Toynbee Hall from attracting the more adventurous and
spirited university men after 1900. The Canon's individualism impeded his appreciation and co-operation with men whose methods and ideals were more social, like
the Fabians and labor unionists. After 1900 Toynbee Hall felt the cooling of
enthusiasm which was willing to take unlimited interest in the individual without
asking " whether it would not be more productive to give one's time to reforms
of administration, by which thousands could be helped." See Picht, *Toynbee Hall*,
p. 98.

between sixteen and twenty-five years old. There was no specific religious work done, and no special Sabbatarian restrictions.[71]

Jane Addams also learned about the university extension movement during her trip to London. In 1867, James Stuart, a Cambridge don, started delivering systematic lectures in northern England. His lectures attracted school teachers and workingmen. These were sanctioned as the equivalent of lectures given at Cambridge by that University in 1873 and by Oxford in 1878. The movement was advanced by the London Society for the Extension of University Teaching, founded in 1876. The year following Miss Addams' visit more than four hundred courses of local lectures were being offered to forty-one thousand men and women. Toynbee Hall, with its well-stocked library and reading rooms, and its connections with the universities, gave " a large place to university extension lectures . . . some of the most learned and eloquent men in England have lecture courses there," Jane Addams explained in 1890. The London Workingmen's College, another popular adult-education enterprise that she learned about, originated in lectures given by Frederick Denison Maurice in 1854 and developed into an organized college when Maurice established a series of classes to help educate the London working classes. Lecturers donated their services.[72]

All of these examples of how to deal with urban disorganization were the object of Jane Addams' attention in 1888. They formed the background of what came to be Hull House. But like so many European inspirations, they did not cross the Atlantic unaltered.

71. The most prominent Sabbath rule at Toynbee Hall prohibited tennis. Albert Shaw, " London Polytechnics and People's Palaces," *Century*, XL (June, 1890), 163–82. See also Robert A. Woods, *English Social Movements* (New York, 1891). Woods returned from London where he studied the same activities Jane Addams did to found Andover House, a settlement in Boston.

72. Jane Addams, " Outgrowths of Toynbee Hall," p. 10, SCPC. The standard history is William H. Draper, *University Extension, a Survey of Fifty Years, 1873–1923* (Cambridge, 1923). See also Herbert Baxter Adams, " University Extension in America," *Forum*, XI (July, 1891), 510–23.

CHAPTER III

HULL HOUSE—THE FIRST DECADE

*I gradually became convinced that it would be a good thing to
rent a house in a part of the city where many primitive and
actual needs are found, in which young women who had been
given over too exclusively to study, might restore a balance of
activity along traditional lines and learn of life from life itself.*

JANE ADDAMS, 1910

Jane Addams and Ellen Starr decided to establish a settlement
in Chicago. Toynbee Hall provided the example by which, and
against which, these young ladies defined their purposes. There
were different problems and obstacles in Chicago than in London.
Could unmarried young ladies use a device formed for university
men? How would they find support for such a project? Would
a settlement be useful? How could they justify moving into an
inconvenient immigrant neighborhood? In the earliest years after
Hull House opened in 1889, the Misses Addams and Starr stressed
the similarity between their own hopes and those which inspired
Toynbee Hall. Later in the nineties, however, they gradually
rejected the English model. Secular, scientific, and pragmatic
ideas displaced the piety with which Jane Addams had originally
justified Hull House. She rejected the inspiration of Ruskin and
Carlyle and their idea of an aristocratic, elite leadership. Miss
Addams came to believe that democracy was the faith that justified
settlements in America. The experiences of the first decade at
Hull House convinced her that a more thoroughgoing democracy
could solve many of the outstanding problems in American life.

In January, 1889, Jane Addams and Ellen Starr took an apart-
ment together in Chicago. They set about to define their intentions, to rally support, and to locate a place that would be suitable
for settling. Since Ellen Starr had taught art at the fashionable
Kirkland School, she knew her way to likely sources of aid. She
was able to arrange interviews with one of the most popular

ministers in Chicago, Dr. Frank W. Gunsaulus, who tested them by asking if their idea of a settlement was a " little training school where young ladies could be instructed how to deal with the poor." The Misses Addams and Starr protested strongly against this description of their idea. They were tired of institutions, they said, and they " simply intended to live there and get acquainted with the people and ask their friends of both classes to visit them. . . ." Dr. Gunsaulus immediately pledged his utmost aid by saying, according to Ellen Starr's report, " Good! The Kingdom of Heaven isn't an organization or an institution." [1]

With this initial success Jane Addams and Ellen Starr tried other religious sources of aid. They called on William M. Salter, the head of the Chicago Ethical Society (founded 1883), who pledged them his " unqualified support." The minister of Dwight L. Moody's church, Mr. Goss, made " all sorts of rash promises." Mr. Goss's brother-in-law, the pastor of the fashionable Fourth Presbyterian Church that Miss Addams attended regularly and in which she taught Sunday school, was anxious to have the prospective settlement located on Chicago's North side. " But we insisted that Dr. Gunsaulus had promised marvelous things for the South side." And Professor David Swing, whose heresy trial had forced his resignation from the pastorate of the same Fourth Presbyterian Church in 1875, promised " money and moral support " whenever needed. Promises of support for what was to become Hull House came from both orthodox and liberal religious sources. [2]

After discussing their plans with these ministers, Miss Addams and Miss Starr set out to study organized charity in Chicago. How did philanthropy work in the city? How would their idea fit in? Who would support a settlement? This early study was rewarded many times over by the wide variety of Chicagoans who supported Hull House, once it was operating. The Misses Addams and Starr got their first important introduction to the world of Chicago philanthropy from their work at the Armour Mission, a non-sectarian educational institution founded in 1886. Bessie Louise Pierce describes the Armour Mission as a " representative " philanthropy, which " provided educational opportunities—including a kindergarten, library, literary societies, and lectures, a free medi-

---

1. Ellen Gates Starr to Mary S. Blaisdell, February 23, [1889], Starr Papers.
2. Jane Addams to Mary Linn, February 26, 1889, April 1, 1889, SCPC.

cal dispensary, a kitchen garden, a sewing or workroom for women, nurseries and bathrooms." [3] Ellen Starr wrote to her sister that the people at the " Armour Mission fairly clamour " to have Jane Addams and herself settle near it. " But I am very much against that, and Jane says she is too. . . . We should simply be swallowed up in a great organization." [4] Both young women had met with the entire board of the Armour Mission in February to present their " scheme." It produced a mixed reaction. The older men tended to think they were vaporizing, Jane Addams wrote her family, but the younger men, especially a Mr. Allen B. Pond, " assured me that I had *voiced* something hundreds of young people in the city were trying to express, and that he could send us three young ladies at once who possessed both money and a knowledge of Herbert Spencer's ' Sociology ' but who are dying from inaction and restlessness." [5]

Search for support soon brought Jane Addams and Ellen Starr in contact with the large Chicago Woman's Club. Members of the club were eager to have a woman's settlement as a child of their club rather than an adjunct of some mission with a board of directors dominated by men. Mrs. J. D. Harvey, one of Miss Starr's acquaintances, called in mid-February to size up Jane Addams. She plunged directly into " the scheme," and after about half an hour of talk came to the point by asking Jane Addams if she wanted to be elected to the Woman's Club.

I told her I should be very glad indeed if it were possible to be elected. She said that they had 360 members too many and that they were trying to restrict it to the election of 1 new member a year. "I came to see you about that. I shouldn't wonder if you would be the one woman." I said that struck me as rather improbable as I was almost a stranger in Chicago. She said " that doesn't make any difference if *I* want you, I am a pretty important member of that club." [6]

Under the powerful sponsorship of Mrs. Harvey, Jane Addams and Ellen Starr were invited that same week to address the Phil-

3. Bessie Louise Pierce, *A History of Chicago*, Vol. III: *The Rise of a Modern City, 1871–1893* (New York, 1957), p. 442.
4. Ellen Gates Starr to Mary S. Blaisdell, February 23, [1889], Starr Papers.
5. Jane Addams to Mary Addams Linn, February 12, 1889, SCPC.
6. Jane Addams to Mary Addams Linn, February 19, 1889, SCPC.

anthropy Committee of the Chicago Woman's Club. Miss Addams spoke and was very well received. The committee later reported to the entire club that " adequate praise cannot be given for the high order of philanthropic work being carried out by . . . Miss Addams and Miss Starr. . . . We strenuously urge all to make it a first duty to become better acquainted with their aims and methods." [7] Endorsement by this committee eventually brought both financial aid and, more important, volunteers to Hull House.

Jane Addams and Ellen Starr also explained their plans to two other women's organizations. The Woman's Christian Temperance Union gave them a polite hearing but only vague promises of support. The Chicago chapter of the Association of Collegiate Alumnae (later the American Association of University Women) was more enthusiastic. After listening to Jane Addams' appeal for assistance, the chapter appointed a committee to provide the project with whatever help it could give.[8]

This search for respectable and fashionable sources of aid was balanced by investigation in a somewhat different direction. In early February, 1889, a man active in city missionary work whom the Misses Addams and Starr had met while visiting an urban mission took them to a Sunday school in the Bohemian quarter, about an hour's ride from Jane Addams' Sunday school at the Fourth Presbyterian Church. The school was conducted by a Mr. Adams who had been a missionary in Prague for ten years. In Chicago on furlough, he was so appalled by the degradation of the Bohemians that he decided to remain in the city. The following Sunday, Jane Addams taught the day's lesson to the only English-speaking class. She reported to her family how " hearing Bohemian all around one created just as ' foreign ' an atmosphere as I ever felt in Europe." [9]

From this beginning, Miss Addams went father afield. As Ellen Starr graphically put it, " Jane thirsts very much for the Anarchists. She is going to hunt up their Sunday schools." About three weeks

7. Cited in Henriette Greenbaum Frank and Amalie Hofer Jerome (comps.), *Annals of the Chicago Woman's Club for the First Forty Years of Its Organization, 1876–1916* (Chicago, 1916), p. 76.

8. Jane Addams to Mary Addams Linn, April 1, 1889, SCPC; Marion Talbot and Lois Kimball Mathews Roseberry, *The History of the American Association of University Women, 1881–1931* (Boston & New York, 1931), p. 108.

9. Jane Addams to Mary Addams Linn, February 19, 1889, SCPC.

later, having first " gotten a letter of introduction to a Mr. Stauber one of the leading anarchists," Jane Addams went to visit one of these anarchist Sunday schools. She found, she wrote, " about two hundred children assembled in a hall back of a saloon with some young men trying to teach them ' free thought without any religion or politics,' the entire affair was quite innocent. I was treated with great politeness and may take a class—it seems to me an opportunity to do a great deal of good—it was all in German." [10]

Besides teaching various Sunday schools, Miss Addams accompanied truant agents on their rounds to discover the areas of the city where school absenteeism was highest. She also was escorted to areas of particularly heavy need by relief officers from the Charity Organization Society.

All these efforts show how, in a few short months, two young women were able to marshal support for their idea of a settlement in Chicago. They gained the endorsement of religious sources, of Chicagoans connected with charitable institutions, of women's organizations, and of those already working almost anonymously in immigrant neighborhoods.

Ellen Starr credited her partner with defining and explaining the purposes of their joint enterprise. She modestly wrote Jane Addams' family how Miss Addams resented " my putting myself out of it in any way. Still I am unwilling to let people suppose that I would ever have worked it out. . . . Jane's idea," she continued, " which she puts very much to the front and on no account will give up," was that those who chose to live in a foreign quarter would benefit far more than the neighbors. " She has worked this out of her own experience and ill health." While recovering from her spinal operation, Jane Addams discovered that taking care of children did not tire her, while small social demands used her up completely. In Baltimore, " after a lecture or a social evening she would feel quite exhausted . . . but after a morning with the colored people in the Johns Hopkins home, she was actually physically better than if she had stayed in bed. . . . Nervous people do not crave rest," Miss Starr summarized, " but activity of a certain kind." [11]

10. Ellen Gates Starr to Mary S. Blaisdell, February 23, [1889], Starr Papers; Jane Addams to Mary Addams Linn, March 13, 1889, Stephenson County Historical Museum.

11. Ellen Gates Starr to Mary S. Blaisdell, February 23, [1889], Starr Papers.

This idea—that charitable service might be therapy for nervously exhausted young ladies—was the one that seemed most newsworthy to people reporting " the scheme." Four months before Hull House opened, when Jane Addams and Ellen Starr were learning about Chicago charities and soliciting support for Hull House, a report entitled " A Chicago Toynbee Hall " appeared in Lucy Stone's *Woman's Journal*.

> One of the chief aims [of Hull House] will be to make it also a retreat for *other* young women who need rest and change, or who desire a safe retreat from the inordinate demands of society, and in whom it is believed that a glimpse of the reverse side of life, of the poverty and struggle of half of the people, will beget a broader philanthropy and a tenderer sympathy, and leave less time and inclination for selfish ambition, or for real or fancied invalidism.[12]

A Chicago clubwoman recounts the beginning of Hull House thus:

> " I remember very well when Miss Addams first brought her plan to our club. I was hurrying from one committee to another, when some one came to walk beside me and began to talk. I paid very little attention until I caught the word: ' A place for invalid girls to go and help the poor.'
> " Now the idea of invalid girls helping the poor! I turned in my astonishment to face a frail, sensitive girl. She looked anything but the reforming extremist type.
> " ' Suppose we sit down and talk about it,' I said. And we did. She told me her plan: to find a neighborhood where help was needed, to live there herself and to muster to her aid such girls as were without a vital interest. You know she had a physiological, psychological theory on that subject, which I still believe is true.' "[13]

The psychological insight which prompted Jane Addams to evolve the plan for Hull House was a part of her fuller critique

12. Leila G. Bedell, " A Chicago Toynbee Hall," *Woman's Journal*, XX (May 25, 1889), 162; my emphasis.
13. Anne Forsyth, " What Jane Addams Has Done for Chicago, a Fight for the Betterment of a Great City," *Delineator*, LXX (October, 1907), 493.

of the responsibilities and failures of college women. They were, she believed, confused about their proper role because there were conflicts between family expectations and the results of college training. So long as the daughter was regarded solely as an inspiration and refinement to the family itself and there was no recognition of "the entity of woman's life beyond the family," the finishing school was quite adequate.[14] After women's colleges were started, the family acquiesced in the ideal of college education without realizing what it meant. At college, a girl's individuality was recognized "quite apart from family or society claims, and she received the sort of training which for many years has been deemed successful for highly developing a man's individuality and freeing his powers for independent action."[15] This education contradicted the family's expectations because the daughter was educated to recognize a social stress and duty outside the family. The college-trained girl was wounded when the family failed to appreciate this duty and asserted authority and control in fields that belonged to her adult judgment outside the home.

When the college woman returned home to the narrower and more concrete claims of the family she had to repress her college training. "She either hides her hurt, and splendid reserves of enthusiasm and capacity go to waste, or her zeal and emotions are turned inward, and the result is an unhappy woman, whose vitality is consumed by vain regrets and desires."[16] The situation, Miss Adams believed, was not simply a conflict between affection for family and trained intellectual convictions. The social claim learned at college was a demand upon the emotions as well as the intellect; the college-trained woman's emotional nature was divided against itself. "When her health gives way under this strain, as it often does, her physician invariably advises a rest." But what she really needed, according to Jane Addams, was "simple health-giving activity, which shall mean a response to all of the claims which she so keenly feels, and which shall involve the use of all her faculties." During her schooling the girl was isolated from "contact with the feebleness of childhood, the

14. Jane Addams, "The College Woman and the Family Claim," *The Commons*, III (September, 1898), 3.
15. *Ibid.*, pp. 3–4.
16. *Ibid.*, p. 4.

pathos of suffering or the needs of old age." Her faculties were trained solely for accumulation, and she learned to " distrust utterly the most human impulses of her nature which would naturally have connected her with the humanity outside of her family and her own immediate social circle." [17]

Hull House offered a solution to these problems. It provided " great opportunities for helpfulness "; it connected wealthy young people with " the starvation struggle, which makes up the life of at least half of the race." For those who had been " cultivated into unnourished, over-sensitive lives " Hull House offered " common labor " which was the great source of " moral and physical health." Miss Addams stressed the usefulness of the settlement, and then noted that " the sense of uselessness and impotence, Huxley declares, is the severest shock the human mind can sustain. . . ." The settlement offered young people the chance " of putting theory into action," of going " where the race most needs aid." If it was natural " to feed the hungry and care for the sick, it is certainly natural to give pleasure to the young and to minister to the deep-seated craving for social intercourse all men feel." [18]

Jane Addams and Ellen Starr always insisted that they had no planned activities when they moved into the house they later named Hull House. [19] The settlement's program evolved gradually. Certainly one of the important concerns of these two young ladies in September, 1889, must have been to explain their motives to their new neighbors, who doubtless wondered why the well-to-do girls had come to South Halsted Street. The first formal activity at Hull House was a reading party. One evening a week, the neighbors were invited in after supper to hear George Eliot's *Romola* read aloud. They chose this novel, perhaps, to appeal to the large number of Italians who lived in the neighborhood. Photographs of Florence, brought back from the 1888 trip, decorated the walls of Hull House. These photographs, and the Misses

17. *Ibid.*, p. 5.
18. Jane Addams, " Outgrowths of Toynbee Hall," pp. 3–5, 8, SCPC; Jane Addams, " A New Impulse to an Old Gospel," *Forum*, XIV (November, 1892), 353, 358.
19. " Miss Culver [Charles J. Hull's heir and owner of 335 S. Halsted St.] has given us the house rent free for four years, amounting to $2880, and we have decided to call the house Hull House. Connect these two facts in any delicate way your refined imagination suggests." Ellen Gates Starr to Mary S. Blaisdell, December 19, 1890, Starr Papers.

Addams' and Starr's fluency in Italian, testified that the ladies appreciated Italian culture.

By using *Romola* as the initial approach to the neighborhood, Miss Addams and Miss Starr shared their literary enthusiasm and also tried to show why they had moved to South Halsted Street. There are many relevant and revealing parallels between the motives of this fictional heroine and the motives of Jane Addams and Ellen Starr. In the novel Romola is inspired to a life of self-sacrificing service among city poor in the first instance by religious devotion. In joining the church as an adult, Romola " thought little about dogmas. . . . She had . . . entered into communion with the Church because in this way she had found an immediate satisfaction of moral needs that all the previous culture and experience in her life had left hungering . . . her submissive uses of all offices of the Church was simply a watching and waiting if by any means fresh strength might come." As a result of her religious commitment, Romola starts to visit and care for the sick and poor, a job for which she had " no innate taste . . . like some women. . . . Her early training had kept her aloof from such womanly labors; and if she had not brought to them the inspiration of her deepest feelings, they would have been irksome to her. But they had come to be the one unshakable resting-place of her mind." She submitted her mind to the Church—represented in the novel by Savonarola—because his preaching constantly showed how these immediate duties fitted into the " wide end of universal regeneration." This was the start of a reason for living for Romola, aside from personal enjoyment or personal affection.[20]

Romola's faith in Savonarola is shattered and she experiences a " new baptism " which is expressed in the language of positivism. " The common life," " the new life of duty," " simple human fellowship as a strongly-felt bond," " the general lot exalted into religious duty " are the phrases which Eliot used in the latter part of the novel.[21] Renewal for Romola comes in a plague-stricken village away from Florence where she " had simply lived, with so energetic an impulse to share the life around her, to answer the call of need and do the work which cried aloud to be done, that the reasons for living, enduring, laboring

20. George Eliot, *Romola* (Chicago, 1885), pp. 365, 366.
21. *Ibid.*, pp. 471, 429, 338, 441.

never took the form of argument." Romola points up the moral of the novel: " It is only a poor sort of happiness that could ever come by caring very much about our own narrow pleasures. We can only have the highest happiness . . . by having wide thoughts, and much feeling for the rest of the world as well as ourselves." [22]

By using *Romola*, Jane Addams and Ellen Starr could illustrate their humanitarian motive yet avoid the language of religious evangelicalism. If anything, Eliot's novel denigrates the Church by emphasizing its authoritarian and superstitious characteristics. *Romola* provides an undogmatic, untheological explanation for humanitarian service. Yet the novel does not deny the religious motive. *Romola* provided the Misses Addams and Starr with an alternative to Protestant evangelical religious language, an important consideration since the Hull House neighborhood in 1889 was more than 90 per cent Roman Catholic.

If Jane Addams and Ellen Starr avoided using an evangelical vocabulary to their neighbors, they did not hesitate to use it to other friends. In a letter to her sister Alice in March, 1889, Jane Addams enclosed a circular describing the College Settlement Association's plan to open a settlement in New York City. " We are modest enough to think that ours is better, is more distinctively Christian and less Social Science." [23] Publicity about the settlement before it opened left no doubt about the piety of its founders.[24] And Miss Addams wrote her partner that she regarded the settlement scheme as a chance to " work out a salvation." [25] Ellen Starr envisioned Hull House as a specifically religious undertaking. Two days before they moved in, she described Jane Addams' beautiful spiritual life and how the plan for Hull House depended on this spirituality. " It is as if she simply diffused something which came from outside herself of which she is the lumin-

22. *Ibid.*, pp. 527, 546.
23. Jane Addams to Alice Addams Haldeman, March 13, 1889, Stephenson County Historical Society.
24. " Is this home [Hull House] to be a place for Christian instruction? Not distinctively so, any more than an Art Institute or a Manual Training School, but truly so, as every home of living disciples of the Lord is such." Mary H. Porter, " A Home on Halsted Street," *Advance* (Chicago), XXIII (July 11, 1889), 500. " The House belongs to the people for all days excepting the Sabbath, when these two weary but unwearied workers rest by worshipping in near churches and aiding in such church-school work as seems to them most requiring assistance." The Rev. J. Forthingham, " The Toynbee Idea," *Interior*, August 7, 1890.
25. Jane Addams to Ellen Gates Starr, January 24, 1889, Starr Papers.

ous medium and I suppose that is precisely what she does do. . . . I don't know how, just at this point, how I should live on my life without her. I couldn't do *this* without her, and I couldn't very well *not* do it. O, my dear, as I told you, I need the outside brace and I've been very mercifully provided with it." [26]

A year's experience at Hull House only deepened Miss Addams' religious convictions. In 1890, she wrote to her stepbrother, " We have seen a great deal of suffering and want this winter and the comfort of Christ's mission to the world—the mind of the Messiah to the race, has been impressed upon me as never before. It seems sometimes as if the race life, at least the dark side, would be quite unendurable if it were not for that central fact." These expressions of concern were not divorced from conventional religious exercise. For the first several years, " Jane Addams led in evening Bible and prayer with everyone on their knees "; and there were regular evening devotions. [27]

Jane Addams made her most enthusiastic evangelical appeal in 1896 when she wrote an explanation of settlement work for the Woman's Christian Temperance Union. She reminded the ladies of the white ribbon that Christ himself had employed a variety of methods. He chose to reveal himself as the Messiah for the first time in accepting a drink from the Samaritan woman, who would today be known as a member of the semi-criminal class. " A simple acceptance of Christ's message and methods is what a settlement should stand for," wrote Jane Addams. The Saviour " intrusted the salvation of the world to a handful of people in whom He aroused a sense of humanity and a conscious- ness of identification with its weakness and sins. He first gave to the twelve young men three years of education; but He added to His marvelous instruction daily association with the lowliest." [28]

By the end of the first decade at Hull House, this religious vocabulary and enthusiasm had become muted in Jane Addams' writing. And with the gradual decline of religious interest came

26. Ellen Starr to Mary E. Allen, September 15, 1889, Starr Papers.
27. The pattern of Toynbee Hall was followed here. No formal religious instruction was permitted, although religious groups could use the rooms. Jane Addams to George Haldeman, December 21, 1890, Stephenson County Historical Museum; Edward L. Burchard to Ellen Gates Starr, January 16, 1938, Starr Papers; Residents' Meeting Minute Book, entry for November 25, 1893, Hull House.
28. Jane Addams, " The Objects of Social Settlements," *Union Signal*, XXII (March 5, 1896), 149.

a more fervent articulation of democratic ideals. The first ten years at Hull House produced a final rejection of the aristocratic models of reform and a gradual abandonment of the vocabulary—and perhaps belief in—religion. There were several reasons for this change toward a more radically equalitarian democratic ideal. Miss Addams discovered differences between the Hull House neighborhood and the Toynbee Hall neighborhood which caused her to reconsider and reject the elitist ideas of English settlements. New residents introduced new ideas and motivations into Hull House activities. Events in the neighborhood and increased knowledge of her neighbors convinced her that her religious motives were interfering with the aims and purposes of the settlement.

Jane Addams gained a new understanding of her neighbors through the brilliantly successful social life at Hull House.[29] There are several explanations for the social accomplishments of the Chicago settlement, which stand in sharp contrast to the failure of similar efforts at Toynbee Hall. The founders of Hull House possessed unusual social tact and sensitivity. They achieved the friendship and understanding of their neighbors rapidly. Jane Addams' unusual ability to enter sympathetically into the experiences of others accounted for much of this success. According to almost universal testimony, Miss Addams was able to appreciate others' points of view without necessarily agreeing with them, and without coercing others toward her own evaluation of those experiences. Francis Hackett, writer and student of nationalism, a Hull House resident in 1906 and 1907, said twenty years later that Jane Addams " had the power to value human beings, to appreciate them, and to feel in terms of them. I do not mean to manipulate them. . . .[30] Miss Addams could apparently sympathize, understand, and evaluate ideas, experiences, ideals, and emotions that were not her own.

Hull House was the institutional expression of Jane Addams' openness to all kinds of ideas and experiences. As one woman put it, " genuine freedom of mind and friendliness of spirit are what have made Hull House possible and are what will decide its future after the day of the great woman who has mothered it

29. During its first year of operation, an average of a thousand people a week came to Hull House, double that number the second.

30. Francis Hackett, " Hull House—A Souvenir," *Survey*, LIV (June 1, 1925), 277.

and around whom it revolves." Few other settlement workers
possessed Miss Addams' readiness to listen to and sympathize with
as wide a spectrum of people and causes. She not only had a
" sense of being identified with others, but also gives others the
sense of being identified with her. This constitutes her democracy
and makes her its most prophetic interpreter." [31]

Miss Addams soon discovered that the Hull House neighborhood differed from what she had seen in East London in ways
that made the assumptions of the English settlements inapplicable.
The condition of the poor was less degraded in Chicago. " There
are also fewer people who expect to remain poor, and they are less
strictly confined to their own districts." Sanitary conditions and
housing were better than in many other cities. Hull House appealed to regularly employed, self-supporting workmen, rather
than to the unemployed and unemployable. These workingmen
neither needed nor wanted charity. " The require only that their
aspirations be recognized and stimulated and the means of attaining them put at their disposal. Hull House makes a constant
effort to secure these means. . . ." The settlement had a particular
appeal, Miss Addams noted, for " people of former education and
opportunity who have cherished ambition and prospects," but
who, for various reasons, had been unable to fulfill them.[32]

During the first decade at Hull House, Jane Addams found that
her original settlement ideals of religion and elite reform inter-
fered with her neighbors' expectations and hopes. She therefore
discarded these principles and replaced them with more democratic
ones firmly rooted in the lives of her immigrant neighbors. Less
than a year after Hull House opened, Miss Addams condescend-
ingly described the

advantage Chicago has over English cities, . . . [in that]
many of the poorest people are foreigners. They are Euro-

31. Ida M. Tarbell, *The Business of Being a Woman* (New York, 1919),
p. 104; Graham Taylor, " Jane Addams—Interpreter, an Appreciation," *Review
of Reviews*, XL (December, 1909), 680.
32. Jane Addams, " Hull-House, Chicago: an Effort toward Social Democracy,"
Forum, XIV (October, 1892), 229–30, 241. The story is told—perhaps truthfully—
that the first person to return the Misses Addams' and Starr's neighborhood call
was Mrs. Mary Pepper Murphey, a graduate in 1864 of Chicago's first high school.
To people like Mrs. Murphey, who already had a good education, Hull House
must have represented a revival of intellectual aspirations long neglected and dulled.
See Edith A. Brown, " Jane Addams and Her Work," *Pilgrim*, VIII (January,
1904), 3–5.

pean peasants direct from the soil. It is much easier to deal with the first generation of crowded city life, than with the second and third. It is more natural, and cast in a simpler mould. . . . Hull House found no precedent at Toynbee Hall for dealing with this foreign life, but one thing seemed clear: to conserve and keep for them whatever of value their past life contained, and to bring them in contact with a better class of Americans.

By 1892 this pride of class had already been shaken as Miss Addams conceded that Hull House residents found " in themselves a constantly increasing tendency to consult their neighbors in the advisability of each new undertaking." [33]

Jane Addams found unsuspected cultural resources among her immigrant neighbors. Immigrants from Greece used the Hull House theater to stage Aeschylus and Sophocles, to the astonishment of the entire city of Chicago. Other Greek immigrants, well-versed in philosophy, established the Hull House Plato Club; on one occasion John Dewey was confounded by the philosophical knowledge of the club members. She soon learned that many Italian and German immigrants knew and loved Dante, Schiller, and Goethe. The Hull House neighborhood contained talented immigrant craftsmen whose abilities had been ignored. Miss Addams discovered how much her neighbors loved to sing and with what pleasure they danced. She found her immigrant neighbors equal to many and superior to some Americans in their love of and respect for learning, and in their enthusiasm for drama, art, literature, and music. Her initial assumption that young college women possessed cultural superiority gave way.

Miss Addams was pushed toward the abandonment of her original religious conviction by the arrival at Hull House of residents whose motives were secular and scientific. Mrs. Florence Kelley, who came to Hull House in late December, 1891, was " the toughest customer in the reform riot, the finest rough-and-tumble fighter for the good life for others, that Hull House ever knew." [34] Mrs. Kelley had divorced her husband and resumed her maiden name. She first boarded her three children with the

33. Jane Addams, " Outgrowths of Toynbee Hall," pp. 12–3; Jane Addams, " Hull-House, Chicago: an Effort toward Social Democracy," p. 237.
34. Linn, *Jane Addams*, pp. 138–9.

Henry Demarest Lloyds, then with Mrs. Russell Wright, the mother of Frank Lloyd Wright and sister of the liberal Unitarian minister, Jenkin Lloyd Jones. Mrs. Kelley started and supervised the long series of scientific investigations which made the Hull House neighborhood a carefully studied social unit. These studies included a chemical analysis of immigrant diet for the U.S. Department of Agriculture, a chapter in the federal Labor Department's 1893 investigation of city slums, a study of the saloon for the *American Journal of Sociology*, a study of the Italian community for the U.S. Bureau of Labor, and some good studies of municipal organization.[35] This scientific interest culminated in the publication in 1895 of *Hull-House Maps and Papers, a Presentation of Nationalities and Wages in a Congested District of Chicago, Together with Comments and Essays on Problems Growing Out of the Social Conditions.* Essays by Hull House residents in this volume dealt with the sweating system, wage-earning children, studies of the Chicago ghetto, the Bohemians, the Italian colony, Cook County charities, "Art and Labor," by Ellen Gates Starr, and "The Settlement as a Factor in the Labor Movement," by Jane Addams.[36]

Mrs. Kelley's interest in the scientific description of social conditions reflected her doctrinaire economic views. She was a socialist and had translated Friedrich Engels' *Condition of the Working Class in England in 1884* into English. "I hold," she wrote to Henry Demarest Lloyd, "to the whole platform of the socialist labor party the world over, that is, the International Socialist Party." Florence Kelley was capable of withering disdain when faced with what she considered sentimental reformers. Eve-

35. W. O. Atwater and A. P. Bryant, *Dietary Studies in Chicago, 1895 and 1896, Conducted with the Cooperation of Jane Addams and Caroline L. Hunt. . . .,* U.S. Department of Agriculture, Office of Experiment Station Bulletin No. 55 (Washington, 1898); "The Slums of Baltimore, Chicago, New York, and Philadelphia," in U.S. Bureau of Labor, *Seventh Special Report of the Commissioner of Labor* (Washington, 1894); "The Italians of Chicago, a Social and Economic Study," in U.S. Bureau of Labor, *Ninth Special Report of the Commissioner of Labor* (Washington, 1897); E. C. Moore, "The Social Value of the Saloon," *American Journal of Sociology,* III (July, 1897), 1–12; see articles by George Hooker on municipal affairs in *Outlook,* LII (September 7, 1895), 382–3; *ibid.,* LIV (October 17, 1896), 685–6; and in *Review of Reviews,* XV (April, 1897), 437–41; *ibid.,* XIX (May, 1899), 575–8.

36. The book is more felicitously written than its title, hereafter cited as *Hull-House Maps and Papers.*

ning prayers disappeared after Mrs. Kelley came to Hull House, and an anonymous writer described her " infinite scorn " of the churches.[37] After Governor John Peter Altgeld secured passage of state legislation regulating the hours and working conditions in specified industries, he offered the position of inspector under the act to Henry D. Lloyd. In refusing (in order to complete *Wealth Against Commonwealth*) Lloyd recommended Mrs. Kelley and Altgeld accepted his suggestion.[38] Her previous investigations stood her in good stead as factory inspector. Backed by the machinery of state government, she actively investigated industrial conditions and prosecuted offenders. Mrs. Kelley's efforts acquainted Jane Addams with reform efforts inspired by secular and scientific motives.

Increasing interest in scientific studies brought a closer relationship between Hull House and the men in the country's first Department of Sociology at the new University of Chicago: Albion W. Small, G. H. Mead, and C. R. Henderson. These lively scholars, and the journal they started in 1895, insisted on the reciprocal relationship between reform and social science, between reformers and social scientists. In the first volume of the *American Journal of Sociology*, the editor, Albion Small, wrote on " Scholarship and Social Agitation." He claimed that scholarship had to " either abandon claims to the function of leadership, and accept the purely clerical role of recording and classifying the facts of the past, or scholarship must accept the responsibility of prevision and prophecy and progress." An active role in planning and effecting reform would " exalt " both scholarship and citizenship, he wrote. " The most impressive lesson which I have learned in the vast sociological laboratory which the city of Chicago constitutes is that action, not speculation, is the supreme teacher." [39] Small offered to publish anything Jane Addams might

37. Friedrich Engels, *Condition of the Working Class in England in 1844*, trans. Florence Kelley Wischewetzky (New York [*ca.* 1887]). Florence Kelley to Henry Demarest Lloyd, June 18, 1896, Lloyd Papers, State Historical Society of Wisconsin; " The Civic Life of Chicago," *Review of Reviews*, XIII (August, 1893), 180.

38. Mrs. Kelley recalled that Lloyd was the man who had recommended her for the job in her " Autobiographical Essays " in the *Survey* in 1926-7. See " I Go To Work," *Survey*, LVIII (June 1, 1927), 273; for a different view see Eugene Staley, *History of the Illinois State Federation of Labor* (Chicago, 1930), p. 105.

39. Albion W. Small, " Scholarship and Social Agitation," *American Journal of Sociology*, I (1895-6), 567, 581-2.

care to submit, although he could give only token payment.⁴⁰

More important to the development of Jane Addams' thought than these men, however, was her close friendship after 1894 with the chairman of the university's Department of Philosophy, Psychology, and Pedagogy, John Dewey. While still at the University of Michigan, Dewey had visited Hull House to speak on " Psychology and History." He wrote to tell Jane Addams of his " indebtedness " for his visit. "While I did not see much of any particular thing, I think I got a pretty good idea of the general spirit and methods. Every day I stayed there only added to my conviction that you had taken the right way. I am confident that twenty-five years from now the forces now turned in upon themselves . . . will be finding outlet very largely through just such channels as you have opened up." ⁴¹ Dewey was a frequent visitor at Hull House after he came to the University of Chicago. He became a member of the Hull House Board of Trustees when the " fatal moment " of incorporation came in 1895. Dewey came to the settlement house to share his enthusiasms and ideas with his close personal friend Jane Addams and also to learn where his ideas and enthusiasms were misguided. " I wish to take back what I said the other night," he once wrote her. " I'm glad I found this out before I began to talk on social psychology as otherwise I fear I should have made a mess of it. This is rather a suspiciously sudden conversion, but it's only a beginning." ⁴²

40. Small did publish an article by Jane Addams in the first volume of his journal, see her " A Belated Industry," *American Journal of Sociology*, I (March, 1896), 536–50. Miss Addams later identified herself professionally with these sociologists. In 1908 she wrote of her attendance at the American Sociological Association: " I simply have to take care of my professional interests once in a while and this little trip was full of inspiration." See Jane Addams to Alice Addams Haldeman, January 7, 1908, Deloach Deposit, SCPC. Weber Linn tells the story of how the University of Chicago faculty voted Jane Addams an honorary degree. Her close friends Mead and Small hurried to Hull House to tell her in advance of confirmation by the board of trustees. Returning later, with tears in their eyes according to Linn, they had to report the trustees' refusal of the faculty recommendation. Linn, *Jane Addams*, p. 160.

41. John Dewey to Jane Addams, January 27, 1892, Frank A. White Papers, Rockford College Archives.

42. Hull House incorporation is characterized as fatal in Jane Addams' invitation to Mary Rozet Smith to become a member of the board, March 26, 1895, SCPC. The board was made up of women afraid of being sentimental and therefore tending to be hard-boiled, and businessmen who were afraid of being hard-boiled and therefore tending to be sentimental; its real purpose was " to say to Miss

The educational efforts at Hull House from which John Dewey learned and which he helped inspire are the subject of the following chapter. Yet Jane Addams' adoption of Dewey's pragmatic ideas and vocabulary must be emphasized at this point. Dewey's emphasis on experiment, experience, and democracy helped displace the original religious and aristocratic motives which had inspired Jane Addams to settle on South Halsted Street.

The displacement of old motives and the development of newer, more pragmatic, more democratic ones became especially marked in Miss Addams' thought after 1894. The severe depression of 1893–4 forced her to take a hard look at all the assumptions and motives of charitable work, especially the established method of relief, charitable visiting. Then in 1894 Jane Addams served on a citizens' arbitration board which tried to mediate the Pullman strike. The failure of this arbitration attempt led her to analyze and compare the motives of the labor movement with Mr. Pullman's philanthropies in his model town of Pullman. During the same period, the political corruption in the Hull House ward—the nineteenth—aroused the residents of the settlement to try to unseat their incumbent alderman. Three unsuccessful aldermanic campaigns convinced Jane Addams that patrician political reformers were, like charity visitors and philanthropic capitalists, basically undemocratic. By 1900 her experience with the depression, the Pullman strike, and the political battles in the Nineteenth Ward had led her to evolve a new and significant ideal

---

Addams, what her friends have always said: ' You are right; go ahead.' " Paul U. Kellogg, " Twice Twenty Years at Hull House; with some Reflections on Neighborhood Work in the United States," *Survey,* LXIV (June 15, 1930), 266. John Dewey to Jane Addams, October 12, 1898, SCPC. Jane M. Dewey—named for Miss Addams—prepared a biography of her father under his direction in 1939 in which she said, " Dewey's faith in democracy as a guiding force in education took on both a sharper and a deeper meaning because of Hull House and Jane Addams." See Paul Arthur Schilpp (ed.), *The Philosophy of John Dewey* (New York, [1939] 1951), p. 30. It is interesting to note that Dewey, like Jane Addams, early analyzed the health of college women. See his " Education and the Health of Woman," *Science,* VI (October 16, 1885), 341–2; " Health and Sex in Higher Education," *Popular Science Monthly,* XXVIII (1886), 606–14; both cited in Lewis S. Feuer, " John Dewey and the Back to the People Movement in American Thought," *Journal of the History of Ideas,* XX (1959), 545–68. Another interesting parallel is in Dewey's description of his educational ideal in *School and Society* (Chicago, 1899), p. 24. He emphasized, in a slightly different context, that Jane Addams got at Rockford, " the idea of responsibility, of obligation to do something, to produce something in the world."

of progressive democracy. She substituted a pragmatic " religion of democracy " for her earlier kind of religion.

By December, 1893, the depression in Chicago had deepened seriously. Crowds of unskilled laborers, originally attracted to the city by the prospect of employment at the World's Fair, were stranded and without jobs. The Hull House tradition against dispensing relief crumbled in the face of the extraordinary distress of that winter. Yet for all the physical suffering, Jane Addams emphasized another aspect of the depression. In a symposium entitled " What Shall We Do for Our Unemployed? " held by the mugwump Sunset Club she urged her listeners to take the unemployed into their confidence. " They are men; they have practical ideas; they would be glad to do their share to remove this trouble of which they are the chief victims. We ought to come together and regard it as a common trouble, and we should consider not what we shall do with the unemployed, but what shall we and the unemployed do together, that we may all as brothers grow out into a wider and better citizenship than we have ever had." [43] This insistence that charity had to be made democratic, that the social life of the city in all its aspects had to be made increasingly democratic, was the first lesson of the severe depression winter.

Miss Addams' idea of democratic charity was not put into practice, however. An Emergency Relief Association—made up of " the better elements "—was formed and Jane Addams served on the committee to assist the physical needs of the unemployed.[44] In the general distress Hull House set up a small labor exchange which rather unsuccessfully tried to locate jobs, and the house broke its long-standing prohibition against distributing coal, food,

43. Jane Addams, "What Shall We Do for Our Unemployed?" *Sunset Club* [*of Chicago*] *Yearbook* (1893/1894), p. 82.

44. Jane Addams' labors on the Committee for the Distribution of Supplies in Kind is recorded in Central Relief Association [of Chicago], *Report to the* [*Chicago*] *Civic Federation, to Its Contributors, and to the Public* (Chicago, 1894). Money spent by the Association was expended " upon the condition that able-bodied men receiving food and lodging shall render an equivalent therefore in labor . . . ," p. 9. " I resigned from the street cleaning committee in despair of making the rest of the committee understand that, as our real object was not street cleaning but the help of the unemployed . . . it was better to have the men work half a day at seventy-five cents than a whole day for a dollar, better that they should earn three dollars in two days than in three days," Addams, *Twenty Years at Hull-House*, p. 161.

and clothing as direct relief. In 1910 Jane Addams recalled the experiences of this winter. She was driven to do the " most serious economic reading I have ever done." In addition, she wrote, it " was also during this winter that I became permanently impressed with the kindness of the poor to each other." [45] The poor themselves contributed the largest amounts of poor relief. Their charity was simple and true, not because it sprang from piety, but because it was democratic.

Miss Addams developed a full critique of urban charities based on this democratic standard. She especially criticized the abuses that crept into charity inspired by religious belief. The Christmas message of good will, Miss Addams observed in 1898, had gradually become institutionalized until it required a distinct effort " to remember that what the message proclaimed above all, was fuller human relations and an untrammeled fellowship; that the message implied democracy rather than philanthropy." So often, she complained, Christmas celebrations widened the space between the classes. Newspaper appeals, in order to excite pity for particular cases, degraded all humanity by sensational stories. These stories were recklessly overstated; they held up the exceptional as the habitual. " Let us not acknowledge that we are divided into two classes, even in order to make a plea that the superior class should overlook the differences at Christmas time. To accent in any way the sense of separation even when done in the name of Philanthropy is to postpone the final realization of the common life." [46]

No relation was changing more rapidly than the charitable relation, Jane Addams wrote in a long article for the *Atlantic* in 1899. The charity visitor—the characteristic feature of the conservative Charity Organization Society movement—was growing perplexed and confused at certain inconsistencies.[47] Miss Addams summarized conservative doctrine about charity in the following way:

45. *Ibid.*, pp. 161, 162.
46. Jane Addams, " Christmas Fellowship," *Unity*, XLII (December 22, 1898), 308.
47. Jane Addams, " The Subtle Problems of Charity," *Atlantic*, LXXXIII (February, 1899), 163–78. The standard work here is Frank Dekker Watson, *The Charity Organization Movement in the United States, a Study in American Philanthropy* (New York, 1922); for a modern appraisal of the inadequacies of this movement see Robert H. Bremner, *From the Depths, The Discovery of Poverty in the United States* (New York, 1956), especially Chapter IX.

the charity visitor was taught that poverty was the result of individual vices or laziness; prosperity—her own and that of others—was the sign of virtue. Thus charity visitors exhorted men to be virtuous, sober, punctual, industrious, thrifty, and saving. Few of these leisured charity workers were self-supporting, yet they proclaimed the virtues of self-support. Few of the visitors were judged solely on their ability to make money, and yet this was the sole test they applied to the poor. This clearly would not do, she wrote, because "democracy has taught us to apply our moral teaching all around, and the moralist is rapidly becoming so sensitive that when his life does not exemplify his ethical convictions, he finds it difficult to preach." [48]

If the charity visitor was perplexed, so were those she visited. The poor were generally willing to lend or borrow anything. Charity was bounded "only by the need of the recipient and the resources of the giver. . . ." The guarded care, the delay and caution with which the visitor gave relief simply outraged the poor man's sense of primitive pity and longing to help his neighbors. To the poor, the charity worker's motives were alien and unreal, if not basically selfish and avaricious. "They cannot comprehend why a person whose intellectual perceptions are stronger than his natural impulses should go into charity at all." [49]

Charity visitors were victimized by their own dogmas, Jane Addams asserted. Instead of studying what a man is and might be, they ruthlessly forced their own bourgeois convictions on the poor. The disproportionate amount of money spent on clothes by working girls was most sensible if one understood the girl's goal of social advancement. The imitation of fashion in cheap clothes was merely the "striving to conform to a common standard which . . . democratic training presupposes belongs to us all." A charity visitor's distress at early marriage among the poor was also quite unreasonable. A workingman's peak income came between the ages of twenty and thirty, not later, as in the class from which the visitor came. The family on relief that spent money on recreation illustrated the greater wisdom of the simple, Miss Addams claimed. The charity worker's failure to understand the legitimate demands of children for pleasure made her less than

48. Jane Addams, "The Subtle Problems of Charity," p. 164.
49. *Ibid.*, pp. 167, 165.

helpful. Her dogmatic misunderstanding of the poor poisoned the whole charitable enterprise.[50]

A more scientific charity, a charity that would become democratic and evolutionary, would correct these dogmatic misunderstandings. "Human motives have been so long a matter of dogmatism," Jane Addams summarized her article, "that to act upon the assumption that they are the result of growth, and to study their status with an open mind and a scientific conscience, seems well-nigh impossible. . . ." But this was exactly what the charitable had to do. When the charity visitor could so identify herself with the poor that she forgot her moralistic preconceptions, she might feel herself "within the grasp of a principle of growth, working outward from within," might feel the "exhilaration and uplift which come when the individual sympathy and intelligence are caught in the forward, intuitive movement of the mass."[51] The people themselves provided the clue for establishing a better and truer charity in America's cities. Dogma and prejudice yielded, in Jane Addams' understanding of charity, to democratic experience.

In interpreting the aims of the labor movement, Jane Addams stressed the same democratic and ethical themes. Her unsuccessful mediation attempts in 1894 gave her material that illustrated again how paternalism delayed progress toward social democracy. As in the field of philanthropy, the corrective was an appreciation of the activities and aspirations of the common people. Miss Addams was always critical of labor violence and was sometimes discouraged by labor's failures, but she was a stronger ally of organized labor than were most Progressives. Much influenced by her friendship with Henry D. Lloyd, she was an early defender of the right, even the necessity, for labor organization. In late 1891 she helped form two women's unions. As noted above, her contribution to *Hull-House Maps and Papers* dealt with the labor movement.

Miss Addams described her experiences in the Pullman strike to the Chicago Woman's Club in late 1894. Her theme was the decline of the older philanthropic motives of industrialists before the idealistic thrust of industrial democracy.

George Pullman had been, she noted, an unusually generous employer, liberal in many respects. This might have succeeded

50. *Ibid.*, p. 169.
51. *Ibid.*, pp. 177, 178.

" if he had had in view the sole good of [his employees and] . . . had called upon them for self-expression and had made the town [of Pullman] a growth and a manifestation of their wants and needs. But unfortunately, the end to be obtained became ultimately commercial and not social. . . ." The original impulse to give his employees the best surroundings was gradually subverted by Pullman's desire for the reputation of a philanthropist. " He cultivated the great and noble impulses of the benefactor, until the power of attaining a simple human relationship with his employes, that of frank equality with them, was gone. . . . He and his employes had no mutual interest in a common cause." [52] Pullman substituted a feeling of gratitude to himself for a sense of responsibility to the community. True greatness, Miss Addams believed, was " the possession of the largest share of the common human qualities and experiences, not . . . the acquirements of peculiarities and excessive virtues." [53]

The old motives of " doing good " to his employees had blinded Pullman to the new glimpses of justice that his employees had caught sight of. Like King Lear, who could not understand his daughter Cordelia moving by principles outside himself, Pullman was unable to watch his employees develop beyond the strength of his own mind and sympathy. Pullman, therefore, never even heard about the ideals of the labor movement, that the injury of one was the concern of all; he failed to grasp the meaning of labor watchwords like brotherhood, sacrifice, and subordination of the individual to the common good. Compared with these principles, the aims of Pullman's liberality—cleanliness, decency of living, thrift, and temperance—were negative and inadequate, according to Jane Addams.

Miss Addams frankly stated that labor's idealism sometimes became ill-directed, that labor's aspirations were sometimes selfishly directed against an employer. But the conscience of her generation was aroused by labor's struggle, and nothing would satisfy that conscience " short of the complete participation of the working classes in the spiritual, intellectual and material inheritance of the human race." Labor unions most clearly embodied the striving for these new ideals of social and industrial

52. This 1894 speech was not published until 1912, see Jane Addams, " A Modern Lear," *Survey* (November 2, 1912), 133, 134.
53. *Ibid.*, pp. 135, 136.

democracy. More than any other organization, she wrote, the labor union met the spiritual requirements of democracy: all men were included in its hopes, all men were recognized as free and equal, and the whole body of men were regarded as the final source of political power.[54]

Political power was a painful subject in the Hull House ward in the 1890's. The Nineteenth Ward was represented by an alderman "whose corruption is noted as abnormal even in his habitat." [55] Johnny Powers' strength lay in his services to his constituents: the number of people holding city jobs exceeded one third of the total registered voters in the ward; Powers was lavish at Christmas time with food and coal and gave generously to all ward charities; and he was always ready to intervene in judicial or administrative procedures on behalf of a constituent. Hull House residents, convinced that Powers' corruption poisoned their attempts to introduce a wider democracy, sparked three opposition campaigns. Each ward was represented by two aldermen elected in alternate years for a two-year term. Two of their campaigns were waged in order to unseat Johnny Powers.

In 1895, the Hull House Men's Club nominated one of their members to oppose Powers' colleague. In a four-way contest— between a Democrat, a Republican, a Populist, and an Independent—the Hull House Independent candidate won. But soon he became Powers' "most loyal supporter." [56] In 1896 Powers was running for his fifth term. After much negotiation, the Hull House forces arranged a fusion ticket with other factions in the district to oppose the Powers machine. The fusion candidate was a member of the Hull House Men's Club and, like Powers, an Irish Catholic immigrant. The colorful campaign brought many influential outside speakers to the Nineteenth Ward. The voteless ladies at Hull House made posters bearings the legend "Yerkes & Powers—the Briber and the Bribed." The Municipal Voters' League, a reform organization formed in January, 1896, to oppose "boodlers" like Powers, spent large sums on publicity and printing. All of this effort brought about a reduction in Powers'

54. *Ibid.*, pp. 136, 135, 137; Jane Addams, "The Significance of Organized Labor," *Machinist's Monthly Journal*, X (September, 1898), 551–2.

55. Julia Lathrop, "Hull House," *Vassar Miscellany*, XXV (May, 1896), 371.

56. Allen F. Davis, "Jane Addams *vs.* the Ward Boss," *Journal of the Illinois State Historical Society*, LIII (Autumn, 1960), 253.

usual majority at the polls, but the Powers machine remained entrenched.[57]

Both Powers and the Hull House ladies started working early for the 1898 campaign. Between 1896 and 1898 "nearly every man who had been prominent in the campaign against Powers received an office or a job. . . ." But Jane Addams was emboldened to try again. A new primary law was in force, a merit system had been adopted in 1895 for city and county offices, a reform mayor had been elected in 1896, and the Municipal Voters' League was stronger than ever, having survived the filing of 987 libel suits, none of which ever came to trial. In 1898 Powers was anxious to be re-elected. Yerkes' transit franchises would come to City Council for renewal in 1899, and this was a good chance to improve the aldermanic salary of $3.00 per meeting. For the first time Powers attacked Hull House directly. "The trouble with Miss Addams is [that] she is just jealous of my charitable work in the ward. . . . Hull House will be driven from the Ward and its leaders will be forced to shut up shop." But the ladies of Hull House had also been active in these two years. The Hull House Men's Club, through its dummy Nineteenth Ward Improvement Committee, established an organization in each precinct of the ward. "Much patient effort," Ray Stannard Baker explained, had been expended " to unite all factions, including the Republican party organization. . . ." Hull House organized all sorts of independent *ad hoc* clubs through which its candidate might be advanced.[58]

Powers' victory over the Hull House nominee—by three thousand votes out of a total of about eight thousand—caused Jane Addams to reflect on why political honesty could not, in an immigrant quarter, displace political corruption. Immigrants preferred the man who did good deeds and helped people, she decided, rather than an abstract appeal to honesty. The reform candidates had been unable to incorporate the simple immigrant

57. The placard plans are included in Jane Addams to Henry D. Lloyd, March 11, 1895, Lloyd Papers, State Historical Society of Wisconsin; Sidney I. Roberts, "The Municipal Voters' League and Chicago's Boodlers," *Journal of the Illinois Historical Society*, LIII (Summer, 1960), 137–43.

58. Davis, "Jane Addams *vs.* the Ward Boss," p. 257; Roberts, "The Municipal Voters' League and Chicago's Boodlers," p. 141. Powers is quoted in Chicago *Tribune*, March 7, 1898, cited by Davis in his article, p. 261; Ray Stannard Baker, "Hull House and the Ward Boss," *Outlook*, LVIII (March 26, 1898), 771.

ideals of goodness into their view of politics. Miss Addams analyzed this disparity and insisted on the value of the demands of her immigrant neighbors. Their demands were to her a valuable criticism of democracy. She became convinced that only by incorporating these immigrant ideals of goodness and helpfulness could American democracy advance. Some of Powers' attempts to help those who lived in the Nineteenth Ward subverted justice, encouraged law-breaking, and undermined confidence in American law. But if the highest ethical demand was to do good, Miss Addams now believed, it was entirely fitting that one should help a man out of trouble just because he was in trouble, irrespective of the law. Some people in the ward realized that they ultimately paid for the alderman's charity. But they preferred to pay rather than " give up the consciousness that they have a big, warmhearted friend at court who will stand by them. . . ." [59]

Powers' favorite form of charity, besides the distribution of tons of coal and food at Christmas and the placement of his constituents in city jobs, was display at funerals. Here he had " the double advantage of ministering to a genuine craving for comfort and solace, and at the same time of assisting at an important social function." Anyone who, while using the carriages the alderman provided, would ask where the money came from, " would be considered sinister." Provision for these archaic rites in an immigrant community " ministers just as truly to a great human need as the musician and artist does." The crucial question was

> what headway can the notion of civic purity, of honesty of administration, make against this big manifestation of human friendliness, this stalking survival of village kindness? The notions of the civic reformer are negative and impotent before it. The reformers give themselves over largely to criticisms of the present state of affairs, to writing and talking of what the future must be; but their goodness is not dramatic, it is not even concrete and human. [60]

The remedy for this corrupt political relationship—like the remedy for the charitable and industrial relationship—was in the

59. Jane Addams, " Ethical Survivals of Municipal Corruption," *International Journal of Ethics*, VIII (April, 1898), 286.
60. *Ibid.*, pp. 281–2.

democratic experience of the common people. For " if we discover that men of low ideals and corrupt practice are forming popular political standards simply because such men stand by and for and with the people, then nothing remains but to obtain a like sense of identification before we can hope to modify ethical standards." If public spirit could be dramatized, the immigrant would quickly embody this higher ideal in his life. " We may learn," she concluded, " to trust our huge and uncouth democracy in its ethics, as we are coming to trust it in other directions. . . ." [61]

Perhaps this is as good a summary as is possible of Jane Addams' first decade at Hull House: learn to trust democracy. The example of Toynbee Hall, theories of elite leadership and religious motives, and the emphasis on individual and industrial virtues succumbed to the lessons of experience. When she collected the essays in which she had described these various experiences and published them in 1902 as *Democracy and Social Ethics*, Miss Addams placed strong emphasis on how democracy was weakened by excluding any group from the democratic ideal. The exclusion of her immigrant neighbors, with their open emotional life of pity and sympathy, was particularly fatal to democracy. The democratic ideal had to include the wisdom and experience of these unsophisticated people, she wrote. *Democracy and Social Ethics* so impressed William James that he called it " one of the great books of the times." He especially praised her sympathetic interpretation of " the religion of democracy." [62]

The experiences of this decade also altered Miss Addams' ideas about settlements. When she reviewed the history of the movement in 1899, she dwelt not on the impulse or motive, but on the *function* of settlements. They dealt with " the most pressing problem of modern life," which was " a reconstruction and a reorganization of the knowledge which we possess. . . ." The settlements, wrote Jane Addams, citing Dewey and James, were places where accumulated knowledge could be applied to life and tried out in experience. " Just as we do not know a fact until we can play with it, so we do not possess knowledge until we have an impulse to bring it into use . . . [to throw our knowledge] into the stream of common human experience." Only when

61. *Ibid.*, pp. 290, 288–9, 274, 291.
62. William James to Jane Addams, September 17, 1902, SCPC.

learning was touched by " the mystic life of the common people " could that learning come alive.[63]

After 1900 Jane Addams broadened the scope of her reform activities. Lack of democracy was not just a neighborhood problem, she discovered, but a national problem. " Lack of faith in the people, lack of faith in all kinds of people, lack of faith that the people contain in themselves a dynamic power which only needs to be used in order to make the world better," was the great menace to twentieth-century America. " We do not yet believe that each soul has within itself a tremendous power " for democratic progress, she declared. We need " to free the [social] forces within ourselves. We will never learn to interpret alien peoples, we will never be able to break through the outside differences, we will never develop in the real democratic direction, so long as we distrust human energy and the power of human thought." [64]

The next two chapters describe how Jane Addams refined and extended her belief in progressive democracy and in the vitality of the life of the common people. She worked actively for educational reform and for increased provision for urban recreation. In both efforts, she asserted her confidence in the powers of human energy and thought, in progress and democracy, and in a higher culture for America inspired by the lives of her neighbors.

63. Jane Addams, " A Function of the Social Settlement," *Annals*, XIII (May, 1899), 324, 329; Jane Addams, " College Women and Christianity," *Independent*, LIII (August 8, 1901), 1855.

64. Jane Addams, " One Menace to the Century's Progress," *Unity*, XLVII (April 4, 1901), 71, 72.

CHAPTER IV

EDUCATIONAL THOUGHT

But we have not yet really begun to enjoy ourselves. We have not yet had full confidence in the wondrous things these children are learning to do. We have not yet learned to teach them as they should be taught, because we do not yet sufficiently reverence their possibilities.

JANE ADDAMS, 1912

The years from 1900 to 1912 were exciting and expansive ones for Jane Addams. Frustrated in her demands for democratic social reforms at the local level, she and other progressives founded a whole series of national reform organizations. Miss Addams worked for educational reform through the National Society for the Promotion of Industrial Education; she labored for city playgrounds through the Playground Association of America. She based her demands for educational reform and urban recreation on the idea of culture. The next two chapters describe her conceptions of culture, and the sources of culture, and show how these conceptions supported her criticism of the schools and her demands for recreational facilities in cities. Through these and other national activities Jane Addams became one of " the most famous women " in America.[1] She spoke authoritatively for American women on the whole range of progressive reforms. In 1912 when the Progressives organized yet another of their voluntary reform organizations—this one a political party—Jane Addams became an important participant in the Bull Moose campaign.

Jane Addams' idea of culture changed during the first decade at Hull House in a way similar to the evolution of her ideas about democracy described in the last chapter. This kind of change was characteristic of the nineteenth century, during which the meanings of the terms culture and democracy changed radically. A recent

1. Lloyd R. Morris, *Postscript to Yesterday, America: The Last Fifty Years* (New York, 1947), p. 35.

study by Raymond Williams points out how the definition of culture, or cultivation, or civilization, was altered in response to new methods of production, and also " to the new political and social developments, to Democracy." [2] Jane Addams' ideas about culture changed as she learned about the new industrial situation and its social consequences in the America of the 1890's.

Her original thinking about the uses and content of culture—as with democracy—originated at Rockford with her reading of Carlyle, Ruskin, and Arnold. These men defined culture as something apart from what they saw around them. Raymond Williams' study begins by examining how the words culture and civilization were defined by these men who were repelled by the mechanistic philosophy of the utilitarians, which they called democracy, and by the materialism of industrial forms. Starting with Carlyle this tradition of social criticism evolved the idea of culture as a separate entity (the body of arts and learning), and also culture as a critical idea, a body of values superior to ordinary values. In this tradition Arnold defined culture as two disparate things: it was " the best which has been thought and said in the world "; and it was at the same time " the study of perfection, . . . a *harmonious* perfection, developing all sides of our humanity . . . [and] a *general* perfection, developing all parts of our society." [3]

These ideals of culture helped to inform and inspire the founding of settlements in England, and Hull House. A settlement, Jane Addams explained in 1890, was an attempt to bring back people of university refinement and cultivation to the sections where working people lived. A settlement disregarded " none of the results of civilization. . . . It rather stands for the fittings of a cultivated, well-ordered life, and the surroundings which are suggestive of participation in the best of the past." Miss Addams stressed the absence of refinement, beauty, and order in the Hull House neighborhood. Her ideal of culture was some-

2. Raymond Williams, *Culture and Society, 1780–1950* (Garden City, 1960), p. xvi. Morton White, *Social Thought in America, the Revolt against Formalism* (Boston, 1957), p. 11, distinguishes between the eighteenth and nineteenth centuries by the latter's " concern with change, process, history, and culture." White's study concentrates on the progressives' " cultural organicism." See also Lawrence A. Cremin's helpful chapter, " Culture and Community " in *The Transformation of the School, Progressivism in American Education, 1876–1957* (New York, 1961).

3. Raymond Williams cites this from Arnold's *Culture and Anarchy,* in his *Culture and Society,* p. 125; emphasis in the original.

thing apart from the industrial environment, absent from and perhaps opposed to the life of her neighbors. This ideal may be taken as her initial reaction to the industrial situation in America in the early 1890's.[4]

Throughout the first decade at Hull House, Jane Addams sloughed off the aristocratic preconceptions with which her settlement had originally been endowed. In the same manner that she found the source and vitality for a new social democracy in her neighbors, Miss Addams came to find true culture among them. In 1897 she cited Tolstoy's ideas about art to explain her own convictions. She told a settlement audience that " music cannot be real . . . painting is only an affection, unless we do it in the name of and for the mass of men . . . [the settlement claims] that we are not only bringing back to the industrial army the things which they ought always to have had, but that by bringing them back we are going, in the end, to have better music and painting, better literature and a higher type of social life; that a service is rendered to both ends of society." [5]

From this beginning Miss Addams came to believe that culture itself had its source in the people, especially the immigrants crowded into American cities. Settlement workers had originally anticipated encountering people more or less unlike themselves, she said. But during the first ten or fifteen years of living in a so-called depressed neighborhood, settlers discovered that their neighbors were " very useful people . . . all kinds of people . . . [who] have in themselves reservoirs of moral power and civic ability. . . ." She told a settlement audience in 1911 that " a new impulse, a new health, a new energy came into the life of the settlement when we began to discover in these crowded and less lovely portions of the city, a certain conservation of historic things, of good music, of artistic handicraft, of those subtle resources of settled society, superior, in Chicago at least, to those which the more prosperous quarters could display." [6] The most

4. Jane Addams, " Outgrowths of Toynbee Hall," p. 11, SCPC.
5. Jane Addams, " Social Settlements," pp. 342–3. See Leo Tolstoy, " What Shall We Do Then? " in *Complete Works* (Boston, 1905), XVII, 268–9 especially. Miss Addams recalled reading Tolstoy with some of her Russian neighbors in her *The Second Twenty Years at Hull House, September 1909 to September 1929, with a Record of Growing World Consciousness* (New York, 1930), p. 409.
6. Jane Addams, " Neighborhood Improvement," in National Conference of Charities and Correction, *Proceedings* (1904), p. 457; Jane Addams' address, University Settlement Society of New York, *Annual Report*, XXV (1911), p. 23.

human qualities, she told a University of Chicago convocation in 1904, were not necessarily those of the cultured and cultivated few. The most human and the best of human culture was " the widespread, the ancient in speech or in behavior, it is the deep, the emotional, the thing much loved by many men, the poetical, the organic, the vital in civilization." The sources of civilization, she said, were primitive domestic customs. Properly interpreted, her neighbors' customs and habits suggested the origins of culture, the " springs, a suggestion of source, a touch of the refinement which adheres to simple things." [7]

These ideas of Jane Addams on the relationship between culture and her " primitive " immigrant neighbors had several sources. In the 1890's, she read, and lectured on, academic studies of primitive societies. These studies, the most important of which was Otis Tufton Mason's *Woman's Share in Primitive Culture*, described the development of culture and civilization and emphasized the role of the woman. Mason credited to women the development—among other things—of food plants and plant medicine, most of the aesthetic arts, all the social fabrics of world civilization, the creation and preservation and spread of language, and " the first device ever made by human being for converting rectilinear into circular motion." Mason concluded that " for the highest ideals in civilization, in humanitarianism, education, and government the way was prepared in savagery by mothers and by the female clan group. . . ." The feminist in Jane Addams must have rejoiced at the work of ethnologists such as Mason. Academic studies may have suggested to her the connection between the skills and arts of primitive peoples and the development of culture.[8]

Jane Addams' ideas of primitivism paralleled those of other Progressive thinkers who critized modern industrial society by recalling primitive culture.[9] Thorstein Veblen, a professor at the

---

7. Jane Addams, "Recent Immigration, a Field Neglected by the Scholar," *University [of Chicago] Record*, IX (January, 1905), 279, 280.

8. Otis Tufton Mason, *Woman's Share in Primitive Culture* (New York, 1894), pp. 279–80, 284. Miss Addams recommended Mason's book to all students in her extension course at the University of Chicago, see *A Syllabus of a Course of Twelve Lectures, Democracy and Social Ethics, by Jane Addams, A.B.* (n.p., n.d.), SCPC.

9. David Nobel has treated primitivism among American Progressives in his *The Paradox of Progressive Thought* (Minneapolis, 1958). For a more general and philosophic discussion of primitivism see George Boas and A. O. Lovejoy, *Primitivism and Related Ideas in Antiquity* (Baltimore, 1934).

University of Chicago after 1894, believed that certain admirable instincts had survived in the industrial workingman. These survivals offered the foundation for a new social order based on science. Modern scientific attitudes were closely related to the instinct of idle curiosity in the " normal man " of preindustrial society, according to Veblen. His description of primitive man was remarkably like Jane Addams' portrait of her immigrant neighbors —peaceful, co-operative, and altruistic. Veblen believed that the forces of industrialism would restore the natural, wholesome, savage traits, traits which were the very sources of civilization.[10]

Henry D. Lloyd also trusted the forces of industrialism to establish a new civilization embodying older values that had been corrupted. Originally, according to Lloyd, man had been a member of a peaceful, co-operative, family-oriented social group. His tory recounted the splintering of these primitive social groups But Lloyd believed, in Professor David Noble's words, that

> at the same time as industrialism was whirling the individual away from the incomplete co-operative groups which had struggled to sustain civilization, it was hammering out . . . the environment that might spell the total salvation of mankind. . . . Industrialism, urbanism, the technological revolution in communications and transportation were reassembling the fragmented individuals into one tightly-knit worldwide community which would have the qualities of the original family group.

For Lloyd the industrial laborers—like Jane Addams' neighbors—were the most likely supporters of the co-operative commonwealth and the social democracy which he prophesied for America.[11]

Like these progressives Jane Addams found a criticism of the industrial and materialistic culture of the 1890's in the primitive cultural traits that European peasants brought to the doorsteps

10. Boas and Lovejoy, *Primitivism*, pp. 214 ff; see also Morton White's discussion of Veblen in *Social Thought in America*, pp. 76–93. Jane Addams included Veblen's *Theory of the Leisure Class* in the bibliography for her extension course, see *A Syllabus of a Course of Twelve Lectures*, SCPC.

11. Noble, *Paradox of Progressive Thought*, p. 151. Lloyd and his wife were early and loyal supporters of Hull House. Jane Addams helped edit a posthumously published collection of Lloyd's essays. See Henry Demarest Lloyd, *Man, the Social Creator*, eds. Jane Addams and Anne Withington (New York, 1906).

of Hull House. Unlike these progressives, however, she did not attempt to construct a theory about a primitive cultural ideal, or about the evolution of primitive cultural traits. Miss Addams knew her neighbors, and she knew that they were not altogether virtuous. She did not believe that civilization was simply the revival or restoration of men's oldest instincts. During the war in 1898, for instance, she saw how easily her neighbors lost what she called their thin veneer of civilization. At an anti-imperialist meeting in 1899 Miss Addams referred to a rising crime rate in the Hull House neighborhood as the result of war's brutalizing effects. " Simple people who read of carnage and bloodshed easily receive its suggestions. Habits of self-control which have been slowly and imperfectly acquired quickly break down under the stress . . . the humane instinct which keeps in abeyance the tendency to cruelty . . . gives way, and the barbaric instinct asserts itself." [12] Because she did not attempt to construct a social theory, Miss Addams did not idealize primitive traits and the savage past in the way some other progressives did. But she did find certain suggestions among her immigrant neighbors of a culture truer and finer than that possessed by many Americans.

Miss Addams believed that the chief cultural instrument in America was the public school. As a democrat she looked on the schools as the chief agency for the preservation and extension of American culture. But, she complained, the schools were failing in their task. Like John Dewey, Jane Addams criticized the schools because their culture had " become entirely detached from experience." [13] Her complaints against the schools were based on the educational experiments at Hull House. The Hull House kindergarten, formed during the first fortnight of the settlement's existence, was her earliest educational project. The kindergarten was soon followed by a creche and nursery which also embodied kindergarten ideas and practices. Jane Addams said in her first explanation of Hull House in 1890 that the settlement stood for Friedrich Froebel's definition of education: " deliverance " of the forces of the mind and body.[14]

12. Jane Addams, " What Peace Means," *Unity*, XLIII (May 4, 1899), 178.
13. Oscar Handlin, *John Dewey's Challenge to Education, Historical Perspectives on the Cultural Context* (New York, 1959), p. 33.
14. Miss Adams' remarks on Froebel are cited by Nina C. Vandewalker, *The Kindergarten in American Education* (New York, 1908), p. 121. Jane Addams,

Chicago had a flourishing kindergarten movement before Hull
House was established. In 1874 Mrs. Alice H. Putnam started a
class to study Froebel's ideas, a class that developed into the
Chicago Froebel Association. News of Chicago kindergartens
reached Jane Addams at Rockford. Mrs. Putnam and her association—with more than two hundred Chicago women enrolled for
instruction—operated from rooms in Hull House from 1894 to
1901. Many other philanthropic institutions in Chicago in the
1890's had kindergartens. One of the earliest public kindergartens
(*ca.* 1881) was at the Pacific Garden Mission, and there was one
at the Armour Mission when Jane Addams and Ellen Starr were
observing Chicago philanthropies in early 1889. *The Kindergarten
Magazine*, with Amalie Hofer as editor, was published in Chicago.[15]

From any one of these sources Jane Addams may have absorbed
Froebel's ideas about social education. An early historian of the
American kindergarten movement, familiar with the Chicago
situation, wrote that " the kindergarten has had far more success
than any other [institution] in dealing with our foreign people."
This same author asserted, " the settlement may not have inten-
tionally preached the doctrines of Froebel, but it has practiced

" Outgrowths of Toynbee Hall," p. 9, SCPC. Mary Jean Miller, " Account of the
Chicago Kindergarten Club," *Kindergarten Magazine*, X (November, 1897), 203 ff,
describes the series of parties and lectures to celebrate Froebel's birthday at Hull
House during 1895–6.

15. Bertha Payne Newell, *Pioneers of the Kindergarten in America* (New York
& London, 1924), has a good chapter on Alice Putnam; see also " Evolution of
the Kindergarten Idea in Chicago, Mrs. Alice H. Putnam and the Froebel Association," *Kindergarten Magazine*, V (June, 1893), 729–33, and " The Chicago
Free Kindergarten Association," *ibid.*, V (June, 1893), 734–8. John D. Hicks,
" The Development of Civilization in the Middle West," in Dixon Ryan Fox
(ed.), *Sources of Culture in the Middle West, Backgrounds Versus Frontier*
(New York & London, 1934), pp. 90–91, suggested that " sometimes [educa-
tional] innovations, such, for example, as kindergartens and manual training
courses, came to the Middle West directly from abroad." See *Rockford Seminary
Magazine*, VIII (April, 1880), 101–4 for a report of the Seventh Annual Chicago
Reunion. The first sentiment offered after the dinner was " the education for
mothers; schools for children, seminaries, colleges, universities for youth, but the
kindergarten for mothers." Annie Howe responded with a short review of Froebel's
kindergarten system. It is interesting that Frank Tracy Carlton used the famous
Rockford word in his *Education and Industrial Evolution* (New York, [1908]
1913), p. 169, when he wrote that " the kindergarten movement is particularly
important because it is really the opening wedge of the great movement which is
now lifting our educational system to higher and broader planes of usefulness,—
usefulness for all classes and ages of students."

them in every phase of its work . . . in the very settlement itself, one may read the philosophy of the kindergarten writ large." [16]

Many Hull House activities were based on the Froebelian idea of self-expression. The shops, the sewing and cooking classes, the music and art schools, and the gymnasium and playground activities all testify to Jane Addams' and Ellen Starr's recognition of the need for varying kinds of self-expression, especially for young people. Their further recognition of this need in adults inspired a whole series of clubs and activities which helped adult immigrants express themselves through manual and fine arts, through athletics, and through intellectual and social activities. Other writers have called attention to the " peculiar unity " between these settlement activities and kindergarten thought and practice. The settlement's aim was to make the immigrant feel at home in America in the same sense that the Froebel kindergarten tried to make the child feel at home in the adult world.[17]

Another Chicagoan was impressed with the applicability of Froebel's educational ideas to American problems. " Froebel's recognition of the significance of the native capacities of children," wrote John Dewey, represented " perhaps the most effective single force in modern educational theory. . . ." [18] Dewey and Jane Addams shared their educational ideas and hopes with each other. Miss Addams was connected with Dewey's project, the University of Chicago Laboratory School, where Froebel's educational ideas were central, just as they were to the settlement.[19]

The laboratory school's curriculum represented Dewey's reaction to the new forces of industrial civilization in the United States in the 1890's. The curriculum centered on what Dewey called occupations. The children performed typical domestic tasks. They raised crops, cooked food, wove cloth, built, furnished, and decorated a house. These industrial activities were designed to show how history and civilization depended on technology and industrial

16. Vandewalker, *Kindergarten in American Education*, p. 110.
17. Woods and Kennedy, *The Settlement Horizon*, p. 132.
18. John Dewey, *Democracy and Education, an Introduction to the Philosophy of Education* (New York, [1916] 1961), p. 58.
19. Dewey explained the ideas that motivated the experiments in the laboratory school in a series of lectures in 1899 which were published as *School and Society*. See Chapter V, " Froebel's Educational Principles," especially p. 117: ". . . in a certain sense the school endeavors . . . to carry into effect certain principles which Froebel was perhaps the first consciously to set forth."

processes. Industrial history, according to Dewey, was not merely a materialistic or utilitarian affair. It was a matter of social intelligence, "the record of how man learned to think, to think to some effect, to transform the conditions of life so that life itself became a different thing." It was "an ethical record as well; the account of the conditions which men have patiently wrought out to serve their ends." [20]

Dewey hypothesized that the child, by re-enacting industrial history, would experience social processes and results on a simple enough level to be able to understand their relationships. Understanding these more simple processes prepared the child to comprehend the complicated society of the contemporary world. Occupations provided "an indispensable instrument of free and active social life." [21] Thus they formed a bridge between the home and the school and integrated the school into the larger world. Occupations were the "instrumentalities through which the school itself shall be made a genuine form of active community life, instead of a place set apart in which to learn lessons." Occupations provided the common spirit and common aims upon which the school, and indeed all social organization, depended. [22]

An address by Jane Addams to the National Education Association in 1897 shows the close relationship between Dewey's ideas on education and her own. She described the school as "a social institution, within which a certain concentration of social interests take place, for the purpose of producing certain social results." After citing a definition of the school by Dewey, Miss Addams said that the ultimate aim of education was "to give the child's own experience a social value. . . ." [23] This was particularly important in schools serving immigrant neighborhoods. But it was in just such neighborhoods that the public schools were most deficient. The immediate impact of immigration, she explained to the teachers, was a splintering of family life. "The family

20. Dewey, *School and Society*, pp. 152–3. Dewey defined occupation in *Democracy and Education*, p. 309, as "a continuous activity having a purpose. Education *through* occupations consequently combines within itself more of the factors conducive to learning than any other method." See also Katharine Elizabeth Dopp, *The Place of Industries in Elementary Education* (Chicago, 1905), based on the experiences of the laboratory school.

21. Dewey, *School and Society*, p. 23.

22. *Ibid.*, p. 14.

23. Jane Addams, "Foreign-Born Children in the Primary Grades," in National Education Association, *Journal of Proceedings and Addresses* (1897), pp. 104, 105.

has no social life in any structural form, and can supply none to the child. If he receives it in the school, and gives it to his family, the school would thus become the connector with the organized society about them." Immigrant parents depended on their children to teach them about American culture and to re-establish whatever structure the family took on in America. The child had to act as both social interpreter and social buffer. He could learn these abilities only at school.[24]

Miss Addams criticized the schools because they separated immigrant children from their parents and their parents' culture. At school the children of immigrants learned "contempt for the experiences and languages of their parents. . . ." American school teachers failed to understand that the immigrant family's experience had been "simple out-door activity, and the ideas they have have come directly to them from their struggle with nature. . . ." This primitive kind of struggle bred a deep family devotion. Teachers too often transformed the child into a smug American by developing his powers "in an abstract direction, quite ignoring the fact that his parents have had to do only with tangible things. . . . This cutting into his family loyalty takes away one of [the child's] most conspicuous and valuable traits. . . ."[25]

In addition to cutting the child off from the culture and affection of his parents, the schools failed to connect him with the industrial culture in which he would almost certainly participate. When the child completed school had he, Jane Addams asked, been given "a consciousness of his social value?" Had the school taught him "to deal more effectively and in a more vital manner with his present life?" Far from doing this, the schools cut their students off from industrial life. "No attempt is made to give a boy . . . any insight into [the factory's] historic significance, or to connect [him] . . . in any intelligible way with the past and future. He has absolutely no consciousness of his social value, and his [industrial] activities become inevitably purely mechanical." To the graduate of the public school industrial labor was tedious drudgery, the senseless manipulation of unrelated materials; once at work the child used "his hands for unknown ends, and his head not at all."[26]

24. *Ibid.*, p. 106.
25. *Ibid.*, pp. 107, 105.
26. *Ibid.*, pp. 108-9.

These unhappy results had come about because the schools ignored industrial history. They ignored " the long struggle of man in his attempts to bring natural forces under human control. . . ." Pedagogically, the schools had ignored a dramatic and graphic approach to the child. Shops and factories contained " vivid and striking examples of the high development of the simple tools which [a foreign child's] father still uses, and of the lessening expenditures of human energy." The study of industrial history would integrate work in factories with " that life which means culture and growth." [27] Culture and growth for the child might come if the schools surrendered their concentration on abstract learning, on reading and writing. " If the little Italian lad were supplied [first] . . . with tangible and resistance-offering material upon which to exercise his muscle, he would go bravely to work, and he would probably be ready later to use the symbols of letters and numbers to record and describe what he had done; and might even be incited to the exertion of reading to find out what other people had done." This kind of education would bring " real joy and spontaneity " into the classroom. The school would be changed, and would feel " the pleasure which comes from creative effort, the thrill of production," not just occasionally, but as " the sustaining motive which keeps it going." [28]

Jane Addams summarized her criticism by opposing " the isolation of the school from life . . . [which] tends to defeat the very purpose of education." The school needed to provide each child with an understanding of the industrialism in which he would soon participate, and thus some " set-off " from the monotony and dullness of industrial labor. The school was supposed to fill each child's mind with " beautiful images and powers of thought, so that he might be able to do this dull mechanical work, and still live a real life outside of it." [29]

The most important development in her educational thought

27. *Ibid.*, p. 109.
28. *Ibid.*, pp. 106-7, 111, 109-10. The democratic theme in Jane Addams thought, discussed in the last chapter, also appears in her educational thought. She believed that the study of industrial history would make the schools more democratic. Such an education would teach each child " to use equally and to honor equally both their heads and hands. . . ." Hateful feelings of class distinction would not grow up in the schools, and no one would distinguish between service to " the commonwealth in the factory or in the legislature." *Ibid.*, p. 109,
29. *Ibid.*, pp. 112, 109-10.

was her rejection of the whole idea that education prepared men for a real life outside the dull monotony of industrial labor. By 1905 she had repudiated any attempt to "find our culture, our religion and our education quite outside" industrialism.[30] This change was a result of a new understanding of her neighbors' educational aspirations and hopes and a new understanding of democratic culture. After a decade of thought and experience Miss Addams came to believe that a culture which lay outside industrial work and the forms of industrial civilizations (the kind of culture advocated by Ruskin, Carlyle, and Arnold) could not be a common possession and, therefore, was not useful for a democracy. This reversal in attitude was clearly exhibited in the changing methods and purposes of the adult education effort at Hull House.

In the early days at Hull House college graduates taught classes that attempted to duplicate undergraduate collegiate courses.[31] The settlement found eager students for those who wanted to share the culture they had acquired at college. These early educational efforts simply assumed the superiority of the culture that a college education signified. There was something patronizing in Jane Addams' remark that information diffused in a social atmosphere, in a medium of fellowship and good will, could be assimilated by the dullest. This patronizing attitude reflects the initial attitude of the ladies of Hull House toward adult education.[32]

By 1897 Miss Addams had reservations about the educational effort at Hull House. "Those of us," she said, "who are working to bring a fuller life to the industrial members of the community, who are looking forward to a time when work shall not be senseless drudgery, but shall contain some self-expression of the worker, sometimes feel the hopelessness of adding evening classes and

30. Jane Addams, "Child Labor Legislation: a Requisite for Industrial Efficiency," *Annals*, XXV (May, 1905), 28.

31. These college extension classes preceeded the active university extension classes sponsored after 1892 by President William Rainey Harper at the newly reorganized University of Chicago.

32. For Miss Addams' attitudes toward college extension classes and her neighbors who took them, see Jane Addams, "How Would you Uplift the Masses?" *Sunset Club* [*of Chicago*], *Yearbook* (1891/1892), pp. 118–21, and Jane Addams, "Hull House, An Effort Toward Social Democracy," pp. 232–4.

social entertainments as a mere frill to a day filled with monoton-
ous and deadening drudgery." A decade later she stated flatly
that " the educational efforts of a settlement should not be directed
primarily to reproduce the college-type culture but to work out
a method and an ideal adapted to adults who spend their time
in industrial pursuits." [33]

Miss Addams made clear the concept of culture she coveted
for her neighbors in a speech to the National Education Association in 1908. She reiterated her conviction that the school's
superficial and mistaken idea of culture too often separated the
immigrant child from his parents. She defined true culture as
" a knowledge of those things which have been long cherished by
men, the things men have loved because through generations they
have softened and interpreted life, and have endowed it with
value and meaning." This ideal of culture was the one the schools
should be teaching; and this ideal was available to teachers in the
beauty and charm of the language, the history, and the traditions
which immigrant parents represented. The real business of the
school was " to give to each child the beginnings of a culture so
wide and deep and universal that he can interpret his own parents
and countrymen by a standard which is world-wide and not pro-
vincial." The cultural resources of immigrant communities, Jane
Addams insisted, were enormous. If teachers could bring the

> handicrafts and occupations, [the immigrants'] traditions,
> their folk songs and folk lore, the beautiful stories which
> every immigrant colony is ready to tell and translate . . . into
> school as the material from which culture is made and the
> material upon which culture is based, they would discover
> that by comparison that which they give them now is a poor
> meretricious and vulgar thing. Give these children a chance
> to utilize the historic and industrial material which they see
> about them and they will begin to have sense of ease in
> America, a first consciousness of being at home.[34]

This development in Miss Addams' ideas about culture and its
impact on her educational ideals explains Hull House's abandon-

33. Jane Addams, " Foreign-Born Children in the Primary Grades," pp. 110–1;
Hull House, *Annual Report* (1906/1907), p. 8.
34. Jane Addams, " Public Schools and the Immigrant Child," in National
Education Association, *Journal of Proceedings and Addresses* (1908), pp. 99–
100, 102.

ment of its summer school at Rockford College. Girls from the Hull House neighborhood were invited to a six-week session at Rockford during the years between 1891 and 1901. The program for 1892 scheduled classes in biology and outdoor study, sketching, needlework, singing, gymnastics, English and letter-writing, Venetian art, and physiology and hygiene. There were reading parties which used George Eliot, modern novelists, Greek plays in English translation, and Ruskin and Morris. Although the summer school provoked some opposition from residents of Rockford, who were used to a rather different kind of student than Chicago school teachers and working girls, Miss Addams' decision to end the summer school was probably part of her growing dissatisfaction with attempts to provide college-type culture for the benefit of her neighbors.[35]

Miss Addams' dissatisfaction with a literary collegiate ideal of education was perhaps stimulated by the exciting educational experiments going on in Chicago in these years. She served on an *ad hoc* citizens' school committee formed at a mass meeting on April 25, 1893, after the appearance of J. M. Rice's damning article, " The Public Schools of Chicago and St. Paul," in the *Forum* for April, 1893. This *ad hoc* committee studied school problems all through the 1890's. Miss Addams' service on this committee brought her into close contact with Colonel Francis Wayland Parker, whose annual battle with a usually hostile Cook County Board of Education over the appropriation for the Cook County Normal School was a continuing struggle on behalf of progressive educational methods. Miss Addams rallied members of Parent-Teachers Associations to testify on behalf of Colonel Parker before the Board of Education. And service on this *ad hoc* committee kept her in touch with the educational experiments at the University of Chicago.[36]

More important than these city-wide services in explaining Miss Addams' changing educational interests, however, was a neighborhood project. The Hull House Industrial Museum was the most

35. The 1892 program is in " Miss Sill's Scrapbook," Rockford College Archives.
36. Rice's article, in *Forum*, XV (April, 1893), 200–15, praised Parker's school in Chicago and practically nothing else. On the Chicago response see Robert L. McCaul, " Dewey's Chicago," *School Review*, LXVII (Summer, 1959), 258–80, and Franklin Parker," Jane Addams of Hull House," *Chicago Jewish Forum*, XIX (Fall, 1960), 13–16.

important educational experiment with which Jane Addams was associated. In her autobiography, she described the sudden inspiration for the museum when she saw one of her neighbors using an ancient type of spindle. Why not arrange the various spinning methods still being practiced in the Hull House neighborhood into a historical sequence? She did so and soon added pictures of various textile processes, maps of early textile trade routes, charts showing how long each process had been in use, lectures on machinery and materials, and even song recitals about weaving. This began a large series of exhibits soon titled the Hull House Industrial Museum, or the Labor Museum, as it was more popularly called.[37] These exhibits, wrote Jane Addams, graphically demonstrated that " history looked at from the industrial standpoint at once becomes cosmopolitan, and the differences of race and nationality inevitably fall away. In the narrow confines of one room, the Syrian, Slav, Latin, and the Celt, show the continuity of industrial development which went on peacefully year by year among the workers of each nation, heedless of differences in language, religion and political experiences." [38]

The Labor Museum had two main purposes. It illustrated the importance and quality of the immigrant's skills and enhanced his prestige in the eyes of his native-born neighbors and Americanized children. At the same time, the museum gave to young people who worked in shops and factories the chance to gain some knowl-

37. Nancy Portia Potishman emphasizes the Labor Museum in her " Jane Addams and Education " (unpublished Master's thesis, Columbia University, 1961). Robert Eugene Tostberg suggests in his " Educational Ferment in Chicago, 1883–1904 " (unpublished Master's thesis, University of Wisconsin, 1960), pp. 196–7, that Dewey originated the idea for the Labor Museum. Dewey did urge in *School and Society*, p. 90, that every ideal school would be equipped with something quite similar to the Labor Museum. The official historians of Dewey's laboratory school, Katherine Camp Mayhew and Anna Camp Edwards, *The Dewey School, the Laboratory School of the University of Chicago, 1896–1903* (New York & London, 1936), p. 195, said that the textile department of the laboratory school was inspired by and utilized ancient spinning methods extant in the city. The parallels between the living exhibits of primitive industrial processes at Hull House and Dewey's use of occupations at the laboratory school show how closely he and Jane Addams shared their educational ideas.

Other departments in the museum, none of which ever achieved the popularity of the textile department, were woodworking, bookbinding, grains, metals, and pottery.

38. Jane Addams, *First Report of the Labor Museum at Hull-House, Chicago, 1901/1902* (Chicago, 1902), pp. 5–9.

edge of the material they were constantly handling at work. In time, Jane Addams hoped, they might become conscious of the social and historic connections of the work. In short, the Labor Museum was designed to bring industrial labor and culture together. "A man often cannot understand the machine with which he works," she wrote in summarizing the museum's first year, "because there is no soil out of which such an understanding may grow, and the natural connection of the workshop with culture is entirely lost for him." Making this connection was one of the tasks of education she wrote, citing her friend John Dewey. "Two sound educational principles we may perhaps claim for the labor museum even in this early stage of experiment—first, that it concentrates and dramatizes the inherited resources of a man's occupation, and secondly, that it conceives of education as 'a continuing reconstruction of experience.' More than that the best 'education' cannot do for any of us." [39]

Through her experiences with the Labor Museum, Jane Addams settled on the educational reforms through which industry and democratic culture could be united: manual training and industrial education. Workingmen, she explained, came into contact with machinery quite as if it had been newly created—just as some of her Italian neighbors looked on the spinning wheel which they saw for the first time in the Labor Museum as a marvelous new invention. Workers had no notion that "the inventions upon which the factory depends, the instruments which they use, have been slowly worked out by the necessities of the race, have been added to and modified until they have become a social possession and have an aggregate value which time and society alone can give to them." Industrial processes were as much a part of culture as anything else which embodied historic human energy and achievement. The crucial point about the Labor Museum, Miss Addams insisted, was that the people who used machinery had only one way to get a consciousness of historic continuity and human interest in life—that way was through a cultural understanding of the machinery they operated.[40]

Miss Addams' autobiographical account of the founding of the Labor Museum stresses the sudden inspiration and lack of

39. *Ibid.*, p. 15.
40. Jane Addams, "Social Education of the Industrial Democracy," *The Commons*, V (June 30, 1900), 20.

precedent for it. The inspiration for the museum, acknowledged or not, was the English arts and crafts movement. She especially drew on the description of industrial guilds in the writings of Morris and Ruskin. Jane Addams rejected much of the anti-machine bias in these two writers but joined them in criticizing the increased meretriciousness and vulgarity of industrial products. A direct imitation of these English movements came through the activities of Ellen Gates Starr. In 1897 she and Jane Addams organized the Chicago Arts and Crafts Society, " probably the pioneer American society of this nature." The society, which met at Hull House, was never very active, and it gradually merged its enterprises with the Labor Museum.[41]

A more direct connection with the English movement was Ellen Starr's decision to learn the art of fine bookbinding. In 1900 she spent six months studying and working under T. J. Cobden-Sanderson at Dove's Bindery, the bindery which serviced the Kelmscott Press. When Miss Starr returned, she established a bindery at Hull House. She lived at Hull House until the late 1920's, supporting herself on the profits from her lovely—and expensive —bookbindings.[42] From Miss Starr, if from no other source, Miss Addams would certainly have been familiar with the idea— quite commonplace in the arts and crafts movement—that industrial products reflected the education and moral life of the nation.[43]

41. Jane Addams, *Twenty Years at Hull-House*, pp. 235–45. Carlton, *Education and Industrial Evolution*, p. 146, gives precedence to the Hull House society. The society published what amounted to an annual report in *Commons*, III (June, 1898), 4. The society's stated aims were to cultivate in its members, and through them in others, a just sense of beauty; to extend the appreciation of the possible beauty of articles of everyday use; to influence the movement toward manual training and art education; to influence sources of design and decoration; to encourage handicraft among the members; to consider industrial conditions with a view to emancipating the workman from undue subservience to his machine; and to hold exhibitions and maintain centers of propaganda.

42. Wallace Rice, " Miss Starr's Book Bindery," *House Beautiful*, XII (June, 1902), 13. In *Commons*, V (June 30, 1900), 21–22, Miss Starr explained that she had grown tired of talking and explaining beautiful things to people living in sordid and ugly places. She had determined to do something. She disclaimed any special talent, but then, she was quoted as saying, " suppose that all the people who had no genius, in the ages when the most beautiful building, carving, bookmaking, silver and smithing, and the like were done, had fallen to talking about the work of past ages, and refused to do any work themselves, how much less we should have now to talk about and to enjoy."

43. Williams, *Culture and Society*, p. 140: " An essential hypothesis in the development of the idea of culture is that the art of a period is closely and

Miss Starr's decision to establish a bindery and to support herself by bookbinding was not for Jane Addams an adequate answer to the separation of industrial labor and culture. Nor was she satisfied with the once-a-week demonstrations at the Labor Museum. If educated, cultivated producers held the key to a more human, a better, industrial product, Jane Addams felt it was only reasonable to work for an extension of educational opportunities.

In 1905 Miss Addams accepted appointment to the Chicago Board of Education. Her three-year term of service did not alter her educational ideas, but only indicated how difficult it was to win public acceptance for new ideas in education. Caught in a bitter political struggle betwen two factions on the board, Miss Addams was unable to make any significant impression on the educational policies of the Chicago school system.[44] It was rather through private, voluntary organizations that Miss Addams made her contribution to educational reform.

Miss Addams was one of the founders, in 1904, and one of the active members of the National Child Labor Committee.[45] The committee's original program contained two demands: uniform, compulsory education laws, and uniform restrictive child labor laws. These two aims were usually coupled as mutually necessary and interdependent. Miss Addams related the demands of the committee to her concern for the type of culture which the public schools taught. " Because we are living in an industrial age we must find our culture through that industry," she told the first annual meeting of the committee. She maintained that " the workman himself is the chief industrial asset, and that the intelligent interest

necessarily related to the generally prevalent ' way of life,' and further that, in consequence, aesthetic, moral, and social judgements are closely interrelated. Such an hypothesis is now so generally accepted, as a matter of intellectual habit, that it is not always easy to remember that it is, essentially, a product of the intellectual history of the nineteenth century."

44. For various interpretations and descriptions of the school board troubles, see Jane Addams, *Twenty Years at Hull-House*, pp. 328–39, and Linn, *Jane Addams*, pp. 224–37. Allen F. Davis, " Raymond Robbins: the Settlement Worker as Municipal Reformer," *Social Service Review*, XXXIII (June, 1959), 140, says that Miss Addams was fearful of losing subscriptions for Hull House and refused to take a forthright stand on some issues because of this fear.

45. Woods and Kennedy, *The Settlement Horizon*, pp. 186–8, suggests that this national committee originated in a child labor committee formed by settlement workers in 1902 with Robert Hunter, head resident of University Settlement in New York City, as chairman.

of skilled men, that power of self-direction and co-operation which is only possible among the free and educated, should be the committee's foremost concern." An extension of the years of education was necessary, Miss Addams said, not only that the child might secure the training and fiber which would later make his participation in industry effective, but also that the child's mind might be trained to take final possession of the machines he would guide and feed. Premature industrial participation, Miss Addams charged, permanently destroyed the " free labor quality " of the producer; it destroyed his powers of originality, invention, and self-direction. Child labor sapped the vitality that carried a person through many years of life. Sending children to work unprepared was " imperilling our civilization." [46]

To help meet this peril, Jane Addams helped found another voluntary organization, the National Society for the Promotion of Industrial Education. This organization, founded in 1906, " came as close as any in the years before 1917 to being an association for the advancement of progressive education." [47] It was a rather mixed group, concentrated in the East, and made up of professional educators, industrialists and capitalists, conservative labor leaders, and social workers. The society held widely publicized meetings, commissioned studies, supported traveling lecturers, and actively lobbied—primarily in the cause of industrial education, but also for the whole spectrum of progressive educational reforms. The society's lobbying efforts were rewarded in 1917 with the passage of the Smith-Hughes Act, which provided federal subsidies for vocational education in secondary schools.[48]

Attempts to agree on the purposes and methods of industrial education filled the society's first years. The organization early endorsed the necessity of publicly supported industrial education and agreed that the secondary school was the level at which its interest lay. Aside from these two agreements, however, there was little unity among the members. Some in the association supported industrial education as the best source of cheap, nonunion

46. Jane Addams, " Child Labor Legislation, a Requisite for Industrial Efficiency," pp. 542, 545, 544, 550.
47. Cremin, *Transformation of the School*, p. 88.
48. For a rather unenlightening study see Robert Ripley Clough, " The National Society for the Promotion of Industrial Education, Case Study of a Reform Organization, 1906–1914," (unpublished Master's thesis, University of Wisconsin, 1957).

labor. Trade-union leaders attempted to control the society because they saw how unregulated industrial education could destroy the apprenticeship system and union control of craft training. For some professional educators, industrial education was merely a pedagogical device which would make the public schools more attractive and interesting to children. Other educators saw in industrial training a new democratic center for the common school curriculum which would help make the schools truer community social centers.

Jane Addams used the term industrial education in the liberal rather than vocational sense. By industrial education she meant general training in the history of industrial processes.[49] " I am not willing to agree," she told a meeting of the society, " that industrial education is one thing, and cultural education is of necessity quite another. Modern industry embodies tremendous human activities, inventions, constructive imaginations and records of devotion. Every factory filled with complicated machines has in it the possibilities of enormous cultural value if educators have the ability to bring out the long history, the human as well as the mechanical development, which it represents." Properly developed, industrial education might furnish deep insights into human culture.[50]

Miss Addams continued to dwell on the relation between culture and the forces of modern industrialism and insisted that only cultivated, educated producers could manufacture a superior industrial product. She came to believe, in addition, that the people themselves possessed the culture to transform industrialism. Her example was German. That nation's technological superiority came from German educators' truer understanding of what culture was. " The Grimm brothers first found in simple people a tremendous human power, a reservoir of charm and beauty and art— all those things which make life worth living. From that time,

49. In this usage Miss Addams followed the lead of one of the pioneers in the American movement for industrial education, C. M. Woodward, who used the phrase to designate studies " which shall impart a culture as truly liberal " as the traditional classic or preprofessional training. See his *Manual Training in Education* (London, 1890), p. 27. In *School and Society*, p. 133, Dewey wrote that whenever " the mastery of certain tools, or the production of certain objects, is made the primary end " of manual training, the educational value was lost.

50. Jane Addams, " Discussion," in National Society for the Promotion of Industrial Education, *Bulletin*, VI, Part 2 (May, 1908), 94.

German educators and statesmen have assumed more and more, that it is their business to uncover and develop that power, and to utilize and protect that source of cultivation which lies in the people themselves." [51]

American educators had been too timid to seize upon the industrial situation and extract its enormous educational value. This lack of courage and initiative "failed to fit the child for an intelligent and conscious participation in industrial life . . . [and the] lack of properly educated men was reflected in the industrial development itself." Education became unreal and far-fetched; industry became ruthless and materialistic. It was "the duty of the state to teach the child to dominate his machine by understanding it. He must know what the machine is about. . . ." Jane Addams was confident that industrial education would "enable the workman to master his machine with his mind as well as his hand, and to supplement the daily grind of the factory with some spiritual power which will humanize and lift the workman. . . ." [52]

Miss Addams never precisely described the way in which industrial education could prepare the worker to master his machine. Nor did she join in the disputes about pedagogical methods which, along with other professional educational matters, soon dominated the proceedings of the National Society for the Promotion of Industrial Education. She did, however, suggest the broad background on which the pedagogy of industrial education should be based. Industrial education had to conform with and utilize the basic instincts of the child, especially the instinct of workmanship. It was, she noted, a child's "instinct and pleasure to exercise all his faculties and to make discoveries in the world around him. . . ." The chief business of the teacher was "merely to direct his [the child's] activity and to feed his insatiable curiosity" by relating the child to his surroundings. [53]

The new pedagogy of industrial education was also to be built on certain social interests of the child. Truancy and quitting school at the legal age of fourteen were primarily the result of the schools' unwillingness to capitalize on the boy's natural interest

51. Jane Addams, "How Shall We Approach Industrial Education," *ibid.*, I (January, 1907), 39.
52. *Ibid.*
53. Jane Addams, "Child Labor Legislation, a Requisite for Industrial Efficiency," pp. 542–3.

and desires, Miss Addams said. At about age fourteen boys demanded that what they did in school should have some direct bearing on earning money, on their being men. Many boys (and also girls) would doubtless remain in school, she continued, were they and their families convinced that the remaining school years had a direct bearing on future wage-earning. The mistake in modern education was that it had "failed to see that this impulse to get ready to play the part of a man and earn money is a worthy educational impulse, quite as suggestive in its line of interest to the educator as the other things are, upon which education has founded itself. . . ." "Study the child," Jane Addams summarized her remarks on pedagogy, "and give him the things he so earnestly desires." [54]

Miss Addams had good precedent for appealing to the child's instinct as the foundation of the new pedagogy. [55] But these instincts needed guidance and nurture. She suggested that educational methods and techniques which would properly develop a child's instincts were being established in charitable work with abnormal children. Working to restore delinquent and psychopathic children provided insights into the processes by which all children learned self-direction and self-control. She cited the placement of orphans in foster homes, where standards of child nurture could be studied and established with some degree of accuracy. Agencies placing orphaned children could gradually

54. Jane Addams, "Discussion," in National Society for the Promotion of Industrial Education, *Bulletin*, pp. 95–6; Jane Addams, "Child Labor and Education," in National Conference of Charities and Correction, *Proceedings* (1908), p. 367.

55. Scientists like G. Stanley Hall and John Dewey described culture as a natural, almost unguided, automatic development of the instincts of children. From psychological investigations in his laboratory at The Johns Hopkins University after 1882 (Dewey was at The Hopkins in these years), Hall concluded that school teachers, the "guardians of the young [,] should strive first of all to keep out of nature's way, and to prevent harm, and should merit the proud title of defenders of the happiness and rights of children. They should feel profoundly that childhood, as it comes fresh from the hand of God, is not corrupt, but illustrates the survival of the most consummate thing in the world; they should be convinced that there is nothing else so worthy of life, reverence, and service as the body and soul of the growing child." G. Stanley Hall, "The Ideal School as Based on Child Study," *Forum*, XXXII (1901–2), 24–5. John Dewey in *Democracy and Education*, p. 52, quoted Emerson favorably "'Respect the child, respect him to the end . . . stop off his uproar, fooling and horseplay; keep his nature and *arm it with knowledge in the very direction in which it points.*'"

discover the prerequisites of care and sympathy necessary for the child's proper development. Thus charitable agencies could learn, through their work with orphans and delinquents, what was necessary for normal education and growth. Care of the feeblest, based on " the primitive emotion of compassion," held suggestions for a new pedagogy which would train and guide a child's natural instincts, and prepare him for industrial life.[56]

Miss Addams was convinced that children who had the benefits of this new kind of education would bring about a new integration of culture and industry. Her optimistic enthusiasm that a child's instincts of workmanship and creativity would flourish under the new education reached a kind of climax in 1912. Educators must look to the children themselves, she recommended to the social-work guild, for the " beginnings of a new life, something much more positive, much more beautiful, much more all-embracing than anything we have yet dealt with. . . ."[57] By 1912 Jane Addams was confident that a child's instincts, with the little guidance of newer educational methods, would create a truly democratic industrial culture in America. In her enthusiasm for such a prospect, Miss Addams glorified the natural instincts of the child.

Self-expression—the old Froebelian emphasis—was the most important emphasis in Miss Addams' optimistic hopes in 1912. " Self-expression is being so rapidly developed, is being so cleverly fostered in all our public schools " that it had to alter both the schools and American social life. This idea, that the child himself was the source of culture and art, was—as Lawrence Cremin has said—a Copernican revolution for the schools. Jane Addams

56. Jane Addams, " Child at the Point of Greatest Pressure," in National Conference of Charities and Correction, *Proceedings* (1912), pp. 26–30.

Jane Addams, " Democracy and Social Ethics," in Andrew C. McLaughlin and Albert Bushnell Hart (eds.), *Cyclopedia of American Government* (New York, 1914), p. 564. Woods and Kennedy, in *The Settlement Horizon*, pp. 270–1, state that the first psychopathic clinic for juvenile criminals, like the idea of a juvenile court, was pioneered by Hull House residents. The Chicago Board of Education established in 1899 a Department of Child-Study and Pedagogic Investigation. Headed by two of Dewey's students, this department concentrated on identifying children with physical and mental defects. The number of special classes and schools for the deaf, dumb, blind, crippled, or mentally retarded expanded rapidly. Tostberg, " Educational Ferment in Chicago," pp. 196–7, asserts that Chicago was the leader in providing such facilities.

57. Jane Addams, " Child at the Point of Greatest Pressure," pp. 26–7.

meant it in just this revolutionary sense. If the child were given opportunity to grow and adapt himself, he would " sweep away our little attempts at charity and correction. . . . We have not yet really begun to enjoy ourselves. We have not yet had full confidence in the wondrous things these children are learning to do. We have not yet learned to teach them as they should be taught, because we do not yet sufficiently reverence their possibilities." [58]

This confidence in the wonderful cultural possibilities of children's instincts characterized Miss Addams' educational thought in the years before World War I. Having worked long and earnestly for educational reform, especially for industrial education, Miss Addams believed that youth's wonderful striving for strength, beauty, and self-development, if unhindered, would reconcile and elevate culture and industrial life.

58. Lawrence A. Cremin, " The Revolution in American Secondary Education," *Teacher's College Record*, LVI (March, 1955), 303; Jane Addams, " Child at the Point of Greatest Pressure," pp. 28, 29, 30.

CHAPTER V

URBAN RECREATION

The spontaneous joy, the clamor for pleasure, the desire of the young people to appear finer and better and altogether more lovely than they really are, the idealization not only of each other but of the whole earth which they regard but as a theatre for their noble exploits, the unworldly ambitions, the romantic hopes, the make-believe world in which they live if properly utilized, what might they not do to make our sordid cities more beautiful and companionable.

JANE ADDAMS, 1909

Few Americans have so glowingly described the hopes of the young as did Jane Addams. She taught other progressives to understand and appreciate youth's striving for pleasure. For her, youth's instinct for enjoyment as expressed in play was a great vital social force that could conquer materialism and work for social righteousness. Miss Addams suffused young people's impulses toward pleasure and play with a high idealism. She believed that play contained the seeds of true culture and true democracy.

Miss Addams' understanding of play had various sources. The Rockford emphasis on physical education has already been described. Some of the literary figures that she read at the seminary also put special emphasis on physical education. In Ruskin's model school the laws of health were the first thing to be learned, along with exercise both indoors and out. " Riding, running, all the honest personal exercises of offense and defense, and music should be the primal heads of this bodily exercise." Perhaps Jane Addams also absorbed the emphasis of phrenologists on healthful exercise and on the laws of physiology and health.[1] She noticed the inclusion of sport in the Toynbee Hall conception of culture,

1. John A. Hobson quotes this from Ruskin's *Time and Tide* in his *John Ruskin, Social Reformer* (Boston, 1898), p. 172; Davies, *Phrenology, Fad and Science*, see Chapter VI, " Phrenology and Education."

and she was anxious to include play and social pleasure in the activities at Hull House.

This emphasis on social pleasure was part of the genius of the settlement movement. Jane Addams recalled the " eager interest " with which those at the first settlement conference in 1893 discussed Lester Ward's *Psychic Factors in Civilization*. Ward wrote that " there may be a positive moral progress in the increase of pleasure, the heightening of enjoyment, and the broadening and deepening of human happiness." This progress depended, according to Ward, on " the emancipation of social energy . . . by perfecting the social mechanism." [2] Settlement workers used recreational activities in order to build whole personalities and organize urban social life. They sponsored musical and theatrical entertainments, receptions, dances and cotillions, games, drills, and athletics. Jane Addams and Ellen Gates Starr were unusually resourceful in organizing these activities, and they found that their Hull House neighbors responded to the recreational opportunities with immediate and continuing enthusiasm. Their response led Miss Addams to reflect on the nature, sources, and uses of play and social pleasure, and on the relation of play to culture.

Jane Addams' emphasis on joy and recreation ran counter to the ideas of some other reformers. The amusement, the sociability, embodied in saloon and dance hall was in itself " a good and legitimate object," she told the ladies of the Woman's Christian Temperance Union. The good fellowship and social life that her neighbors found in these places needed to be transferred to other neighborhood institutions rather than prohibited.[3] Hull House activities were designed, at least in part, to do just that; the social activities of Hull House had simple fellowship and social pleasure as their aims. Boys' and girls' clubs constantly held dances, theatricals, debates, and parties of one sort or another. " The public always asks of a Hull House club what it is studying," wrote a resident. " The [Hull House] club is such a one as

2. Jane Addams, " Graham Taylor—Pioneer in Sociology," *Chicago Theological Seminary Register*, XVIII (November, 1928), 17; Lester Ward, *Psychic Factors in Civilization* (Boston, [1892] 1906), pp. 113, 114.

3. Jane Addams, " The Objects of Social Settlements," p. 148. See also a Hull House resident's analysis of the saloon and alternatives in E. C. Moore, " The Social Value of the Saloon," pp. 1–12.

hundreds of sociable people in Chicago join; Hull House offers it a pleasant room for its meetings, and a director who devises some things which its members could not devise for themselves." [4] The formal educational efforts included a spring social given by each class and a reception for all the students who had completed one of the college extension courses.

Jane Addams' ideas about play developed in the same fashion as her ideas on education. Based on her experiences at Hull House, she came to believe that play could inspire a higher and more democratic culture in American cities. She evolved a more pragmatic attitude toward the experiences of her neighbors and discovered what she believed to be primitive cultural resources among the immigrants.

She revealed her changing ideas about recreation most clearly in her writings about the theater. The stage provided training in " manners and personal refinement and courtesy " which could not be given by direct instruction and made these lessons more palatable by entertaining as well as instructing, she wrote in 1902.[5] In later years, this original emphasis gradually gave way to a view of the theater as a pragmatic testing ground for social relations. Jane Addams derived her new ideas partly from her experience with the Hull House Players, a semiprofessional little-theater group, formed in October, 1901. Membership was limited, and so highly prized that members who moved from the Hull House neighborhood frequently made long trips back to continue to participate. The Hull House Players performed the works of dramatists such as Ibsen, Shaw, and Galsworthy. William Butler Yeats once lectured to them.[6] Miss Addams noted that the stage was becoming the most popular teacher of public morals. For the playwrights, almost alone among moralists, had to " reduce their creeds to action. . . . It would be a striking result if the teachings of the contemporaneous stage should at last afford the moral

4. Madge C. Jenison, " A Hull House Play," *Atlantic Monthly*, XCVIII (July, 1906), 84.

5. Jane Addams, " What the Theatre at Hull-House Has Done for the Neighborhood People." *Charities*, VIII (March 29, 1902), 284.

6. Laura Dainty Pelham, " The Story of the Hull-House Players," *Drama*, VI (May, 1916), 249–62. Constance D'Arcy Mackay, an early historian of the little-theater movement, emphasized the preponderance of " ideological " drama at Hull House in her *The Little Theatre in the United States* (New York, 1917), pp. 115–9.

platform . . . [for] social reform." [7] Since ideals had to be reduced to action, Miss Addams wrote citing Aristotle, the stage offered a place where " things may be tested [vicariously], where society and the individual may find out the relation of settled methods and certain modes of living. . . ." Miss Addams called attention to the drama coming out of the New York City ghetto, which carried forward speculation on the " readjustment of the industrial machine that the primitive sense of justice and righteousness may secure larger play in social organization." [8]

Jane Addams came to see the theater as a significant resource for the formation of a more democratic culture in America. The theater could unite men, she said, because it appealed to man's primitive emotions. She cited Simon Patten's remark that the theater was the only place in the city that offered " memory food." The stage represented the basic emotions of love, jealousy, revenge, and daring. Participation in these ancestral and primitive emotions, even though based on illusion, was valuable, she maintained. The theater was thus able to bring men together in a common mood and to unite them through a mutual interest in elemental experience. [9]

The idea that the theater provided emotional participation which was both recreative and universally appealing suggested a whole new conception of play to Miss Addams. She explored more closely the relationship between play and culture. In 1907 she told how play embodied the experience of the race, especially the most primitive activities and experiences. " We have a multitude of games founded upon religious festivals, upon the manoeuvers of war, and of the chase, upon harvesting grain and treading the grapes, upon love making, upon trial by combat, upon the processes of primitive industry." Such games might provide a common cultural basis for all Americans. These games could be further

7. Jane Addams, " The Reaction of Moral Instruction upon Social Reform," *Survey*, XXII (April 3, 1909), 19.
8. Jane Addams, " Recent Immigration, a Field Neglected by the Scholar," p. 281; Jane Addams, " Child Labor on the Stage," *Annals*, XXXVIII, Supplement (July, 1911), 60–5.
9. Jane Addams, " Public Recreation and Social Morality," *Charities*, XVIII (August 3, 1907), 493. For a more modern treatment of the theater's effects on immigrants see Reuel Denney, *The Astonished Muse* (Chicago, 1957), p. 246, which suggests that theaters provided a new democratic language, and that movies socialized the immigrant.

adapted toward the primitive customs upon which they were based,
Miss Addams said, and the adaptation "would bring the game
nearer the universal type and therefore make more valuable [the
game's] recreative quality." [10]

The Hull House neighbors provided an instructive example in
the value of recreation. Even when on relief, and over the objection of the charity visitor, immigrant families spent money on
amusements. Jane Addams justified such expenditure: "As the
danger of giving no legitimate and organized pleasure to the
child becomes clearer, we remember that primitive man had games
long before he cared for a house or for regular means." [11] Immigrants realized this truth, she said, because the process of immigration stripped a person of all save the universal characteristics
of man. The simple immigrant who embodied the most basic
qualities of human personality connected play and culture quite
easily and naturally.

From play's roots in primitive emotion and activity Jane Addams
hoped a higher culture might evolve, a culture based on play.
Time to play in youth, Miss Addams cited scientists as saying,
was "the guarantee of adult culture. It is the most valuable
instrument the race possesses to keep life from becoming mechan-
ized." Especially for those whose later life would be one-sided
and mechanistic, a full period of childhood should be guaranteed,
so that "he may cultivate within himself the root of that culture
which can alone give his later activity a meaning. . . . Unusual
care must be taken to secure to the children their normal play
period, that the art instinct may have some chance and that the
producer himself may have enough coherence of character to
avoid becoming a mere cog in the vast industrial machine." [12]

Culture was not mere learning, Miss Addams remarked in 1905;
culture was the power of enjoyment, the power to play with a fact,
to get pleasure out of it. No one without this power, however
learned, was cultivated. "Some of us see that in the crowded
districts of our cities the one thing which stands for culture as

10. Jane Addams, "Public Recreation and Social Morality," p. 493. In a
telling metaphor, Miss Addams compared primitive customs with the "unspecified
cell" of evolutionary science.
11. Jane Addams, "The Subtle Problems of Charity," p. 173.
12. Jane Addams, "Child Labor Legislation, a Requisite for Industrial Efficiency," pp. 547, 548.

against mere mechanical learning, the thing which will keep life from becoming commonplace and dead, is the constant play of little children with each other." " Aesthetic feelings originate from the play impulse," Miss Addams believed, and " the constant experimentation found in the commonest plays are to be looked upon as ' the principal sources of all kinds of art.' " [13] Children, through their play, overcame differences in language, religion, dress, and manner. And, as Miss Addams noted elsewhere, " the definition of the cultivated man must always be that of the man who is able to forget differences of dress and language, of manner and other superficial distinctions because he is able to perceive and grasp the underlying elements of identity and comradeship." [14]

Jane Addams accompanied her theorizing about play with deeds that ultimately inspired Chicagoans to construct the finest park system in America.[15] In 1892 Hull House opened a small playground on three-quarters of an acre of land leased to Miss Addams rent free by William Kent. " It was open to both children and youths," said the historian of the American play movement. " The sand garden type of apparatus, sand pile, swings, building blocks, and giant slide, was provided for the younger children, while the boys of adolescent age played handball and indoor baseball. An experienced kindergartner and a policeman supervised the play-

13. Jane Addams, "Work and Play as Factors in Education," *Chautauquan*, XLII (November, 1905), 25; Jane Addams, " Child Labor Legislation, a Requisite for Industrial Efficiency," p. 548. John Dewey cited Matthew Arnold as the source for his statement that the ability of a mind to play freely about a subject, a playful attitude of mind, was a sign of culture. See his, " Play," in Paul Monroe (ed.), *Cyclopedia of Education* (New York, 1913), IV, 726.

14. Jane Addams' speech in University Settlement Association of New York, *Annual Report*, XVI (1902), 55. For a more extensive and systematic treatment of this relationship between play and culture, see Johan Huizinga, *Homo Ludens, a Study of the Play-Element in Culture* (Boston, 1955).

15. I have constructed my narrative of the development of recreation in Chicago from the following sources: Elizabeth Halsey, *Development of Public Recreation in Metropolitan Chicago* (Chicago, 1940); Graham R. Taylor, " Recreational Developments in Chicago Parks," *Annals*, XXXV (1910), 304–21; *Chicago Recreation Survey* (Chicago, 1937); Clarence E. Rainwater, *The Play Movement in the United States, a Study of Community Recreation* (Chicago, 1922); E. B. DeGroot, " Recent Playground Development in Chicago," *American Physical Education Review*, XIII (1908), 462–7; Charles Zueblin, " Municipal Playgrounds in Chicago," *American Journal of Sociology*, IV (1898–9), 145–8; Sadie American, " The Movement for Vacation Schools," *ibid.*, 309–25; and Charles Zueblin, *American Municipal Progress* (New York, 1916).

ground, the latter detailed by the city, usually umpired the indoor baseball game." In 1893 Hull House built a gymnasium to replace the makeshift indoor play area—once used as a saloon—which was so popular with the neighbors. These privately supported efforts provided the model for subsequent, and grander, public efforts.[16]

Public support for play in Chicago came first through the school board, which in 1892 established the position of Supervisor of Physical Education and provided for the first gymnasium ever built in an American public school at North-West Division High School. In 1897 the board allowed the West Side District of the United Charities—the district that included Hull House—to use school grounds for a summer playground. That same year, the school board decided to add playgrounds and gymnasiums to schools that had been constructed without them. Two years later the school board opened the play areas of six schools for summer use under the direction of the Vacation Committee of the Chicago Woman's Club. The Chicago Federation of Settlements urged the school board not only to allow school facilities to be used, but to take the initiative in establishing and supporting play-grounds and vacation schools.[17]

The most important public facilities for recreation in Chicago were created by various park districts. In 1895 the Illinois Legis-lature passed a general enabling act that permitted one hundred voters to petition a county judge to form a park district. Such districts had a locally elected board empowered to levy taxes and borrow against future taxes. In 1899 Mayor Carter Harrison formed a Special Chicago Park Commission which encouraged the formation of park districts in the city and the creation by these districts of small neighborhood parks. By 1910 Chicagoans had spent, or had committed themselves to spend, over ten million dollars for city parks. The landscaping and architecture for all the parks was done by Daniel H. Burnham and the Olmsted brothers, architects and planners of the 1893 Chicago World's

16. Rainwater, *Play Movement*, p. 56; Zeublin, *American Municipal Progress*, p. 302. Indoor baseball was played out of doors with a large soft baseball which allowed the game to be confined to a smaller area.

17. For the report of the federation's committee which lobbied for these purposes and of which Jane Addams was a leading member, see *Commons*, III (October, 1898), 11.

Fair, and the same men who were most active in the "city-beautiful" movement and in city planning.[18] Theodore Roosevelt enthusiastically described Chicago's parks as "one of the most notable civic achievements of any American city."[19]

The settlements in Chicago provided much of the inspiration and experience on which the city's park system was built. Graham R. Taylor, son of the founder of a Chicago settlement and secretary of the Chicago Playground Association, was too modest when he said guardedly that for "some of the social and recreative lines [of the public parks] the work of the social settlement undoubtedly afforded in some degree a prototype." Edward B. DeGroot moved from his post as Hull House playground leader to Director of Gymnastics and Athletics for the South Park District. The Chicago School of Civics and Philanthropy, created by local settlement people and led by Graham Taylor, was one of the few places where professional recreational training was available.[20]

Settlement people also helped found the Playground Association of America in 1906 in order to spread their ideas of play and the example of the Chicago park system throughout the country. The association recognized Miss Addams' local leadership in Chicago by electing her vice-president. Professional recreation leaders, settlement residents, philanthropists, and municipal officers and reformers were present at the organizational meeting in Washington. Men and women active in city planning, municipal art programs, and other progressive municipal reforms identified themselves with the association and its agitation for city parks and playgrounds.[21] The first national meeting of the association was held in Chicago. As an officer, familiar with the local playground movement, Miss Addams addressed the association on a practical topic: the uses of play.

18. The Burnham Plan, the most important city plan for Chicago, was completed in 1908. For a recent study of Burnham and F. L. Olmsted, and their relation to urban reform, see Ray Lubove, *The Progressives and the Slums, Tenement House Reform in New York City. 1890–1917* (Pittsburgh, 1962), pp. 217 ff.

19. Roosevelt is quoted thus in Graham R. Taylor, "How They Played at Chicago," *Charities and The Commons*, XVIII (August 3, 1907), 473.

20. Taylor, "Recreational Developments in Chicago Parks," p. 336. Several Hull House residents worked on the New Deal survey of city recreation.

21. See H. S. Curtis, "How It Began," *Recreation*, XXV (May, 1931), 71, and Howard Brauscher, "Early Days of the Playground Association of America," *Recreation*, XXV (May, 1931), 72.

Play or recreation—Jane Addams used the words interchange-ably—had two main uses in the modern city. Play could unite isolated city dwellers through mutual social interest, and play was the method through which men could express their indi-viduality. Thus provision for recreation could defeat the devices for keeping men ignorant of each other, with which the modern city was filled, and at the same time liberate city dwellers by revealing each individual's unique character.

Miss Addams stressed that recreation allowed individuals to realize and develop their individuality. Scientists, she wrote, told how the imaginative powers—the sense that life possessed variety and color—were realized most easily in moments of pleasure and comradeship. It was then that individual differences and varia-tions were disclosed. " Only in moments of recreation does . . . [our] sense of individuality expand; . . . [we] are then able to reveal, as at no other time, that hidden self which is so important to each of us." Playgrounds gave the opportunity " to express, as nowhere else, that sense of being unlike one's fellows. . . ." This assertion of individuality was also the path of social progress. " The variation from the established type," wrote Jane Addams, " is at the root of all change, the only possible basis for progress, all that keeps life from growing unprofitably stale and repetitious." [22]

She believed that urban culture—the civilization of the cities—depended on provision for recreation. The city offered rich cul-tural opportunities for varied social relationships, she wrote in 1912. But in order that each city dweller might avail himself of this great gift, the city had to organize and structure its social life, and this was where recreation could make a major contribution. Play was the antidote for the poisonous loneliness and solitude that filled the modern city. It was the " prime motive " uniting children and drawing them into a comradeship which discovered and revealed and respected human differences and human varia-tion. " A true democratic relation and ease of acquaintance is found only among the children of a typical factory community because they readily overcome differences of languages, tradition and religion, which form insuperable barriers to adults." On city

22. Jane Addams' page, *Ladies' Home Journal*, XXX (July, 1913), 19; Jane Addams, " Recreation as a Public Function in Urban Communities," *American Journal of Sociology*, XVII (March, 1912), 616; Jane Addams, *Spirit of Youth and the City Streets* (New York, 1909), pp. 8–9.

playgrounds, according to Jane Addams, children could learn the techniques and methods of knowing each other, of revealing themselves to each other, in short, of consciously living together in the crowded human city.[23]

These remarks show Jane Addams' identification of culture with the city. Indeed she idealized the city. It was the place, she said citing Aristotle, "where men live a common life for noble ends." The human city was a place of freedom and at the same time a place of "companionship in a larger measure than can be obtained elsewhere. . . . You exalt and intensify your own self-consciousness as you see it revealed in like-minded people who are living in this vast concourse [of the city] but who could not be found at all if the concourse were smaller." Jessie Binford, long-time Hull House resident, relates that many of the residents in the years before 1917 journeyed into the open countryside on Sundays, " just to be in the country—some wanted to paint, others to walk." The head resident did not accompany them. When they returned she would ask whether they had had a good time, and ask what they had managed to find to do all day—in the country. It " just did not appeal to her," Miss Binford says.[24]

In 1907 Miss Addams wrote of the " dreariness of American farm life. . . ." Later, in 1913, she stressed the disadvantages of a rural upbringing. The country child had never learned to do things with other people; he was inclined to be set in his ways, to lack alertness and ability. Those who grew up in the country and moved to the city had great difficulty learning how to know other people and revealing themselves to others; they had great difficulty playing. To Miss Addams urban recreation was not, as Morton and Lucia White assert, a nostalgic " effort to recapture some of the natural, almost biological features of rural community living." Rather, play was the instrument for bringing about a purer democracy and a higher morality to the life of American cities.[25]

Many members of the Playground Association of America inter-

23. Jane Addams, " Child Labor Legislation, a Requisite for Industrial Efficiency," p. 548; Jane Addams, " Child at the Point of Greatest Pressure," p. 28.

24. Jane Addams, *Newer Ideals of Peace* (New York, 1907), pp. 92, 9–10; Jane Addams, " Child at the Point of Greatest Pressure," p. 28; letter, Jessie Binford to author, May 21, 1962.

25. Jane Addams, *Newer Ideals of Peace*, pp. 66–7; Morton and Lucia White, *The Intellectual Versus the City, from Thomas Jefferson to Frank Lloyd Wright*

preted play as training in democratic morality.[26] Miss Addams
developed this theme on several occasions. More than once she
explained how public games prepared young men for political
democracy. Playground activities embodied ideals of fair play
which were also the rules upon which democracy was founded.
On the playground each boy had to accept rules that embodied a
rude sort of justice. The relevance of such rules to democracy
was especially important, Miss Addams noted, because modern
patriotism had to be based "not upon a consciousness of homo-
geneity but upon a respect for variation, not upon inherited
memory but upon trained imagination." [27]

Miss Addams was quite specific about how play was related
to more just human relations in politics. Corrupt politicians continued in power, Miss Addams wrote, perhaps recalling her campaigns against Alderman Powers, by utilizing those old human
notions of personal affection, desire for favors, fear of ridicule,
and loyalty to comrades. The leader of a gang of boys, just like
a political boss, appealed to these motives. The playground could
alter this pattern. A group of boys, Miss Addams assured readers
in the *Ladies' Home Journal*, would not continue to play in the
streets and alleys and poolrooms—with their illicit pleasures—

(Cambridge, Mass., 1962), p. 150. See *Twenty Years at Hull-House*, pp. 16–18,
for Jane Addams' wonderful description of her own rural youth. This conventional
rural lyric, which appears in so many autobiographies by Progressives, only emphasizes Jane Addams' absorption in the life of the city. Miss Addams was in the Henry
George tradition of urban reform which identified the city with never democratic
and cultural ideals. Brand Whitlock said that Tom Johnson knew "intuitively that
the city in all ages has been the outpost of civilization, and that if the problem
of democracy is to be solved at all it is to be solved first in the city." Sam Jones's
dream was "a city in which there were the living conceptions of justice, pity,
mercy, consideration, tolerance, beauty, art, all those graces which mankind so long
has held noblest and most dear." See Brand Whitlock, *Forty Years of It* (New
York, 1914), pp. 172, 366, and Frederick C. Howe, *The City, the Hope of
Democracy* (New York, 1906), especially Chap. XVI "The City Beautiful."
    26. See the association's president, Luther Halsey Gulick, "Play and Democ-
racy," *Charities and The Commons*, XVIII (August 3, 1907), 481–6; Joseph Lee,
an active member of the association, "Play as a School of the Citizen," *Charities
and the Commons*, XVIII (August 3, 1907), 486–91; Henry S. Curtis, the asso-
ciation's secretary-treasurer, "Playground Training," *American Physical Education
Review*, XVI (May, 1911), 302–8. See also Mary E. McDowell, "Recreation as
Fundamental Element of Democracy," *Playground*, VII (August, 1913), 191–5.
Many of these people drew on an essay by Josiah Royce, "Some Relations of
Physical Training to the Present Problems of Moral Education in America," in his
Race Questions, Provincialism and Other American Problems (New York, 1908).
    27. Jane Addams, "Recreation as a Public Function in Urban Communities,"
p. 616; Jane Addams' page, *Ladies' Home Journal*, XXX (August, 1913), 19.

after they had discovered the "fascinating apparatus" of the playground. Once on the playground, the gang leader would find his special power of manipulation gone. For success on the playground went to the boy who could best meet competitive athletic standards, standards that depended on personal prowess alone. Boys on the playground, Miss Addams continued, learned to detest exploitation, to despise pleas for special treatment. Thus the rules of the playground were preparation for future political participation, "the basis for a new citizenship [that] in the end will overthrow the corrupt politician." [28] Team spirit, respect for rules and for the standards of athletic achievement—however absurd these specific rules and standards seemed to adults—were analogues to a higher social morality and a purer democracy for American cities.

In 1909 Jane Addams published a lyric to play, *The Spirit of Youth and the City Streets*. This book was her favorite among all those she wrote. It represents her mature ideas on the origins and psychology of play. The background for her inquiry into the origins of play was the work of academic scientists. Her friend William James listed the play instinct along with twenty-eight others in his *Psychology*. She probably knew of G. Stanley Hall's analysis of play: "the motor habits and spirit of the past of the race persisting into the present. . . ." [29] Miss Addams was also familiar with Karl Groos' book, *The Play of Man*, published in 1901, in which he interpreted play as the method by which crude childish faculties were prepared for adult tasks. She settled on none of these explanations, however. Rather she emphasized that play was self-expression and self-assertion of man's nature, particularly man's erotic nature. This original explanation of play was her most important contribution to the movement for urban recreation. It is certainly the most interesting aspect of her thought about play. [30]

Jane Addams described how play revealed erotic and sensuous

28. *Ibid.*; see also G. Stanley Hall, *Youth. Its Education, Regimen, and Hygiene* (New York & London, 1907), Chap. VI, "Play Sports, and Games," in which Hall says that play at its best is merely a school of ethics.

29. G. Stanley Hall, *Adolescence, Its Psychology, and Its Relations to Physiology, Anthropology, Sociology, Sex, Crime, Religion and Education* (New York, [1904] 1920), I, 202.

30. When other members of the Playground Association of America used the idea that play was "a vicarious expression of the sex impulse," they cited Miss

elements of the human personality that were frequently hidden or disguised or repressed. She knew nothing of Freud's work, yet she understood the mechanism of repression. She explained a wide variety of deviant behavior as the consequence of repression of sexual drives for which the normal outlet was play. The city's irresponsibility about play ignored the fact, she wrote, that "amusement is stronger than vice and that [amusement] . . . alone can stifle the lust for [vice]. We see all about us much vice that is merely a love for pleasure ' gone wrong,' the illicit expression of what might have been not only normal and recreative pleasure, but an instrument in the advance of a higher morality." [31]

She described in *Spirit of Youth* the difficulties the city boy found in expressing, either in his job or in his leisure, " the sudden and furious bursts of energy, his overmastering desire to do things ' without being bossed all the time. . . .' "

> He discovers that in whatever really active pursuit he tries to engage, he is promptly suppressed by the police. After several futile attempts at self-expression, he returns to his street corner subdued and so far discouraged that when he has the next impulse to vigorous action he concludes that it is of no use, and sullenly settles back into inactivity. He thus learns to persuade himself that it is better to do nothing, or, as the psychologist would say, " to inhibit his motor impulses." [32]

But Miss Addams was convinced that such inhibition was futile. In 1901 she had written—citing unnamed psychologists as authorities—that under the influence of strong emotions, such as fear, certain elements of self could be prevented from coming into action. But these elements were only stupified or drugged. Sooner or later they asserted themselves in all their old power. " All such inhibitive measures must in the end be futile," she concluded. On the same topic in *Spirit of Youth* Miss Addams wrote that

Addams; see Henry S. Curtis, *Education through Play* (New York, 1915), p. 73. For two modern treatments that roughly parallel Miss Addams' idea see Robert W. White, " Motivation Reconsidered, the Problem of Competence," *Psychological Review*, LXVI (1959), 292–333; and Franz Alexander, " A Contribution to the Theory of Play," *Psychoanalytic Quarterly*, XXVII (1958), 175–93.

31. Jane Addams, " Public Recreation and Social Morality," p. 494.
32. Jane Addams, *Spirit of Youth*, pp. 109, 110–1.

" the love of pleasure will not be denied, and when it has turned into all sorts of malignant and vicious appetites, then we, the middle aged, grow quite distracted and resort to all sorts of restrictive measures. We even try to dam up the sweet fountain itself because we are affrighted by these neglected streams. . . ." [33]

Miss Addams reviewed the offenses for which young girls and boys had been brought before the Cook County Juvenile Court. Many of these offenses were crimes of great imagination, excitement, and adventure, characteristics that were " basic " to youth and that " will be evinced by each generation of city boys. . . ." Most of the fifteen thousand juvenile criminals in the court in 1908 " had broken the law in their blundering efforts to find adventure and in response to the old impulse for self-expression." An adult with the most rudimentary notion of prudence could not have imagined or committed these juvenile crimes, which were characterized by recklessness and bravado. " Only the utilization of that sudden burst of energy belonging partly to the future could have achieved them, only the capture of the imagination and of the deepest emotions of youth could have prevented them! " [34]

The deepest emotions, Miss Addams suggested, were those that expressed man's sensual and erotic life. [35] The " fundamental sex susceptibility " suffused the world with its deepest beauty and meaning; it furnished the momentum toward all art. This was revealed most clearly by youth during puberty, that basic experience which had so many varied, remote, and indirect expressions. At puberty a boy's instincts urged him to action yet frightened him by their novelty and undefined power. Mastering these instincts was difficult because at the time of their arousal, youth's sense of self-control and discrimination was least educated. Young people's senses were singularly acute during early adolescence, Miss Addams wrote. Youth stood helplessly open to the world.

33. Jane Addams, " Respect for Law," *Independent*, LIII (January 3, 1901), 20; Jane Addams, *Spirit of Youth*, p. 6.

34. Jane Addams, *Spirit of Youth*, p. 70. On Cook County Juvenile Court, the first in America, championed by Hull House residents, see Herbert H. Lou, *Juvenile Courts of the United States* (Chapel Hill & London, 1927).

35. In trying to appeal to her neighbors after a day of sense-dulling labor, Miss Addams reported in 1897, only the highly sensuous could penetrate. " Only music with a real swing or a sensuous appeal " could arouse neighbors from their exhaustion. See Jane Addams, " Social Settlements," p. 341.

It was nothing short of cruel, she insisted, to overestimate the senses of the young and inexperienced as the modern city did. Youth's power to appreciate developed far ahead of his power to express himself, she declared.[36]

Mastering the erotic instincts was doubly hard for city youth because the modern city retarded the imagination while stimulating the senses. Thus the city brutalized and finally broke the connection between the sex impulse and increased human and social consciousness. Urban youth, Jane Addams noted, had developed no capacity for recreation demanding mental effort or muscular skill; nor had they the necessary discipline for any consecutive recreational effort. They were reduced to seeking that which depended on vagrant sight, sound, and taste; they interpreted the strong drives of puberty in purely selfish ways.[37]

The history of civilization, Miss Addams summarized in 1909, was the effort to substitute some sort of ideal for the driving force of blind appetite. "In failing to diffuse and utilize this fundamental instinct of sex through the imagination, we not only inadvertently foster vice and enervation, but we throw away one of the most precious instruments for ministering to life's highest needs." Unless the twentieth-century city tried to return to the hopelessly outmoded rural model—where community restraint and genuine social control existed—it had to go down the path of freedom for the young, freedom made safe by knowledge and habits of self-control.[38]

Play could provide the discipline, instruction, and guidance toward self-control, she maintained. Sound advice to young men in regard to the physical changes of adolescence "emphasizes a clean mind, exhorts an imagination kept free from sensuality and insists upon days filled with wholesome athletic interest." Play could also relate individual drives to the welfare of others. Miss Addams singled out the folk dances of her immigrant neighbors as ideal instruction in self-control: "These old forms of dancing which have been worked out in many lands and through long

36. Jane Addams, *Spirit of Youth*, p. 16; see also Jane Addams, *A New Conscience and an Ancient Evil* (New York, 1912), Chap. IV.

37. Jane Addams, *Spirit of Youth*, Chap. II. Compare G. Stanley Hall, "The Ideal School Based on Child Study," *Forum*, XXXII (1901–2), 35: ". . . at no stage of life [as adolescence] is the power to appreciate and apprehend so far ahead of power to express."

38. Jane Addams, *Spirit of Youth*, p. 29.

experiences, safeguard unwary and dangerous expression and yet afford a vehicle through which the gaiety of youth may flow. Their forms are indeed those which lie as the basis of all good breeding, forms which at once express and restrain, urge forward and set limits." [39]

Jane Addams held the highest hopes for the transforming power of modern youth once they were adequately protected and provision had been made to secure their play. The children themselves would transform culture and politics, just as she hoped they would transform education. Playing children would bring a new righteousness to industry, would purify democracy, would, in short, invigorate and elevate American culture. Her hopes for this transformation lay not with professional recreation leaders, but with the children themselves. In the peroration of *Spirit of Youth*, she described her apocalyptic vision of the "august moral resources" contained in the new spirit of youth. These resources could bring order out of chaos, beauty out of confusion, justice and kindliness and mercy out of cruelty and inconsiderate pressure. Youth had a great power for direct action, an ability to stand free from fear, to break through life's trammelings. Most of all, youth desired to improve the world. Young people impatiently insisted on strenuous and vital action to right the world's wrongs and injustices. The modern city, Miss Addams mourned, had isolated these desires of youth. No effort had been made to channel and discipline them, to make them operative in the life of the city. Yet these desires were the only thing that could make democracy work. America had, she insisted, only one court of last appeal against the materialism of culture. This court was "the wonderful and inexplicable instinct for justice which resides in the hearts of men,—which is never so irresistible as when the heart is young. We may cultivate this most precious possession, or we may disregard it." America could "either stand stupidly staring as [the divine fire of youth] sinks into a murky fire of crime and flares into the intermittent blaze of folly or we may tend it into a lambent flame with power to make clean and bright our dingy city streets." [40]

39. Jane Addams, *A New Conscience and an Ancient Evil*, pp. 105–6; Jane Addams, *Spirit of Youth*, pp. 15–6.
40. Jane Addams, *Spirit of Youth*, pp. 161–2. Richard C. Cabot, a Boston physician, wrote in his *What Men Live By* (Boston, 1914), p. 90, that since Miss Addams' *Spirit of Youth*, men have come "to think of recreation as something holy."

CHAPTER VI

CLIMAX AND DISSATISFACTIONS: THE PROGRESSIVE CAMPAIGN OF 1912

We [Americans] do not unite for action because we are not stirred to act at all, [thus] the protective legislation in America is shamefully inadequate . . . it is easy to unite for action people whose hearts have been filled by the fervor of that willing devotion which religion always generates in the human heart, from whatever creed it may be preached.

JANE ADDAMS, 1909

Jane Addams' confidence in the ability of man to master and transform his environment, to bring order and beauty and justice to his social relations reached a climax in 1912. The Progressive party seemed to consolidate reform efforts in which she had participated through many separate organizations. She was drawn into the party, and later into the campaign, by the party's endorsement of woman suffrage and its demands for social and industrial justice. She was also attracted to the party by its flood of optimism, enthusiasm, and moral fervor which persuaded many progressives that their long, separate labors were about to be realized. For Jane Addams, 1912 was the year of greatest hope, and the years immediately after were filled with dissatisfaction.

Although not a militant suffragette, Miss Addams entered national politics because she believed that women needed the franchise. Ever since her Rockford days she had favored woman suffrage, and by 1912 she was convinced that many of women's traditional activities were conducted outside the home as matters of public policy. Political agencies conducted these traditional activities less efficiently and humanely because women could not vote. And women who were cut off from their old jobs of protecting the home, educating children, and humanizing social and industrial relations were becoming social and moral reactionaries.

120

Jane Addams placed women's votes in the larger context of democratic self-government. She specifically rejected the arguments for woman suffrage based on the doctrine of natural rights. Such arguments were the " traditional women's rights clamor." Arguments from natural rights were " too barren and chilly " to convince men of the twentieth century; they were the " platitudes of our crudest youth." The whole doctrine of inalienable rights was an empty dignity, a " moral romanticism." The twentieth century, she wrote, had found a more passionate democratic creed —the evolutionary idea of human rights gradually won in the process of history itself. It was this idea of democratic self-government as an evolutionary concept that inspired Miss Addams' demands for woman suffrage. The history of self-government was " merely a record of human interests which had become the subject of governmental action, and of the incorporation into the government itself of the classes who represented the new interests. . . ." Since women's traditional concerns had become the objects of governmental action, it was appropriate to give women the vote.[1]

Government in the twentieth century was concerned with large areas of social and economic life, in Miss Addams' analysis, and primitive societies had much to tell modern man about effective governmental organization. If democratic self-government were to be inaugurated by the advanced men of her day, Jane Addams believed that they should conduct the most careful research into " those early organizations of village communities, folk-motes, and mirs, those primary cells of both social and political organization where the people knew no difference between the two, but quite simply met to consider in common discussion all that concerned their common life. They would investigate the craft guilds and *artels*, which combined government with daily occupation, as did the self-governing university and free town." The idealistic founding fathers of America, the " advanced men " of the eighteenth century, were " unconscious of the compulsions of origins and of the fact that self-government had an origin of its own. . . ." The founders, Miss Addams maintained, had depended on property rights and English law, on " penalties, coercion, com-

---

1. Jane Addams, *Twenty Years at Hull-House*, p. 340; Jane Addams, " Recent Immigration, a Field Neglected by the Scholar," p. 275; Jane Addams, " Votes for Women and Other Votes," *Survey*, XXVIII (June 1, 1912), 367.

pulsion, and remnants of military codes to hold the community together . . . rather than a well-grounded belief in social capacity and in the efficiency of the popular will." [2]

Jane Addams blamed the failures of democratic self-government in America—" the shame of the cities "—on the failure of the founders to provide a vehicle for the " vital and genuinely organized expression of the popular will." Government was becoming remote and unreal because it refused to deal with the actual life of the mass of men. The devotion, comradeship, zeal, and *esprit de corps* that might have been won by government had been absorbed in America by voluntary organizations, because these organizations dealt with the real issues of life. " A government has always received feeble support from its constituents," Miss Addams declared, " as soon as its demands appeared childish or remote. Citizens invariably neglect or abandon civic duty when it no longer embodies their genuine desires." [3]

The admission of women to the electorate, she thought, would revive democratic self-government. Women would demand that government concern itself with the chief problems of life in the modern city—primitive human-welfare problems—which had traditionally been women's concern. If one could connect these " primordial " problems, " these old maternal anxieties, which are really the basis of family and tribal life, with the candidates who are seeking offices it would never be necessary to scold either man or women for remaining at home on election day." [4]

Women needed the experience that political participation brought in order to avoid becoming indifferent to social problems. " For women's voice to be effective in all our enlarged housekeeping, she needs full suffrage; and if she needed it for nothing else, she has claim to share the fullest social civic life for the sake of her own mental development." The denial of the ability to remedy the adverse conditions of city life caused women to lose interest in these conditions. For, as Miss Addams put it, the " ability to perform an obligation comes very largely in proportion as that obligation is conscientiously assumed." Unen-

2. Jane Addams, " Problems in Municipal Administration," *American Journal of Sociology*, X (January, 1905), 426, 427.

3. *Ibid.*, p. 427; Jane Addams, " Recent Immigration, a Field Neglected by the Scholar," p. 283.

4. Jane Addams, " Modern City and the Municipal Franchise for Women," *Woman's Journal*, XXXVII (April 7, 1906), 53–5.

franchised women increasingly lost touch with new standards and ideals in housekeeping—either individual or municipal housekeeping. The voteless woman was doomed to "moral idleness," an idleness which retarded all kinds of social and political progress.[5]

Thus Jane Addams regarded woman suffrage as an instrumentality rather than a right. She argued for the ballot by describing how the community might be improved if women could vote. With equal suffrage, women's homebuilding instincts, their love of order, and their passion for details would be reflected in industrial adjustment and reform.

> Those affairs which naturally and historically belong to women, . . . are constantly overlooked and slighted by our political institutions. . . . To turn the administration of our civic affairs wholly over to men may mean that the American city will continue to lag behind in those things which make a city healthful and beautiful. . . . If women have in any sense been responsible for the gentler side of life which softens and blurs some of its harsher conditions, then certainly they have a duty to perform in our American cities.[6]

For the Bryn Mawr graduating class of 1912, Miss Addams elaborated this argument. The discipline of college training only sharpened women's desire to oversee the performance of their traditional activities. She listed the special contributions that college women—when enfranchised—could make to the community. A college woman who had specialized in economics would get sweatshop and tenement-house work outlawed, industrial laboring conditions licensed and inspected, minimum-wage boards and maximum-hours legislation for women's work, the prohibition of night work, the protection of childbearing women, and all the new legislation embodied in employers' liability acts. A college woman who had specialized in economics would also demand, according to Miss Addams, that labor unions be granted legal status, that free employment bureaus be established, that trade-training be available free, that the liquor traffic be regu-

5. *Ibid.*, p. 16; Jane Addams' speech, Madison, Wisconsin, January 23, 1912, reported in Chicago *Tribune*, February 4, 1912, Sec. IX, p. 1; Jane Addams' speech, "Communion of the Ballot," November, 1912, typescript, SCPC; Jane Addams, "Pragmatism in Politics," *Survey*, XXIX (October 5, 1912), 12.
6. Jane Addams, "Woman Suffrage and the Protection of the Home," *Ladies' Home Journal*, XXVII (January, 1910), 21.

lated, that industrial arbitration and conciliation apparatus be established, and that scientific management be adopted by industry.

The college woman with scientific training, were she to get the ballot, would want to apply bacteriological tests to the milk supply, to foods, and to the public water supply in order to assure their purity and safety. She would insist on measures to prevent infant mortality and to care for newborn infants—such measures as the prevention of blindness, regulation of midwifery, control of contagious diseases, vaccination and the administration of tetanus antitoxin, care of tuberculosis, and medical supervision of school children. Such college-trained women, Miss Addams suggested, would also want to concern themselves with the sanitation and ventilation of housing, the disposal of wastes, and the prevention of industrial diseases.

The college woman trained in the liberal arts, because she had no ballot, was prevented from getting care for dependent children, pensions for mothers, care for the aged, poor, and homeless, and care for mental defectives. Without the vote, no one listened to her protests about the conditions of jails and penitentiaries, of police stations, or to her suggestions for the gradual elimination of prostitution. The liberal arts graduate would probably concern herself with the extended care of young girls—raising the legal age of consent and establishing juvenile courts. She would, Miss Addams was sure, work for the suppression of gambling, the protection of immigrants, for decent advertising, municipal art, and for more useful public facilities like baths and washhouses.

The college woman who immediately married and established a household needed the franchise most of all, Jane Addams asserted. For without the vote she could take no part in forming the laws regulating marriage and divorce, defining legitimacy, or protecting a married woman's legal rights. She would be unable to influence laws governing nonsupport, exemption and homestead laws which would protect her in case her husband went bankrupt, or laws regarding coguardianship. Without the ballot the married woman was unable to influence public provision for the education of her children and their recreation—child labor laws, vocational guidance, industrial education, and playgrounds.[7]

7. Jane Addams, "The Civic Value of Higher Education for Women," *Bryn Mawr Alumnae Quarterly*, VI (June, 1912), 59–67.

Jane Addams' desire to possess the instrumentality of the ballot gained immediacy and urgency as the need for reform was increasingly acknowledged. By 1912 she believed that the case for these various reforms had been proved, and that the American people, perhaps even a majority of the male voters, were ready to endorse them. Miss Addams' convictions that the time was ripe for a consolidated national effort in the name of reform and for the granting of the most effective instrument toward reform—woman suffrage—drew her into partisan politics.

As an officer of the National American Woman Suffrage Association and as a well-known advocate of equal suffrage, Jane Addams requested a hearing from the platform committee of the Republican national convention when it met in Chicago in June, 1912. The committee summoned her by telephone one evening and gave her one hour's notice of her scheduled appearance. When Miss Addams arrived somewhat breathlessly, with a hastily gathered group of Chicago suffrage leaders, she "was told that she might have five minutes (later extended to seven) and present one speaker. . . . There was confusion and noise in the room and the attention of the committee was distracted. The platform contained no reference to woman suffrage." [8]

Plans for another political convention held Jane Addams in Chicago into August in 1912. Theodore Roosevelt, deprived of the Republican nomination, allowed a new party to form around his desire to humiliate Taft. Jane Addams was asked to join the Roosevelt party, which seemed to promise considerably more sympathy for many of the causes to which she was committed than any other political organization.[9] She knew Roosevelt stood for woman suffrage because she listened to him—some said convinced him to—endorse equal suffrage publicly for the first time.[10]

8. Elizabeth Cady Stanton, Susan B. Anthony *et al.* (eds.), *History of Woman Suffrage* (New York, 1881–1922), V, 705.

9. Jane Addams, "Lessons of the Election," *City Club [of Chicago] Bulletin*, V (November 27, 1912), 362: "When I found a party that went just about as far as I did, and when, moreover, I was asked to join it—and of course to be 'asked' is always an important element in a woman's career—I was very happy indeed to do so."

10. In March, 1911, according to Hull House lore, Roosevelt visited Hull House and rode with Miss Addams, Charles E. Merriam, and Grace Abbott to a mass meeting of immigrants who had just received their second papers and were therefore entitled to vote. Conversation in the car turned to woman suffrage. Miss Addams opined to the Colonel that "it might work almost as well as manhood suffrage has worked." At the meeting Roosevelt endorsed equal suffrage for the first time

She also knew that after the Republican convention Roosevelt had seen a special report by the committee on industrial standards of the National Conference of Charities and Correction. The committee had been appointed in 1909, when Jane Addams was elected the first woman president of the conference. Paul U. Kellogg, committee chairman in 1910, explained how the committee furnished a focus and common platform for the agitations conducted separately by groups such as the National Child Labor Committee, the National Consumer's League, the Woman's Trade Union League, the American Association for Labor Legislation, and the National Tuberculosis Association. All these organizations were concerned with defining minimum social and industrial standards. The time had come, Kellogg asserted, to frame standards " definite enough so that a public legislator, or a business manager, who disregards these standards may know that he offends as definitely as the man who disobeys generally accepted rules of health or violates the ordinary canons of decency." The committee's report, submitted in 1912, presented not a " declaration of social ideals . . . [but] the sub-basement floor which we regard as positively the lowest stratum that should be tolerated by a community interested in self-preservation." [11] The report urged minimum-wage boards, a living minimum wage, the eight-hour day, the six-day week, safety and health regulations, the right to a home, abolition of child labor (the minimum age was 16), abolition of sweatshops, and social insurance against sickness, unemployment, industrial accidents, and old age. Kellogg wrote Jane Addams that he had had a session with Roosevelt at Oyster Bay in July. Roosevelt " took over the Cleveland program of standards of life and labor almost bodily, and it was, as you know, incorporated in the Progressive platform." [12]

with Miss Addams' quip. See Linn, *Jane Addams*, p. 273; Edith Abbott, " Grace Abbott and Hull House, 1908–1921," *Social Service Review*, XXIV (December, 1950), 502; Correspondence File " A ", National Federation of Settlements. Roosevelt's changing attitude toward equal suffrage, and his growing support as it seemed like an issue that could win him political support is revealed in E. E. Morison *et al.*, eds., *Letters of Theodore Roosevelt* (Cambridge, Mass., 1951–4), VI, 240, 1341–2, and VII, 594–5.

11. Paul U. Kellogg, " Report of the Committee on Occupational Standards," in National Conference of Charities and Correction, *Proceedings* (1910), p. 374; " Report of the Committee of Standards of Living and Labor," in *ibid.* (1912), p. 377.

12. Kellogg, " Report of the Committee of Standards of Living and Labor," pp. 388–94; Paul U. Kellogg, " The Industrial Platform of the New Party,"

Miss Addams did indeed know that the report had been incorporated into the Progressive platform, for she was an important member of the party's platform committee.[13] The meetings of this committee were one of the most extraordinary features of this extraordinary convention. Open hearings were scheduled; all delegates, or anyone in Chicago, were invited to appear and offer suggestions. Chester Rowell, editor of the Fresno (California) *Republican*, wrote eloquently about the direct democracy of this platform-writing process. He described these proceedings of the committee as a " new thing in platform making." Even a cursory glance would convince one that it was " new in its comprehensiveness, new in its definiteness, and new in its sociological tone. . . ." Another newspaperman gave this picture of the committee:

> The whole Progressive Party was made up of enthusiasts, and of course the [platform committee] was similarly composed. Every member of it believed, with the utmost sincerity, in his own proposition. There was only a tattered minimum of possibility of compromise in such a committee. They fought all day . . . and they fought all night. They remained in the committee room, and had their meals brought into them there. They argued and discussed and debated. They wrote out their ideas in a thousand phraseologies. But they could not agree.[14]

Survey, XXVIII (August 24, 1912), pp. 668–70, referred to by Jane Addams in *Second Twenty Years at Hull House*, p. 27. Jane Addams, Julia Lathrop, Florence Kelley, Alice Hamilton and others were members of the committee for a one-year term. For Roosevelt's use of the committee report compare Theodore Roosevelt, " Confession of Faith," in *Works* (National ed., New York, 1926), XVII, 266–7, with Owen R. Lovejoy, " Report of the Committee of Standards of Living and Labor," in National Conference of Charities and Correction, *Proceedings* (1912), p. 377.

13. After Taft's nomination, a group of Roosevelt intimates was designated to draw up a tentative platform: Gifford Pinchot, William D. Lewis, Chester Rowell, and later George W. Kirchwey. In Chicago in August, William Allen White, James R. Garfield, and Charles McCarthy were added. One delegate from each state was elected by the convention. The full committee invited Herbert Knox Smith, George Record, Samuel McC. Lindsay, and Jane Addams to join them.

14. Chester Rowell, " The Building of the Progressive Platform," *California Outlook*, XIII (August 17, 1912), 5. Rowell failed to mention the continuous control Roosevelt exercised over the whole platform proceedings. He approved each plank before the committee adopted it. Oscar King Davis, *Released for Publication, Some Inside Political History of Theodore Roosevelt and His Times, 1898–1918* (Boston, 1925), p. 330.

Jane Addams described the meetings of the platform committee as a moving religious experience. In the committee, she felt "keenly the uplifting sense of comradeship. . . ." In the convention itself "all dogmas and group egotisms were dropped, or rather, melted down by overwhelming good will and enthusiasm." The convention was "a curious moment of release from inhibitions, . . . reticent men and women . . . [spoke] aloud of their religious and social beliefs, confident that they would be understood. . . . there was a quick understanding of those hidden scruples which we were mysteriously impelled to express." The sound of the convention was "not unlike the psychic uproar which accompanies a great religious conference when the sword of the spirit bursts through its scabbard." The men and women at the Progressive convention were "haunted by the same social compunctions, animated by like hopes, revealing to each other mutual sympathies and memories. . . . For three days together they defined their purposes and harmonized their wills into a gigantic cooperation." [15]

Meetings of the platform committee, Miss Addams wrote, were much like meetings of the American Economic Association, the Civil Service Reform League, the American Sociological Society, the Men and Religion Forward Movement, or the National Conference of Charities and Correction. She was confident that reform proposals advocated by these small "cults" were finally going to be tried out as national political programs. Members of voluntary organizations, Miss Addams said, had all experienced the frustration and disappointment of detached and partial effort. The Progressive party offered the opportunity to test the validity and vitality of reform measures on a national scale.[16]

15. Jane Addams, *Second Twenty Years at Hull-House*, pp. 3, 31-2; Jane Addams, "Progressive's Dilemma—The New Party," *American Magazine*, LXXV (November, 1912), 14. Compare William Allen White's metaphoric description of 1912 in *The Autobiography of William Allen White* (New York, 1946), p. 428, "the American people were melting down old heroes and recasting the mold in which heroes were made."

16. For "cults" see Jane Addams, "Lessons of the Election," p. 361, Jane Addams, "My Experiences as a Progressive Delegate," *McClure's Magazine*, XL (November, 1912), 12. The personnel of these voluntary organizations overlapped considerably. In 1912 the American Sociological Society had 600 members, 162 of whom also belonged to the 2,400-member American Economic Association. One hundred and thirty-nine members of the large National Conference of Charities and Correction (3,300 members) belonged to the American Economic Association.

Along with these descriptions of harmony and the achievement of a unified national program of reform, Miss Addams also noted the difficulties of the platform committee sessions. She used her own personal example to describe how difficult it had been for her to " swallow " the platform demand for two new battleships a year and how she opposed the plank endorsing the fortification of the Canal Zone. In justifying her acceptance of the platform, she did not underemphasize her pacifist convictions nor her activities in the peace movement. But, she asserted, deaths from industrial causes far outnumbered the casualties in even the most destructive wars. Fifteen thousand men were killed and half a million men crippled in industry each year in America, she reported. This injury to and loss of life was enough to carry on the American Civil War and the Russo-Japanese War simultaneously. Perhaps, Miss Addams mused, no one could oppose war in her generation " so long as we stultify ourselves by our disregard of the shocking destruction in industry." One had to choose which righteous principles had to wait, she wrote, and " when a choice was presented to me between protesting against the human waste in industry or against the havoc in warfare, the former matter made the more intimate appeal. . . ." [17]

In addition to these difficult matters, Miss Addams had to accept Roosevelt's disagreeable decision that the Progressive party in the South would exclude Negroes from all active membership or control. Without power to alter Roosevelt's decision through the platform committee, Jane Addams criticized the convention's action admitting white delegations only from disputed southern states in a statement to newspaper reporters. " Some of us are very much disturbed that this Progressive Party, which stands for human rights, should even appear not to stand for the rights of negroes." The party which championed the cause of the disadvantaged and helpless could not consistently deny " the right of the negro to take part in this movement." Colonel Roosevelt's plans for breaking up the Solid South were " statesmanlike," Miss Addams was quoted as saying, but the rights of Negroes could be

---

Four of the 47 delegates at the annual meeting of the National Civil Service Reform League in 1912 were also members of the National Conference of Charities and Correction.

17. Jane Addams, " My Experiences as a Progessive Delegate," p. 14.

preserved without interfering with these plans and without excluding Negroes. When Roosevelt refused to heed this appeal,
Jane Addams returned to the platform committee where she wrote
or inspired a draft plank on Negro rights which she urged to be
included in the platform. During an all-night session of the
committee, the plank was refused. Miss Addams was in deadly
earnest; Roosevelt recalled later that " it was on this very matter
that Miss Jane Addams came very near leaving the Progressive
party. . . ." [18]

However difficult it was for Miss Jane Addams to swallow
Roosevelt's militarism and however much she regretted his decision to exclude Negroes from the party in the South, the
enthusiasm of the platform committee meetings and the acceptance
of the plank advocating woman suffrage which she had written
persuaded her to second Roosevelt's nomination. Her speech was
brief. She said that she was " stirred by the splendid platform "
which pledged the party to so many humane causes. The platform
represented earnest conviction and high hopes; it pulled upon
one's faculties and called " to definite action." [19] Miss Addams

18. Miss Addams is quoted in New York *Tribune*, August 6, 1912; Theodore
Roosevelt to Raymond Robbins, August 12, 1914, in Morrison *et al.* (eds.),
Letters, VII, 801. The struggle over Negroes in the party provoked widespread
newspaper comment. Miss Addams was less disturbed about Roosevelt's decision
when she wrote to Lillian Wald urging her to join the Bull Moose party: the
" Negro situation was really much better than the newspapers make out. . . . On
the whole I am sure we are making for social righteousness and I haven't a shadow
of regret." See Wald Papers, August 14, 1914 [misdated], New York Public
Library. Since Jane Addams had helped found the National Association for the
Advancement of Colored People, W. E. B. DuBois, editor of the association's
magazine, asked her to justify her endorsement and support of a lily-white party,
lily-white in the South, at least. Progressives all believed, Jane Addams assured
readers of the *Crisis*, that no man was good enough to vote for another. The
Progressives had made the race issue a national rather than a sectional one, and
" possibly this is all we can do at the present moment." Jane Addams, " The
Progressive Party and the Negro," *Crisis*, V (November, 1912), 31.
19. Others have described the platform differently. Donald R. Richberg, *Tents
of the Mighty* (New York, 1930), p. 30, said there " was room on that platform
for anyone who had seen Peter Pan and believed in fairies." The *Nation's* " Tatler "
wrote in 1916 that " no one human mind could have compassed such a hodge-
podge . . . and the leaders of the movement did not hesitate to crack a jest on the
fact in private." See *Nation*, CII (February 3, 1916), 134. An embittered Amos
Pinchot said that the platform was a " catch basin "; it has been constructed " on
the theory that the more hooks baited, the more fish would be caught." He accused
the platform committee of putting in " wordy paragraphs on almost everything,
from the shorter catechism to how to build a birchbark canoe." Amos R. Pinchot,

eulogized Roosevelt as one of the few public figures "who has responded to the social appeal." The party needed a "leader of invincible courage, of open mind, of democratic sympathies, one endowed with power to interpret the common man and identify himself with the common lot." Thus Miss Addams "heartily" seconded Roosevelt's nomination.[20]

The *Literary Digest* reported Jane Addams "was easily the most conspicuous figure present, save, of course, one." Judged by the applause, Miss Addams was a close second. When Roosevelt was nominated there was a great cheer. "It was no mild, perfunctory cheer; it was a cheer from Cheersville, one that had been suppressed for six weeks in the bosom of the multitude, and when the people unclasped it, the cheer jumped into joyful proportions and became a real circumstance." But, this same writer recalled twenty-five years later, "not even the Colonel got much more rousing cheers than Jane Addams, when she rose to second his nomination. The Colonel was there on the platform, and I saw his eyes glisten with pride and exultant joy that she was fighting under his banner. I have rarely seen him happier than he was at that moment."[21]

The end of Miss Addams' speech was the signal for another huge demonstration. A large yellow banner reading "Votes for Women" was thrust into her hands. In attempting to regain her seat with this unwieldy banner, Miss Addams was intercepted by some of the delegates from Oregon who formed a column behind her and started a march through the aisles. Under a

---

History of the Progressive Party, 1912–1916, ed. Helene Maxwell Hooker (New York, 1958), pp. 200, 172, 201.

20. Miss Addams' seconding speech was inserted in the U.S., *Congressional Record*, 62nd Cong., 2nd Sess., August 12, 1912, XLVIII, Part 12, Appendix, 564–5. Benjamin P. Dewitt, *The Progressive Movement, a Non-Partisan, Comprehensive Discussion of Current Tendencies in American Politics* (New York, 1915), p. 85 wrote: "The most significant incident connected with Roosevelt's nomination was the seconding speech made by Jane Addams of Chicago. This speech was the entrance of women into national politics in a new sense, and, in addition to giving tremendous impetus to the suffrage movement, drew to the Progressive party the support of thousands of women in those states where women have the right to vote."

21. *Literary Digest*, XLV (August 17, 1912), 244; William Allen White, dispatch for George Adams syndicate, Chicago, August 7, 1912, SCPC, and his *Autobiography*, p. 484; Jacob Riis was reported as saying that the "name of Jane Addams . . . brought forth almost as much applause as the mention of Colonel Roosevelt's name." St. Louis *Post-Dispatch*, October 24, 1912.

headline " Uproar Stirred by Jane Addams," the Chicago *Tribune* reported the next day that " women in the audience stood up waving their handkerchiefs and screaming approval. The women delegates joined the procession and delegations from several states participated." [22]

Miss Addams actively campaigned for the Progressive party. During October and the first week in November she traveled more than 7,500 miles to address Progressive rallies. From October 1 to 17, she was in Wisconsin, Michigan twice, the New York City area, Indiana, and back to Chicago. From October 20 to November 5, she was in Oklahoma, Kansas, Nebraska, Minnesota, the Dakotas, Colorado, Kansas again (at the importunity of William Allen White), and back to Chicago on election day. Miss Addams was responsible for making her own engagements and travel arrangements for her speaking tour, which, like the others that constituted the Progressive campaign, lacked firm central direction or co-ordination.

For these appearances, she composed a basic speech which she varied only slightly during the campaign. In it she argued for the various social and industrial reforms and for woman suffrage. She reviewed for her audiences the platform demands for legislation to prevent industrial accidents, occupational diseases, overwork, and involuntary unemployment. The platform further called for minimum safety and health standards through the exercise of public authority, including federal control over interstate commerce and the taxing power. The prohibition of child labor, minimum-wage standards for women and a general prohibition of night work, and the eight-hour day for women were also demanded. Progressives pledged themselves to institute a six-day week for all wage earners, and the eight-hour day in continuous (twenty-four-hour-a-day) industries. The platform also included planks seeking the abolition of convict contract labor and the application of prisoners' earnings to support their dependent families. Publicity for hours, wages, and conditions of labor was urged, plus the establishment of a Department of Labor. In addition the Progressive platform called for " standards of compensation for death by industrial accident and injury and trade disease which will transfer the burden of lost earnings from the

22. Chicago *Tribune*, August 8, 1912.

families of working people to the industry, and thus to the community; the protection of home life against the hazards of sickness, irregular employment and old age through the adoption of a system of social insurance adapted to American use. . . ." And Jane Addams assured audiences across the country that " by the test of my own experience I can confirm the need for almost every one of the social and economic measures advocated by the Progressive party. . . ."[23]

Women were vitally interested in these social and economic questions, Miss Addams insisted in her campaign speeches. Drawing on her own experiences, she pointed out that she had entered partisan politics because the line between politics and philanthropy was constantly shifting. She had long been concerned with repairing the evil effects of child labor, sweatshop conditions, economic depression, and destitute old age.

> In joining a political party I merely followed the various philanthropic undertakings which this party's platform had declared to be matters for political action. I cannot see that I am doing any differently than when I went before the Illinois legislature. . . . I am working for the same thing that I was working for then, only another and wider and more efficient instrument has been offered me.

The best instrument for these reforms, Miss Addams reiterated, was woman suffrage. Politics would be " infinitely benefited if women were taking a natural and legitimate share in the development and in the administration of governmental activities." Women who had started welfare services frequently saw them languish and fail when taken over by the government. These women needed the ballot to protect useful services. Also, many " beneficent measures "—and here she frequently summed up several platform planks—remained unenacted because voteless women could not insist that the state provide them.[24]

23. The platform also contained a mild endorsement of the unionization of labor: " We favor the organization of the workers, men and women, as a means of protecting their interests and of promoting their progress." On platform see George Henry Payne, *Birth of a New Party*. . . . (n. p., 1912), pp. 307–8.

24. Miss Addams subscribed to a clipping service. The clippings for October and November, 1912, contain the speeches which I have drawn on, at SCPC. Quotations are from Jane Addams' page, *Ladies' Home Journal*, XXX (January, 1913), 25; Jane Addams, statement, New York *Tribune*, September 28, 1912;

Jane Addams campaigned more energetically for the Progressive platform than for the Progressive candidate. She responded to a reporter's question whether it was the platform alone in which she was interested: "It is the platform we women care about, the platform which embodies so much that we desire. But with a platform there must be candidates, and we are very glad," she added with a smile, "to have so distinguished a man to lead our cause." Miss Addams certainly wanted the party to go farther than Roosevelt did. Teddy Roosevelt, in responding to one of Gifford Pinchot's many letters complaining about the conservatism of party chairman George Perkins, wrote that "on the [Progressive party] platform I disagreed with him [Perkins] much less than I disagreed, for instance, with such high-minded people as McCarthy of Wisconsin and Jane Addams." In 1930, Miss Addams recalled that "in spite of our belief in our leader, I was there, and I think the same was true of many others, because the platform expressed the social hopes so long ignored by the politicians; although we appreciated to the full our good fortune in securing on their behalf the magnetic personality of the distinguished candidate."[25]

Jane Addams campaigned not so much to elect Theodore Roosevelt as to publicize certain principles. A political campaign, she wrote in October, 1912, was "but an intensified method of propaganda. . . ." The day following the election, the erstwhile campaigner was quoted as saying she

had expected from the beginning that Mr. Wilson would be the next President of the United States. The candidacy of Mr. Roosevelt and the principles enunciated in the Progressive platform afforded the opportunity for giving wide publicity to the necessity for social and industrial reforms, and it is my belief that Mr. Wilson as President . . . will give heed to the necessities of the people as they have been made so plainly apparent. . . . I am not disappointed in the result. It is my expectation and belief that Mr. Wilson will give the country a wise and capable administration.

Jane Addams, "Why Women Are Concerned with the Larger Citizenship," in Shailer Mathews (ed.), *Woman Citizen's Library* (Chicago, 1913-4), IX, 2130, 2137.

25. New York *Tribune*, September 28, 1912; Roosevelt to Pinchot, November 13, 1912, in Morison *et al.* (eds.), *Letters*, VII, 640; Jane Addams, *Second Twenty Years at Hull-House*, p. 31.

The discussion of the Progressive platform, with its demands for social and industrial justice, was a political novelty, according to Jane Addams. " At moments we believed that we were witnessing a new pioneering of the human spirit, that we were in all humility inaugurating an exploration into the moral resources of our fellow citizens." Miss Addams assured politicians that the campaign would " not only enlarge our concept of truth, but . . . give it a chance to become humanized and vital." Politics, like philosophy, was " not sufficient unto itself," she said quoting William James. Politics, especially progressive politics, had to plunge " eagerly into reality, into science, into life, there to be refreshed and rejuvenated." [26]

Thus Miss Addams believed that the Progressive campaign was successful even though Roosevelt was defeated, because it had created great enthusiasm for reform. This was " the last lesson of the campaign . . . the enormous amount of enthusiasm . . . to grapple with the social questions." Jane Addams' name was especially associated with one expression of this Progressive enthusiasm. Many Progressive rallies featured the singing of a Jane Addams Chorus, which was designed to duplicate the enthusiasm of the Progressive nominating convention. The singing and noise at that Chicago convention had in it " something inspired; spiritual, almost uncanny. It caught one by the throat." [27] To achieve this inspiring noise on the hustings the Progressive National Committee published a special edition of its " Progressive Battle Hymns " for use of these choruses under the title " Jane Addams Songbook (10¢)." [28]

This excitement was admirable because it had been attached

26. Jane Addams, " Pragmatism in Politics," p. 12; *Chicago American*, November 6, 1912; Jane Addams, *Second Twenty Years at Hull-House*, p. 33; Jane Addams, " My Experiences as a Progressive Delegate," p. 13.

27. Richard Harding Davis, " The Men at Armageddon," *Colliers*, XLIX (August 24, 1912), p. 10.

28. These choruses were all female, usually had a large number of voices, sometimes over a thousand. The standard garb for their appearances at Progressive rallies was a plain, full-length, white dress. The songbook included hymns, popular songs, and campaign songs. In the last category were " Roosevelt " to the tune of " Maryland, My Maryland," " We Stand at Armageddon " to the tune of " The Warin' of the Green." Hymns included " God for Us," " Work for the Night Is Coming," and an adaptation of " Follow, Follow, We Will Follow Jesus," to " Follow, Follow, We Will Follow Roosevelt," copy of " Jane Addams Songbook (10¢)" at SCPC.

to the cause of reform, Miss Addams stated. "There is a tremendous advantage in numbers when it comes to enthusiasm, good-will and humanitarian zeal, and if we could only direct the moral energy of which this country possesses so much into the same channels at the same time, there is almost nothing we could not accomplish." And this was what the Progressive campaign had started. The overwhelming enthusiasm of the campaign "seemed to indicate a breaking down of the lines that formerly separated the religious, the political, the philanthropic and the civic interests, so that for the moment they were merged." [29]

This extraordinarily exciting campaign represented the optimistic climax of Jane Addams' hopes for reform. In 1912 she was "quite sure" that if the public discussed and understood reform plans "they would quickly be put into operation." Certain difficulties and dissatisfactions, however, soon undermined her high confidence. She was to find the years 1913 and 1914 gloomy indeed when compared with the exaltation of October and November, 1912. Miss Addams was never able to regain the confidence and enthusiasm of the Progressive campaign.

Jane Addams left Chicago in February, 1913, for six months in Europe, where she attended an international suffrage meeting in Budapest as part of her vacation. Back at Hull House she found that the prosperity of the campaign year had ended and hard times had returned. Thirty-six years later Edith Abbott recalled Miss Addams' reaction to this neighborhood crisis of unemployment: "'I don't know what to do and haven't even a law to propose as a remedy,' Miss Addams said in her confession of failure." The fund that Hull House secured to pay for work— mostly street cleaning, as in 1893—was infinitesimal.[30]

Economic failure was coupled with disintegration of political hopes. The Progressive party had organized elaborate research and educational departments after November, 1912, and Jane Addams had associated herself with these enterprises. But efforts to form a Progressive bloc in Congress were unsuccessful, and this deprived the party of any very effective influence on national legislation. The Progressives were badly split over the problems of leadership and philosophy. Many of them wanted to go farther

29. Jane Addams, "Lessons of the Election," pp. 363–4.
30. Edith Abbott, "Grace Abbott and Hull House," 1908–1921," p. 508.

and faster than Roosevelt and his Wall Street friend, George Perkins. Roosevelt was in poor health and was unable or unwilling to give much direction to party affairs. Disaffected Progressives continued to bicker with him over his retention of Perkins as party chairman. John Kingsbury wrote Miss Addams three weeks before she left the country quoting one of the disgruntled Progressives: " The Colonel has become suspicious of the whole social worker crowd except Jane Addams, and he is afraid of her, and we must depend on her to save the situation." [31] The " situation " in the Progressive party rapidly disintegrated and with it went the hopes for a transformed politics.

Thrown back from efforts at reform through a national political party, Miss Addams might have resumed her highly successful neighborhood work at Hull House. But in this area, also, she found certain dissatisfactions creeping in after the high enthusiasm of the Bull Moose campaign. The settlements were coming under increasingly strong attack in these years as outmoded instruments of neighborhood improvement and the settlement movement was losing much of its early vitality. Miss Addams had consistently maintained that the settlement was a place for experiment, not an administrative agency. Settlement workers had always asserted that public provision for social services was preferable to private support. " It is better that a public building, like a school, become a center of a neighborhood, than a quasi-private building like a settlement," Miss Addams had written in 1906. " Hull House has always held its activities lightly, as it were, in the hollow of its hands, ready to give them over to whomsoever would carry them on properly. . . ." As if in response to these statements, the voters of Illinois in 1911 allowed the Chicago school board to open Chicago schools as social centers. Two years later, twenty-four schools were opened, and fifteen more were added by 1916. Old friends of the settlements like John Dewey felt that schools should replace the settlements

---

31. For a good description of the collapse of the Progressive party, see George E. Mowry, *Theodore Roosevelt and the Progressive Movement* (Madison, 1946), pp. 284–303. John Kingsbury to Jane Addams, January 12, 1913, SCPC. Roosevelt wired Miss Addams, February 4, 1913, " Understand you will be in New York on the twelfth if so it is very important that you should be at the [Progressive party's] Lincoln dinner as a guest. I am afraid that your absence from the dinner were you in New York would give rise to serious misunderstanding. Earnestly hope you will be at the dinner if only for a short time." At SCPC.

because in the latter something was done for the public " by
people who are better off financially than they are. But giving a
community facilities that it lacks for special classes and recreation
through the public school puts the work on a different basis." The
few public schools that were being operated as settlements illustrated, Dewey wrote, that " the schoolhouse is the natural and
logical social center in the neighborhood. . . ." [32] Other agencies
in Chicago were by 1913 providing many services originated by
the settlements. The Chicago park districts furnished better
recreation facilities than settlements could afford. The public
schools had made increased provision for vocational and manual
training, and they had made a start in providing art and music
education.

The settlement movement by 1912 had worn out many of its
original purposes. Addressing the National Conference of Charities and Correction in that year, Jane Addams urged members of
the social work guild to discover new challenges.

> Certainly we have reached the point that we will not allow
> anyone to die if he can be saved, . . . but are we clear as to
> the end in view? Having obtained that, what shall we do
> next? Because it is after all a negative thing to make over
> a quarter of a city, . . . in order merely to keep children alive.
> It is well so far as it goes, but it is not after all sufficient,
> and we look about to see the next step, the one beyond the
> mere negative salvation of human life.[33]

Nor had the settlements, Miss Addams mused, been getting their
full share of eager young people. Had the student volunteer
movement or the socialists drawn off the young college students
who used to come to the settlements, she wondered? " Whereas,
in the early 'nineties we felt as if we had been in the van, . . . in

32. Jane Addams, " Social Settlements in Illinois," in Illinois State Historical
Library, *Publication*, XI (1906), 168; Jane Addams, " Hull House," in William
D. P. Bliss (ed.), *New Encyclopedia of Social Reform* (New York, 1908), p. 589.
On the 1911 vote, see Charles Zueblin, *American Municipal Progress*, p. 254. The
rapid expansion of community centers in Chicago is fully explained in Rainwater,
The Play Movement, pp. 147–57. For Dewey, see John Dewey and Evelyn Dewey,
Schools of Tomorrow (New York, 1915), especially Chapter VIII, " The School
as a Social Settlement." I have quoted from pp. 209, 224.
33. Jane Addams, " Child at the Point of Greatest Pressure," p. 26.

1910 it came to pass that we were beginning to be looked upon as among the conservative agencies in the community, at least some of the young people felt that we were slow, and were not keeping up with the procession." [34]

What Jane Addams missed among younger social workers was the spontaneity, the direct emotional response, the enthusiasm of the earlier years. Instead of the enthusiasm of the Progressive campaign which united reform impulses, she saw a growing professionalism which dissipated reform energy. In lobbying for federal support for industrial education, the National Society for the Promotion of Industrial Education increasingly concerned itself with the establishment and definition of professional teaching goals, a task in which Jane Addams had little desire to participate. As Lawrence Cremin notes, " as professionalism moved inexorably forward, fewer men and women like Jane Addams, Jacob Riis, Theodore Roosevelt, and Walter Hines Page concerned themselves directly with educational reform. . . ." [35] In 1909 the Playground Association of America published a tentative normal course of play in order to establish professional standards for the training of playground leaders. The question of whether school authorities or a special park board should control city parks, and similar questions, increasingly absorbed the association's time and effort. Professionalization seemed to Jane Addams to divide reform and to kill the emotional sources for reform enthusiasm.

These discouragements, however, were as nothing compared to the incredible news that war had broken out in Europe in the summer of 1914. This seemingly impossible cataclysm jarred Jane Addams as did no other event in her mature years. Her personal response to the war came on top of these recent discouragements. Miss Addams was soon totally absorbed in the problems of war and peace.

34. Jane Addams' address at twenty-fifth-anniversary dinner for the New York University Settlement, in *Annual Report*, p. 22.
35. Cremin, *The Transformation of the School*, p. 184.

CHAPTER VII

NEUTRALITY

*As women we are the custodians of the life of the ages and
we will no longer consent to its reckless destruction. We are
particularly charged with the future of childhood, the care
of the helpless and the unfortunate, and we will no longer
endure without protest that added burden of maimed and
invalid men and poverty-stricken women and orphans which
war places on us.*

*We have builded by the patient drudgery of the past the
basic foundation of the home and of peaceful industry; we
will not longer endure that hoary evil which in an hour
destroys, or tolerate that denial of the sovereignty of reason
and justice by which war and all that makes for war today
render impotent the idealism of the race.*

JANE ADDAMS, 1915

The uncertainties and discontents Jane Addams felt in the years
after 1912 were swallowed up in the catastrophe of August, 1914.
The outbreak of war persuaded her that the struggles for domestic
reform dwindled to unimportance when compared with this world
crisis. Miss Addams became a leader of American opposition to
the war and to preparedness. She also became the focus for the
hopes of European women that America might aid in halting
the war.

Miss Addams had early related pacifism and internationalism to
the social welfare interests for which she labored. She believed that
war destroyed democracy and culture. As the enormity of the war
in Europe became apparent, Jane Addams' work for peace crowded
out other long-standing commitments. The pacifism that had been
diffuse before 1914 came to absorb her wholly. After 1914 she
organized all other interests around the themes of peace and of
war's horrible consequences for democracy and civilization. Jane
Addams led the campaign in America to offer some sort of

neutral mediation to the European belligerents. When the old peace organizations held back, she formed several new groups, which publicized the idea of neutral mediation and tried to build public support for it.

Throughout her entire career Jane Addams wrote about and worked for peace. Her changing conceptions of peace paralleled the evolution of her thought on social welfare and reform. In the earliest days at Hull House, she based her belief in non-resistance to evil on religion. One of the motives embodied in the settlement movements was "a certain renaissance going forward in Christianity." And, she emphasized, the "early Christians were preeminently non-resistant." The settlement tried to practice this religious attitude; the founders of Hull House, Miss Addams wrote, felt "that it would simply be a foolish and an unwarrantable expenditure of force to oppose and to antagonize any individual or set of people in the neighborhood; . . . [that the] residents should live with opposition to no man. . . ."[1]

Her conception of peace was strongly influenced by Leo Tolstoy. Through a personal visit to him and avid reading of his books, she identified herself with the nineteenth-century European movement which desired "to get back to the people, to be identified with the common lot."[2] She read Tolstoy's *My Religion* soon after graduating from Rockford, and her own religion reflected an appreciation of his book. During 1893, along with Russian refugees in the neighborhood, she studied Tolstoy's theory of nonresistance. Most important, however, was Tolstoy's *What Then Must We Do?* Many years later Jane Addams called it "A Book That Changed My Life." It was not so much a prose work, she wrote, as one of life's "vital experiences."[3]

In *What Then Must We Do?* Tolstoy described his unsatisfying attempts at charitable relief in Moscow during a depression winter. This experience led him to believe that all attempts at charity and amelioration were false. How could a person retain anything for himself when others had nothing? How could one

1. Jane Addams, "A New Impulse to an Old Gospel," pp. 354, 355.

2. Jane Addams, "Americanization," American Sociological Society, *Publications*, XIV (1919), 210. See also Lewis S. Feuer, "John Dewey and the Back to the People Movement in American Thought," *Journal of the History of Ideas*, XX (1959), 545–68.

3. Jane Addams, *Second Twenty Years at Hull-House*, p. 409; Jane Addams, "A Book That Changed My Life," *Christian Century*, XLIV (October 13, 1927) 1196.

be a good man " just a little? " Tolstoy's remedy was to leave the city, to reject the literature and art and science which the city stood for, and to embrace a life of common labor. His ridicule of charity challenged Jane Addams to justify her activities at Hull House, especially during the terrible depression winter of 1893–4.[4]

Tolstoy's challenges induced Jane Addams to visit him at Yasnaya Polyana while she was on a European vacation in 1896. The visit did not satisfy her. Tolstoy, in peasant garb, direct from working in the fields, asked about her stylish dress which, he said, contained enough expensive material to clothe several children, and about her income as an absentee owner of a farm. A witness reported that there was no unpleasantness in these prickly questions and her answers; but Jane Addams wrote of her " misgivings " about the visit. These misgivings centered on Tolstoy's pacifism. Nevertheless the meeting had made a " profound impression " on her, she said. In the months following, she read " everything of Tolstoy's that had been translated into English, German, or French. . . ."[5] The impact of the visit lay not so much in what Tolstoy had said, but in his example—" the life, the gentleness, the Christianity of the soul of him. . . ." Tolstoy's radical stand threw all such efforts as that of settlements into the " ugly light of compromise and inefficiency—at least so it seemed to me—and [this] perhaps accounts for a certain defensive attitude I found in myself."[6]

Miss Addams found confirmation for an increased pragmatism in her thought in Tolstoy's life. He had formulated a new moral

4. Leo Tolstoy, " What Shall We Do Then? " in *Complete Works* (Boston, 1904–1905), XVII, p. 87. See *ibid.*, p. 333, for Tolstoy's assertion that the salvation from evil for men of the wealthy class rests with women.

5. Aylmer Maude, " A Talk with Jane Addams and Leo Tolstoy," *Humane Review*, III (October, 1902), 216; Jane Addams, *Twenty Years at Hull-House*, p. 275.

6. Maude, " A Talk with Jane Addams and Leo Tolstoy," pp. 216–7. In *Twenty Years at Hull-House*, Jane Addams described the most instructive, if temporary, result of her visit to Tolstoy: her decision to spend two hours a day baking bread in an effort to share in the common labor of the world. Soon this resolution seemed " utterly preposterous. . . . The half dozen people invariably waiting to see me after breakfast, the piles of letters to be opened and answered, the demand of actual and pressing human wants,—were these all to be pushed aside and asked to wait while I saved my soul by two hours' work at baking bread." Perhaps Tolstoy was " more logical then life warrants," she mused. " Could the wrongs of life be reduced to the terms of unrequited labor and all be made right if each person performed the amount [of labor] necessary to satisfy his own wants. . . ." See pages 276–7, 274.

insight, and he had reduced it to action. Moral principles that were not put into action, she said, were not really believed. No start on a solution to vexing social problems was possible until new moral insights were formulated and tested in action. That was the most important thing about Tolstoy, she said in 1902. He had put the simplicity and naturalness and utter sincerity of his nonresistance into action.[7]

Based on this pragmatic example of nonresistance, Jane Addams believed that social sentiment was evolving away from war toward peace. When America embarked on an imperialistic war in 1898, she analyzed the evolutionary growth of peace sentiment. Peace, she said tentatively to an anti-imperialist audience, was " the unfolding of life processes which are making for a common development . . . a rising tide of moral feeling which is slowly engulfing all pride of conquest and making war impossible." The war frustrated this evolution. War threw back social progress and confused the new, developing moral feelings that supported this progress, she asserted. The growing belief that each life was sacred gave way as barbarism replaced the more humane instincts. War turned the imagination away from humanitarian concern for the common life, and diverted the courage and toil of industry to bravery and endurance in destruction and brutality.[8]

The evolutionary conception of peace was a most important one for Jane Addams. She elaborated this suggestion to a Chautauqua audience three years after the end of the Spanish-American War. Some people, like Tolstoy, she said, appealed for peace because war was wretched, squalid, and sordid. Some people opposed war because it cost so much. She opposed war, she said, because she believed in human solidarity, in the worth of each human life, and in the obligation to build up civilization. Wars would not cease because they were sordid and expensive. " When we once surround human life with the same kind of heroism and admiration that we have surrounded war, we can say that . . . war will become impossible."[9] Jane Addams suggested that war sur-

7. Jane Addams, "Count Tolstoy," *Chautauqua Assembly Herald*, XXVII (July 11, 1902), 5.
8. Jane Addams, "Democracy or Militarism," Central Anti-Imperialist League of Chicago, *Liberty Tract*, I (1899), 36.
9. Jane Addams, "Count Tolstoy," p. 5; Jane Addams, "Democracy or Militarism," p. 38; Jane Addams, "The Interest of Labor in International Peace," Universal Peace Congress, *Official Report*, XIII (1904), 145.

vived because people failed to understand that " the same strenuous endeavor, the same heroic self-sacrifice, the same fine courage
and readiness to meet death may be displayed without the accom-
paniment of killing our fellow men." Peace workers needed
fewer theoretical and sentimental appeals. They needed something
active and practical. Miss Addams was searching, she told a peace
congress in 1904, for " a moral substitute for war, something
that will appeal to the courage, the capacity of men, something
which will develop their finest powers without deteriorating their
moral nature, as war constantly does."

The Americans who were working out this pragmatic displacement of war, she continued, were men at the bottom of the social
ladder. It was the laboring man, the producer, who was naturally
opposed to the destruction of war. "We shall come to the point
some day when all human labor will be considered so valuable,
and human life so important, because it contributes to the great
process of civilization, that we will not allow any man . . . to be
shot down, nor allow him to go forth to kill his fellow man." [10]

Just as Jane Addams discovered the sources of a true and vital
democratic culture among her immigrant neighbors, she also
gained from them new ideals of, and hopes for, peace. They
were, for example, appropriating the paraphernalia of war for the
purposes of peace and human dignity. Almost every Sunday some
Italian Benefit Society held a parade with flags, uniforms, and
drums, to celebrate the " little wall between themselves and starvation and a pauper's grave." Hopes for peace and a substitute
for war lay in activities like these. For, " if the race once discovered the excitement and the pleasure and the infinite moral
stimulus and the gratification of the spirit of adventure to be
found in the nourishing of human life, in the bringing of all the
world into some sort of general order and decent relationship one
with another " men would no longer think of war as their only
joy and pleasure.[11]

This idea of immigrants substituting the nurture of life for the
war spirit was most important for Jane Addams. As the hopes and
dreams of her neighbors were " a prophecy of the future development in city government, in charity, in education, so their daily

10. Jane Addams, " The Interest of Labor in International Peace," pp. 145, 146.
11. Ibid., pp. 262, 261.

lives are a forecast of coming international relations." In 1907 Miss Addams wrote *Newer Ideals of Peace* in which she explained how the lives of her neighbors held the clues to an advancing social morality that would eventuate in world peace. Immigrants, she wrote, were reduced to the " fundamental equalities and universal necessities of human life itself "; their social relations were based on the most " basic and essential likenesses of their common human nature. . . ." The immigrants in American cities had " an unquenchable desire that charity and simple justice shall regulate men's relations." Their " sense of pity, their clamor for personal kindness . . . [demanded] the abolition of degrading poverty, disease, and intellectual weakness. . . ." These ideals and desires were intangible, Miss Addams admitted, but they had " the strength and irresistible power of those ' universal and imperious ideals which are formed in the depths of anonymous life. . . .' " A newer morality and the newer ideals of peace were discovered in " the pathetic strivings of ordinary men, who make up the common substance of life," the compassionate hopes and aspirations of the unsuccessful and defeated. It was " natural," she wrote, that the synthesis of a new internationalism " should be made first at the points of greatest congestion." Not in the future, she said in 1907, but " at this moment there is arising in these cosmopolitan [immigrant] centers a sturdy, a virile, and an unprecedented internationalism which is fast becoming too real, too profound, too widespread, ever to lend itself to warfare." [12]

In this interpretation of her neighbors' aspirations toward peace, Jane Addams revealed a significant facet of her personality. She described the " devotion to unselfish aims," the disinterestedness, of her neighbors, who themselves did not set geographic or racial or even national bounds to their hopes and aspirations. The compassion and kindliness of these immigrant quarters broke through every " tribal bond." Disinterested emotion and action were also at the heart of her own personality. In *Twenty Years at Hull-House* she wrote that " disinterested action was like truth and beauty in its lucidity and power of appeal." Impersonal emotion was for Jane Addams the truest and most dependable motive of

---

12. Jane Addams, *Newer Ideals of Peace*, pp. 16, 14, 17, 13, 236, 20; Jane Addams, " New Internationalism," National Arbitration and Peace Congress, *Proceedings*, I (1907), 215, 214.

reform. For her, emotion could be so deeply felt and understood that it became formal and impersonal. The immigrants' growing demands for social and industrial reform and for peace expressed their disinterestedness, she claimed.[13]

Miss Addams believed that disinterested reform provided a moral equivalent to war by protecting and building up human life. In arguing for the suffrage prior to 1912, she had emphasized women's special role in promoting reform and, since reform was the method for displacing war, in eliminating the war spirit. Jane Addams developed a philosophy of women's special contribution to the cause of peace. Primitive women had been the industrialists, while men had done the fighting. This had taught men how to co-operate, Miss Addams believed, but it had also instilled in them some unfortunate traits. "It may always be harder for a body of men to go out to do things, to reform, than it will be for women. They are not quite free from the fighting instinct yet." Primitive women, on the other hand, had never learned to co-operate, because their domestic tasks isolated them from each other. But modern industrialism, as it absorbed many of women's traditional activities, was also breaking into their domestic isolation. "The ancient family affection, that desire to protect and rear little children which [women] have expressed so long in isolation, . . . [was now being] socialized and be[ing] brought to bear as a moral force on the current industrial organization." As the earliest industrial workers and as the traditional industrial organizers, women were the natural people to reform and organize industry toward more humane goals. If industrial incentives were ever to "seem as strenuous, as heroic, as noble as well worthwhile" as wars, industry had to be reformed and humanized. Women had to organize themselves for reform and service so that "woman's traditional work will go forward worthy of its domestic beginnings, [and so] that the wolfish eagerness of the chase and of the battlefield shall be mitigated by the defense of the weak and the education of the young." Women

13. Jane Addams, *Newer Ideals of Peace*, pp. 235, 12; Jane Addams, *Twenty Years at Hull-House*, p. 151; Jane Addams, "Speech at the Winnetka Memorial Meeting, February 12, 1905," in *Jessie Bross Lloyd, September 27, 1844–December 29, 1904* (n. p. [Chicago], n. d. [1905]), pp. 57–8; Alice Hamilton has stressed the impersonal relations among the women at Hull House in her *Exploring the Dangerous Trades, the Autobiography of Alice Hamilton* (Boston, 1943), p. 61.

ought to be able, Miss Addams said, " to bring a distinct factor into the peace of the world. We [women] ought to make it clear that bodies of people can act together without [men's] fight spirit, without the spirit of competition, without the spirit of rivalry. . . ." [14]

Jane Addams' reform activities can be interpreted partly as her search for a substitute for the war spirit. She continually insisted that the life of each man needed to be expanded, raised in value, nourished. Only then would war be displaced. Thus she worked tirelessly to reform education and industrial conditions so that workers might find comradeship, glamor and ritual, pleasure and self-expression, in their work. Jane Addams expressed the idea of industrial reform as a substitute for war clearly in her reluctant acceptance of the Progressive platform planks that demanded military preparations. "It was a serious matter to appear to desert the [peace] cause. . . ." she wrote. She reread her peace appeals before voting for the platform and found that she " consistently pursued one line of appeal. I contended that peace is no longer an abstract dogma, but that marked manifestations of ' a newer dynamic peace ' are found in the new internationalism promoted by men of all nations who are determined upon the abolition of degrading poverty, disease and intellectual weakness. . . ." It was not, Miss Addams said, so much a choice between progressive reform and peace, as the realization that the pursuit of peace was futile "so long as we stultify ourselves by our disregard of the shocking destruction in industry." [15]

The events of August, 1914, did not immediately shatter her optimistic hopes for peace and reform. Disbelief, a feeling of complete and ludicrous unreality, was her immediate reaction. [16] She defended the peace movement as a limited success after war broke out. She wrote that when hostilities began, neutral nations condemned war, and the belligerents all apologized for it. Was that not a sign, she asked readers of the *Ladies' Home Journal*, that " public sentiment has at last turned against war. . . ." It was

14. Jane Addams, "Woman's Special Training for Peacemaking," American [National Arbitration and] Peace Congress, *Proceedings*, II (1909), 253-4; Jane Addams, "New Ideals of Peace," 107, 110.
15. Jane Addams, "My Experience as a Progressive Delegate," p. 14.
16. Jane Addams, *Second Twenty Years at Hull-House*, p. 118.

only a matter of time, she thought, before international arbitration became normative.[17]

At the beginning of the conflict, Jane Addams was primarily concerned with how the hostilities interrupted the social and industrial reforms she had hoped would provide an alternative to war. Other settlement workers, with similar pragmatic ideas of the equivalents to war, were also concerned with the war's effects on progressive reform. Along with Jane Addams, Paul U. Kellogg and Lillian Wald helped organize one of the early American responses to the European war, a round table conference at the Henry Street Settlement in New York City in September, 1914. The initiative for this informal meeting came from Kellogg, editor of the *Survey*. He was discouraged, he wrote Jane Addams, by the silence of the older peace societies in the face of this unprecedented bloodshed. Kellogg wrote that Nicholas Murray Butler and the rest of the conservative peace people were " reluctant to do anything because of [Wilson's] . . . desire that we shall not be involved. But for the very reason that those in the seats of the mighty cannot act—and also perhaps for the very reason that we are not of that sort—it would seem to me that humbler folk, by joining our voices together, could make these tidings [of peace] heard by the common people of the world." Lillian Wald explained the purpose of the conference as " a means by which, in humbleness and quiet, some of us who deal with the social fabric may come together to clarify our minds and, if it seems wise, to act in concert." [18]

When Jane Addams arrived in New York to attend the Henry Street conference, she was interviewed by reporters. She discussed the " inconsistency" of war. Human sensibilities were more acute, comradeship and friendliness between nations were more developed, than at any time in man's history. " Either we ought not to have equipped ourselves with these fine sensibilities or we ought not to face the horrors now confronting us." Miss Addams despaired of social reform during the struggle. She dismissed

17. Jane Addams, " Is the Peace Movement a Failure?" *Ladies' Home Journal*, XXXI (November, 1914), 5.

18. Paul U. Kellogg to Jane Addams, September 11, 1914, SCPC; Lillian Wald to William Dean Howells, September 22, 1914, copy at SCPC; for Miss Wald's recollected account of this meeting see her *Windows on Henry Street* (Boston, 1936), pp. 288–90.

her work for abolishing child labor as an "idle thought" compared with the human suffering and destruction in the trenches. A 25 per cent infant mortality rate was a "little thing," she was quoted as saying, when compared to the wholesale slaughter of thousands of men a day.[19]

The men and women who met at Henry Street Settlement in September and again in midwinter published a strident indictment of war. Their joint statement stressed the humanitarian and welfare measures that war negated. Social workers, the report said, were thrown back from "social development to the back eddies of salvage and relief. . . ." The Henry Street report also stressed the point Miss Addams had made to newspaper reporters: war contradicted the international sympathy and comradeship developed through world travel and world-wide communications. The nurture, fulfillment, conservation, and ascent of human life were all blocked and frustrated by war, the conferees asserted.[20]

Before the Henry Street conference had published these sentiments, or formally organized itself, women in Europe had organized to protest against the war. One of these protests originated with a Hungarian journalist and suffrage worker, Rosika Schwimmer.[21] When the conflict broke out, she shifted her considerable energies into organizing antiwar sentiment and circulated a petition calling for neutral mediation under the leadership of President Wilson. With several hundred thousand signatures on her petition, Madame Schwimmer arrived in America on September 6 to present it to the President. Taken in hand by Mrs. Carrie Chapman Catt, an officer of the International Women's Suffrage Alliance, Madame Schwimmer and Mrs. Catt interviewed both the President and Secretary of State. Having done as much as she could in Washington, Rosika Schwimmer set out on a cross-country speaking trip and called on women to protest against war and to demand the vote so that they could make their protest

19. New York *Evening Post*, September 30, 1914.

20. Jane Addams, *et al.*, "Towards the Peace that Shall Last," *Survey*, XXXIII (March 6, 1915), Part II, unpaged. The conference ultimately organized itself as the American Union against Militarism, the civil liberties bureau of which became independent, and after the end of the war became the American Civil Liberties Union.

21. Miss Addams had met Madame Schwimmer at the 1913 Budapest congress of the International Women's Suffrage Alliance. In 1914 Madame Schwimmer was the international press secretary for the alliance.

heard. She also urged women to demand the creation of international institutions that would make any recurrence of war impossible.[22]

Another European suffrage worker came to America in 1914 to urge a special women's protest against war. Mrs. Emmeline Pethick-Lawrence undertook an American lecture tour during which she indicted the governments run by men that had brought European civilization to the brink of collapse.[23] "No picture, however overdrawn, of women's ignorance, error, or folly could exceed in fantastic yet tragic horror the spectacle which male governments are furnishing history today. . . . The failure of male statecraft in Europe is complete." Mrs. Pethick-Lawrence objected to entrusting peace to the very men whose intrigues, ambitions, and secret diplomacy had brought on the Great War. Women on the other hand were "the natural custodians of the human race" who had "one passion and one vocation, and that is the creation and preservation of human life." She urged the women of America to organize "a campaign of preparation for peace . . . of awakening and educating public opinion with regard to the supreme value of human life." Only through organization could women bring pressure on the men in government toward a constructive and creative peace. It was, Mrs. Pethick-Lawrence said, "vital to the interests of the human race itself that the mother half of humanity should now be admitted to articulate citizenship," not for industrial and social reform, but for peace.[24]

The speaking efforts of these two unusual women inspired Jane Addams to aid in organizing the ephemeral Chicago Emergency Federation of Peace Forces in December, 1914. This federation was composed of various local organizations—civic, reform, and political. With the aid and advice of the secretary of the Chicago

22. Reported in "Women and War," *Outlook*, CIX (March 24, 1915), 676–7.

23. Emmeline Pethick-Lawrence had been released from prison in the summer of 1914. She had taken part in Emmeline Pankhurst's militant suffrage campaign. Mrs. Pethick-Lawrence repudiated the violence of these tactics, and concerned herself with the cause of peace. She was one of the earliest members of the Union for Democratic Control and urged the extension of suffrage to women as the first step in making governmental policy more responsive to popular control. She arrived in this country in late October, and was Jane Addams' guest when she spoke in Chicago.

24. Mrs. F. W. Pethick-Lawrence, "Union of Women for Constructive Peace," *Survey*, XXXIII (December 5, 1914), p. 230; and her "Motherhood and War," *Harper's Weekly*, XIX (December 5, 1914), 542.

Peace Society, Louis Lochner, the federation invited delegates to a national peace meeting. " Every public organization in the United States whose constitution, so far as we could discover, contained a plank setting forth the obligations of internationalism " was included. A tentative peace program accompanied the invitations. The program's first point was the petition Rosika Schwimmer had presented to President Wilson in September. Other proposals were culled from the platforms of European organizations opposed to the war, organizations like the Union for Democratic Control, the Swiss Ligues de Pays Neutres, the International Peace Bureau in Belgium, Anti-Oorlog Rad in Holland, and the Socialist party.[25]

The wide publicity and the arguments of the dramatic Madame Schwimmer and Mrs. Pethick-Lawrence aroused other organizational efforts. These European women prompted Carrie Chapman Catt to ask Miss Addams " to join her in sending informal invitations to all the national women's organizations which had standing peace committees to send delegates to a congress of women in Washington on January 10 and 11 [1915]." [26] Miss Addams and Mrs. Catt invited women from organizations representing a wide spectrum of political and social opinion. These sponsors hoped to construct a minimum program which women's organizations could use as a united basis for action.

Delegates responding to Jane Addams' and Mrs. Catt's invitations founded the Woman's Peace party in Washington on January 10, 1915. Miss Addams was elected chairman and delivered a keynote address. She reminded the ladies that even in the heat of the suffrage battles she had not maintained that women were better than men; " but we would all admit that there are things concerning which women are more sensitive than men, and that one of these is the treasuring of life." Using the report of the Henry Street conference as her text, she pointed out that women were discovering the various ways in which war denied the protection, the nurture, the fulfillment, the conservation, and the ascent of human life. Infant mortality rates rose in every country

25. "National Efforts Crystallizing for Peace," *Survey*, XXXIII (January 9, 1915), 393–4.
26. Marie Louise Degen, *The History of the Woman's Peace Party* (" Johns Hopkins University Studies in Historical and Political Science," Vol. LVII; Baltimore, 1939), p. 338.

at the start of mobilization. No country could support the aged and infirm when thousands of its splendid youth were being crippled or killed. From the ideal of protecting the lives, health, and welfare of its citizens, the state had fallen back into a tribal ideal. "Women have a right to protest against the destruction of that larger ideal of the state in which they had won a place, . . . and to deprecate a world put back upon a basis of brute force— a world in which they can play no part." Thousands of women, Miss Addams continued, had become convinced of the sanctity of human life as an accepted tenet of civilization. They had deemed war forever impossible. But all that was now overturned; women had to begin all over again to establish the belief that human life was sacred above all else that the planet contained.[27]

Applying themselves to this task set by their presiding officer, the members of the Woman's Peace party endorsed a revised version of Madame Schwimmer's petition. An English instructor at the University of Wisconsin, Julia Grace Wales, refined Madame Schwimmer's suggestion of a neutral conference into a more detailed plan for neutral mediation. Miss Wales suggested that an international commission of scholars might serve as a body to mediate the war. Without a preliminary armistice, such a commission would circulate various peace proposals to the belligerents. The commission would not be diplomatic, since delegates would be without the power to commit their governments. The individuals of the commission could originate proposals, or receive proposals from any quarter. Two rather vague principles were to govern peace plans circulated by the commission: terms that humiliated any of the parties were unacceptable; plans that embodied compromises which might cause future wars were also unacceptable.[28]

27. Jane Addams, "What War Is Destroying," *Advocate of Peace*, LXXVII (March, 1915), 65, 64.

28. Walter I. Trattner, "Julia Grace Wales and the Wisconsin Plan for Peace," *Wisconsin Magazine of History*, XLIV (Spring, 1961), 203–13, suggests that Miss Wales's plan was in a sense "an attempt to extend the Wisconsin Idea— drawing upon technical experts to help the state formulate public policy—to the realm of international relations." See page 205. The plan was known variously as Continuous Mediation Without Armistice, and as the Wisconsin Plan for Peace. The Wisconsin state legislature endorsed it and forwarded it to the U.S. Congress. See U.S., *Congressional Record*, 63rd Cong., 3rd Sess., 1915, LII, 3631–4. Women's Peace Party, *Program for Constructive Peace, January 10, 1915*, SCPC.

Both the Woman's Peace party and the Chicago Emergency Federation of Peace Forces were attempts to rally and unify peace sentiment in America. Jane Addams led both organizations. These early peace groups were like the voluntary associations that progressives had organized before the war. And just as the National Conference of Charities and Correction had attempted to establish minimum industrial standards, these organizations which Jane Addams led tried to establish a minimum peace program. But war loomed much larger than child labor or urban recreation ever had, and Miss Addams decided to combine the prewar strategy of the progressives with visits to the political leaders of the warring countries.

While Jane Addams was presiding at the meeting of the Chicago Emergency Federation of Peace Forces in late February, 1915, she received a cablegram inviting members of the Woman's Peace party to an international peace congress of women from both neutral and belligerent countries. The invitation was signed by Dr. Aletta Jacobs, the leader of a group of European women who knew each other through the international suffrage movement. Dr. Jacobs proposed a peace meeting because the 1915 biennial suffrage congress had been cancelled by the hostess organization in Berlin. Dr. Jacobs insisted that war should not be allowed to divide women on issues which transcended national differences and she asked Jane Addams to preside at the congress.[29]

The Woman's Peace party accepted Dr. Jacobs' cabled invitation, and on April 16 an American delegation set sail for The Hague. On the twelve-day crossing—for the last five days of which they were detained in the English Channel—the forty-two delegates (five more women joined the delegation in Europe) studied and revised the preliminary program of the congress. Miss Wales was a delegate, and the American delegation proposed to substitute her plan for the truce idea suggested by the congress sponsors. The other proposals adopted by the Woman's Peace party in January were also proposed as additions to the preliminary program for The Hague congress.[30]

29. Chrystal Macmillan, " The History of the Congress," in International Congress of Women at The Hague, 28th April–1st May, 1915, *Report* (Amsterdam, 1915), pp. XXVI–LXVIII.
30. Each delegate paid her own expenses to the congress, see Jane Addams, *Peace and Bread in Time of War*, p. 13. For a description of these events see

The congress opened on April 28 with 1,136 delegates from twelve countries in attendance. More than one thousand of the delegates were from Holland. In her presidential address, Jane Addams tried to clarify why German, Belgian, English, Italian, Hungarian, Dutch, American, and Scandinavian women were meeting together. At a moment when internationalism seemed to have broken down, she said, the delegates wanted to express the basic solidarity of women. They wanted to declare "the reality of those basic human experiences ever perpetuating and cherishing the race, and courageously to set them over against the superficial and hot impulses which have so often led to warfare." The nurture and cherishing of the race was stifled, Miss Addams said, by the lack of international institutions to promote peace and social progress. She hoped the peace congress would mark the first step in the establishment of such institutions.[31]

The only membership requirements of the congress were that delegates had to believe " *a.* That international disputes should be settled by pacific means; *b.* That the parliamentary franchise should be extended to women." These two requirements made plain the close connection between the prewar suffrage movement and these efforts for peace. For Jane Addams, who had identified democratic reform and peace from her very early days, this connection must have seemed a familiar one. The congress resolved not to discuss two topics: responsibility for, and conduct of, the war; or any proposals for the "humanization" of war. The congress resolutions—many of which came from the floor—included a statement of liberal peace terms, endorsement of various means of democratic international co-operation, and a strong demand for the representation of women in both national and international political life.[32]

Emily G. Balch, "Journey and Impressions of the Congress," in Jane Addams, Emily G. Balch, and Alice Hamilton, *Women at The Hague, the International Congress of Women and Its Results* (New York, 1915), pp. 1–21. Louis P. Lochner accompanied the women as lecturer, and as a ghost writer for the daily stories Jane Addams promised to file with the New York *Times,* see Louis P. Lochner, *Always the Unexpected, a Book of Reminiscences* (New York, 1956), p. 52.

31. Jane Addams, "Presidential Address," International Congress of Women at The Hague, 28th April–1st May, 1915, *Report* (1915), pp. 19, 21.

32. International Congress of Women at The Hague, 28th April–1st May, 1915, *Report,* p. 33. The congress adopted the following platform as principles of a permanent peace: no transfer of territory without the consent of the people residing

The congress adopted Rosika Schwimmer's motion (seconded by Julia Grace Wales) urging " the neutral countries to take immediate steps to create a conference of neutral nations which shall without delay offer continuous mediation. The Conference shall invite suggestions for settlement from each of the belligerent nations and in any case shall submit to all of them simultaneously, reasonable proposals as a basis of peace." This was the most difficult question for the women of the congress to resolve. Some were reluctant to ask for peace if there were any doubts about its justice. Others felt the congress would be a failure without a demand to end the war. These difficulties " were met by putting into one resolution the demand for an end to the bloodshed, for the beginning of peace-negotiation and for the establishment of peace based on the principles of justice adopted by the Congress." The congress not only asked neutral nations to call a conference but, on a further suggestion by Madame Schwimmer, resolved to send " envoys to carry the message expressed in the Congress resolutions to the belligerent and neutral nations of Europe and to the President of the United States." [33]

According to Dr. Alice Hamilton, Jane Addams originally disapproved of this kind of publicity. Madame Schwimmer's proposal, Dr. Hamilton wrote, was " hopelessly melodramatic and absurd and we said that Miss Addams would never consent to go about from court to court presenting resolutions. Then as she

---

therein; the right of conquest not to be recognized, autonomy and a democratic parliament not to be refused any people. Future international disputes should be referred to arbitration and conciliation; social, moral, and economic pressure should be brought against those refusing to co-operate in arbitration. The ladies demanded democratic control of foreign policy, including equal representation of men and women. They also urged the calling of a third Hague conference after the war, and the establishment of a permanent international court and a permanent international conference to plan and execute proposals for international co-operation. The congress delegates argued for universal disarmament by international agreement, and the nationalization of all arms and munitions manufacturing. The women at The Hague also urged free trade, free seas, and the opening of trade routes on an equal basis to all. They endorsed the proposition that foreign investments should be at the risk of the investor. All secret treaties were to be void, and legislative endorsement was to be necessary for all treaties in the future. And finally, " This International Congress of Women declares it to be essential, both nationally and internationally, to put into practice the principle that women should share all civil and political rights and responsibilities on the same terms as men." *Ibid.*, pp. 37–41.

33. *Ibid.*, pp. XLVI, 37, 41.

talked to the foreigners she [Jane Addams] saw that in their eyes it was both dignified and important and she consented. . . ." Her acquiescence was the beginning of one of the most unusual incidents in the many efforts to halt the war. Miss Addams and Dr. Jacobs set out to present the resolutions of the women's congress to the governments of Great Britain, German, Austria and Hungary, Italy, France, and Belgium. A second group of envoys from the congress visited Scandinavia, Russia, and the Netherlands. Private conferences with liberals in England buoyed Jane Addams' hopes of success for her mission. She talked with Graham Wallas, H. N. Brailsford, Norman Angell, and F. W. Jowett while waiting to interview Sir Edward Grey and Prime Minister Asquith. She wrote to Mary Smith that " some of the wisest men we met were in favor of the pilgrimage so that I am going on with a keen heart." [34]

During May and June, Jane Addams and Aletta Jacobs presented the congress resolutions to statesmen of the belligerent countries. They interviewed Lord Asquith and Grey in London and Chancellor Bethmann Hollwegg and Foreign Minister Jagow in Berlin. In Vienna the two envoys presented their appeals to Count Stuergkh and Count Burián. Later they spoke with Count Tisza in Budapest. On June 4 and 5, Dr. Jacobs and Miss Addams saw Baron Sonnino and Prime Minister Salandra in the Italian capital. They were received by Théophile Delcassé and René Vivani in Paris on June 12 and 14. On the fifteenth they interviewed d'Avignon in Havre, where the Belgian government-in-exile was located.[35] They received serious and courteous treatment from everyone they interviewed except Delcassé. On occasion Miss Addams was received with honors. Anti-militarist groups in several countries held mass meetings which she was invited to address. In each country, the delegation from The Hague congress tried to establish contact with groups and individuals who were opposed to the war.

34. Alice Hamilton to Louise DeK. Bowen, May 16, 1915, SCPC; Jane Addams to Mary Rozet Smith from Amsterdam, May 19, 1915, SCPC. For the men Miss Addams consulted in England see " Women and Peace," *Christian Commonwealth*, XXXV (May 19, 1915), 418, 420, and Graham Wallas to Jane Addams, May 14, 1915, SCPC.
35. In addition they spoke with Loudon and Cort van der Linden at The Hague, and with Hoffman and Motta in Berne. The envoys, along with Dr. Alice Hamilton who accompanied them, had a personal audience with Benedict XV and a long interview with Cardinal Gaspari, Papal Secretary of State.

The most emphatic response to their presentation of the congress resolutions came from Count Stuergkh. To the apology that perhaps their mission seemed foolish, he replied forcefully that theirs were " the first sensible words " he had heard in his office in ten months. Miss Addams was greeted in Hungary with something approaching a celebration. Count Tisza received them in a cordial manner, and, according to Miss Addams' notes, told them that " the Hungarians were getting nothing out of the situation. Let Germany settle with the Belgians. He [Tisza] would welcome [peace] negotiations." Other interviews ranged from noncommital to discouraging.[36]

While Dr. Jacobs and Miss Addams were visiting the belligerent countries, a second group from the congress was interviewing government leaders in the neutral countries and Russia. Rosika Schwimmer, Emily G. Balch, Chrystal Macmillan from England, and Madame Cor Ramondt-Hirschman of Holland traveled to Scandinavia and Russia. They tried to discover if any single country would initiate a neutral conference or whether these European nations might join to initiate a conference, whether American co-operation might become the decisive factor in forming a neutral conference, and whether these countries would join if America took the initiative.

The ladies' interview with the Swedish prime minister was the most encouraging. Eager that Stockholm be the site of final peace negotiations, Wallenberg was led to say that Sweden would take the initiative in calling a neutral conference " if he had sufficient evidence that it would be not unacceptable to the belligerents." Pressed hard, he said that sufficient evidence could be a lady bringing a little note from a chief representative on either side. In St. Petersburg the peace envoys got Sergei Sazonov to approve a statement which said that calling a neutral conference would not be an unfriendly or an unacceptable act, although he remarked that he did not feel it would produce results. Confronted with this billet in a second interview, Wallenberg first disputed the ladies' recollection of his remarks, then asserted that Sazonov's pessimism about results made the statement valueless. To allay fears like those of Wallenberg—that calling a neutral conference might be construed as unfriendly or unacceptable to

36. Dr. Degen's study covers these events fully; see her *History of the Woman's Peace Party*, pp. 92 ff.

the belligerents—the congress envoys decided to revisit Berlin and London. Jagow wrote for the ladies a guarded statement: " Germany would not be unfriendly to calling a conference of neutrals, but it would be doubtful if practical results would come from such a conference." The British government responded to a second visit by stating officially that it "would not place any obstacles in the way of formation of [a neutral conference offering mediation] or make any protests against its existence if it should come into being." These assurances were inadequate for Prime Minister Wallenberg, and for officials in Denmark, Norway, Sweden, and the Netherlands to whom the ladies communicated their information. Neutral Europe was waiting for action from America.[37]

Jane Addams returned home in early July to present the results of her own and her colleagues' travels in Europe to President Wilson. She knew about the slighting press notices of The Hague congress. Upon landing Miss Addams told a newspaper reporter somewhat defensively that the congress envoys " were not looked upon as meddlers [in Europe]; no one thought we were amusing. The movement was taken there more seriously than it has been taken here. The newspapers of Europe accepted it as something to be reckoned with." The Americans who had pooh-poohed the women's efforts should know, she said, " that in almost every European country the most distinguished men admitted freely that the task of making peace is women's work." [38]

The Woman's Peace party, with other peace groups, rented Carnegie Hall on July 9 to hear Jane Addams' report. She was cautious in her claims. She returned from the warring countries, she said, with no desire to let loose any more emotion. What was most needed was some careful understanding, some human touch in the complex situation. No government, Miss Addams said, saw any hope that a neutral conference could end the war; and no country could ask for or admit its willingness to receive peace negotiations. The nation initiating such action, Jane Addams said, would be considered weak and would be punished at the

37. Report of Emily G. Balch to Jane Addams, July 3, 1915, SCPC; Memorandum by Rosika Schwimmer and Chrystal Macmillan [August 2, 1915], SCPC; Sir Eric Drummond to Chrystal Macmillan, July 22, 1915, SCPC.
38. Edward Marshall, " Jane Addams Points the Way to Peace," New York *Times Magazine* (July 11, 1915), p. 1.

negotiating table. But, she said, all the foreign offices agreed that if neutral peoples who commanded the respect of these diplomats could be got together " to study the situation seriously and to make propositions, one, two, three—even if they were turned down over and over again until something was found upon which negotiations might commence, *there is none of the warring countries that would not be glad to receive such service.* Now that came to us unequivocally." [39]

Miss Addams was guardedly optimistic. One hopeful sign was the growth of a pragmatic pacifism among the younger men of Europe. She had discovered in each country a difference in the way the generations regarded the war. " The older men believed more in abstractions . . . [and] when they talked of patriotism they used certain theological or nationalistic words, . . . [which] meant more to them than they did to the young men. . . ." The younger generation felt that the war did violence to their highest ideals. Many of Europe's " young men had come to take life much more from the point of view of experience; . . . they were much more—pragmatic . . . [and they took] life much more empirically. . . ." In the trenches they tested the slogans of Victorian statesmen, and they found that war " was not what they wanted to do with their lives." It seemed clear, Jane Addams said, that there had grown up a generation in Europe, and in America, which " had revolted against war. It is a god they know not of, that they are not willing to serve; because all their sensibilities and their training upon which their highest ideals depend, revolt against the whole situation." [40]

A second hopeful sign which Jane Addams reported from her visit to European statesmen was the division of each belligerent country into two groups, a military party and a civilian party. She believed that the civilian parties in Europe, reinforced by youth's revolt against war, were strong enough to support a beginning of peace negotiations. Her whole neutral mediation strategy presupposed a large civilian group in each belligerent country.[41]

39. Jane Addams, " The Revolt against War," *Survey*, XXXIV (July 17, 1915), 356.

40. *Ibid.*, pp. 357, 358. For another American's formulation of the " cold staring skepticism of youth " faced with war, see Randolph Bourne, *Untimely Papers*, ed. James Oppenheim (New York, 1918), p. 59.

41. Miss Addams reflected the analysis of British liberals like John Hobson, Norman Angell, and H. N. Brailsford with whom she had spoken in England.

Although military men and civilians were fiercely united at that moment, she reported, in all of the countries there were two differing approaches to the war. The military party demanded a military solution; the civilian party deprecated the exaltation of militarism and feared the possibilities which increasing army control was bringing. As loyal as the military men, these civilians saw the safeguards of civil life crumbling, censorship being imposed. They longed for a nonmilitary settlement; they believed " with all their hearts that the military message is the wrong message. . . ." The number of those who feared the army and hoped for a negotiated settlement, Jane Addams believed, was growing. To a friendly New York *Times* reporter, she remarked that " we came away impressed with the belief that probably all of the thinking civilian population would welcome advances looking to some settlement and that the most practical and acceptable advance would be some form of conference of neutrals guided by the United States." [42]

Miss Addams did not specify the precise form that a commission for neutral mediation should take, nor its precise function. She characterized the kind of mediation she advocated as scientific rather than diplomatic. Mediation in the old sense was sure to fail, she asserted. Leaving peace to the professional diplomats who had let Europe slip over the brink into war was foolish. She suggested rather vaguely that the mediation commission might perform other than diplomatic functions. " Effective American work for the peace of the world . . . must mean the organization for the purpose of some thing bigger than yet has been planned, not designed to try its hand at ' stopping the war. . . .' " Miss Addams urged that a neutral commission be formed of those who were experts in international life, those who had had international experience so long and so unconsciously that they could view the European situation not in nationalistic terms, but disinterestedly, in terms of " human life and human experience as it has been lived during the last ten years in Europe." If men of international temper and experience could come together to make repeated

See Charles Roden Buxton (ed.), *Towards a Lasting Settlement* (London, 1915), and Laurence W. Martin, *Peace Without Victory, Woodrow Wilson and the British Liberals* (New Haven, 1958).

42. Jane Addams, " The Revolt against War," p. 356; Marshall, " Jane Addams Points the Way to Peace." p. 1.

propositions to the various governments from the social and human standpoints, it might be the beginning of a way out, Miss Addams said. A continuous conference of neutral powers, standing ready to act when the opportunities arose, " might be of immense value." [43]

Jane Addams' trip to the war capitals did not reveal the best way to organize such a commission. On July 20 she reported to some of the men and women who had gathered at Henry Street ten months before. Paul Kellogg wrote that Miss Addams was " far from self-confident and cocksure that she knew the way. . . ." She was emphatic that the diplomats of Europe were discredited. " What was needed was a new deal. The people want to do the real thing; not play with counters as would be the case in an official diplomatic conference." The Henry Street group was divided over the kind of neutral conference that would be most effective, some urging an official conference—under the sponsorship of the United States government—others favoring a privately initiated and supported group. Some argued for a neutral conference concerned only with the defining of the rules of sea law, others wanted to include general issues. Those at Henry Street were also undecided whether it should be a large or small conference and whether it should include all neutrals or only neutrals in this hemisphere. Jane Addams felt it would be a mistake to have an official conference of delegates. It was " a mistake to exalt the governments too much; . . . science, commerce, the great international activities are at a standstill because of the quarrel of the governments. . . . Why assume that the governments are all that there is of Europe? " She hoped somehow to get " some small group of people together who could act as negotiators, going back and forth in the same way that negotiators have settled strikes. Several ways are open to create such a group; and Miss Addams has not settled with any finality on the one which she feels like committing herself to." [44]

It seemed to Miss Addams that the decision about these alternatives had been taken out of her hands when she received the report

43. Jane Addams, " The Revolt Against War," p. 358; Marshall, " Jane Addams Points the Way to Peace," p. 1.
44. Paul U. Kellogg to Louis Lochner, July 21, 1915, Lochner Papers, Wisconsin Historical Society; Minutes of Peace Meeting at Henry Street Settlement, July 20, 1915, Emily G. Balch Papers, SCPC.

of the second group of congress envoys. They had argued publicly for an official mediation commission and had circulated a detailed preliminary proposal to neutral governments in Europe. As president of the congress, Jane Addams felt committed to this approach and thought she should not publicly endorse different proposals. She requested Lillian Wald to omit her name from some of the material being circulated by the Henry Street group.[45] During the next months, she worked diligently to publicize the women's congress proposals for a neutral mediation commission of official delegates. She used her considerable talents for publicity to try to build public support for an official conference.

A neutral conference would foil the censorship of all peace proposals that had been imposed by the militarists, she argued. Even in England, where the whole process of government depended on free public opinion, the modification of government policy through public discussion was almost impossible. Miss Addams described how men in all European countries who wished to discuss " the essential and indispensable condition for ceasing the conflict," who wished to start building the likemindedness on which peace would ultimately rest, were ignorant of each other. A neutral conference would provide a mechanism through which these isolated men might find each other. For, she said, proposals from a neutral mediation commission would become matters of international moment. Patriots on both sides could discuss such proposals. Thus a neutral commission could restore the disrupted communications between the minorities on both sides who opposed a crushing military solution to the original causes of the war.[46]

Miss Addams also argued for a neutral conference by stressing the changes in the nature of the conflict. She realized earlier than most Americans, earlier than Secretary of State Lansing or President Wilson, that the war in Europe was revolutionary. In a prophetic statement, she wrote:

> If this war is to be ended by public negotiations and by discussion on the part of the people themselves of the terms of peace, it can only be done through some such clearing-

45. Jane Addams to Lillian Wald, September 24, 1915, Wald Papers, New York Public Library.
46. I have summarized Jane Addams, " Peace and the Press," *Independent*, LXXXIV (October 11, 1915), pp. 55–6.

house as a conference of neutral powers would afford. Otherwise people will know nothing of the terms of peace until these are practically ratified; and the only way popular opposition could then express itself would partake of the character of revolution.

Moreover, the situation in Europe was growing more complex with each passing day. " The enthusiasm for continuing the war," she wrote, " is fed largely on a fund of animosity growing out of the conduct of the war. . . ." Soon the original causes of the war would be so overlaid with hostility, falsehood, passion, and misunderstanding that no solution save crushing military defeat would be possible. It was urgent, she wrote repeatedly, that mediation be offered before peace became impossible.[47]

This sense of the perils of hesitation moved Jane Addams and her colleagues to try to get the national administration to act. Lansing, Colonel House, and President Wilson were the prime targets of this peace campaign, and Jane Addams was its leader. She called on both Wilson and House in July. Lillian Wald and Jane Addams and others saw Lansing in early August. Emily Balch talked with House and Wilson in mid-August. Jane Addams revisited the President after Miss Balch. In September, Dr. Aletta Jacobs and Miss Balch saw Wilson, House, and Lansing. Because none of these visits produced a positive response or commitment, Miss Balch, Dr. Jacobs, and Miss Addams released a manifesto to the newspapers describing the projected neutral conference on October 15. These congress envoys described their visits to European chancellories, which had convinced them that " the belligerent governments would not be opposed to a conference of neutral nations . . . [a conference which] might provide the machinery which would lead to peace." The neutral governments " stand ready to cooperate with others in mediation." Yet America hesitated. " The excruciating burden of responsibility," they wrote aiming straight at the White House, " for the hopeless continuance of this war . . . rests on the wills of those neutral governments and people who . . . cannot, if they would, absolve themselves from their full share of the responsibility for the continu-

47. Jane Addams, " The Conference of Neutrals," *Survey*, XXXV (January 22, 1916), p. 495; Jane Addams, " The Food of War," *Independent*, LXXXIV (December 13, 1915), p. 430.

ance of war." Jane Addams, Lillian Wald, and Rosika Schwimmer saw Colonel House on November 21, and the Colonel told them plainly that the President could not act officially in the matter. The final episode in the women's urgent attempts to influence Wilson was on November 26, when the Chief Executive received Mrs. Philip Snowden and Rosika Schwimmer. On that day twelve thousand telegrams arrived at the White House, all of them urging the President to act. Wilson again expressed sympathy and readiness to act, when the time was propitious.[48]

The advocates of a neutral conference got a variety of excuses from the officials to whom they talked. The most revealing interview was between Wilson and Dr. Jacobs on September 15. She quoted the President as saying

> the U.S. were now in such great difficulties with the belligerents that a definite answer [to Dr. Jacob's plea for calling a neutral conference] in one way or another was impossible . . . about his attitude towards peace he could not say a word. Every-day that attitude could be changed, according to the circumstances and even a quite unofficial statement in one way or another could bind him in a certain degree. He want [sic] to remain free to act in the best way as he sees the things himself.[49]

Neither Lansing nor House was quite candid with Jane Addams and her fellow advocates of action because neither was quite certain of Wilson's mediation ambitions and plans. After William Jennings Bryan resigned in June, 1915, Lansing and House had persuaded Wilson that secret negotiations were the better method to bring about a situation favorable to an American offer of mediation. Both Lansing and House after mid-1915 shared the conviction that America must eventually enter the war on the side of the Allies, and both men were also convinced that any American mediation offer not approved in advanced by the Allies would be a fatal mistake. Into this complicated situation Jane Addams brought her report from the European statesmen. She

48. The manifesto is included in *Women at The Hague*, pp. 162, 165–6. Mrs. Henry Ford contributed $8,000 to the Woman's Peace party to solicit telegrams to Wilson.
49. Aletta Jacobs to Jane Addams, September 15, 1915, SCPC.

stated that Sir Edward Grey had told her that the belligerents " could not begin negotiations, that was for the neutrals "; she had remarked to him that the neutrals thought they had to wait for the right moment, to which Grey " indicated his astonishment by asking when did they think that the right moment would come." Lansing contradicted, and House dismissed, Miss Addams' report which called into question both men's diplomatic strategy. And although the President did not share the convictions of his closest advisers about the inevitability of American entry into the war, he pursued their strategy which surrendered to the Allies the initiative in calling for efforts at mediation.[50]

By the end of 1915 many of Jane Addams' associates in the drive for mediation were discouraged over the possibilities for an officially sponsored conference. These women were bewildered and confused by Wilson's refusal to act. They also recalled the peace party's resolution of January, 1915, which pledged them to work for an unofficial conference if an official one could not be obtained. Rosika Schwimmer obtained an appointment with Henry Ford in November, about three months after Ford had announced his conversion to pacifism. Impressed by Madame Schwimmer's stirring appeal, Ford volunteered to finance a neutral conference. Ford's hasty and abrupt offer took the party and its president by surprise. Ford conferred with Miss Addams and other party officials in New York City on November 22, chartered a ship— the " Oscar II "—that night, and spoke with President Wilson on the twenty-third. Ford reported to the women later on the same day that the President had refused his request to appoint a neutral conference to be transported in the " Oscar II." But Wilson assured Ford that he was within his rights if he wished to finance a private venture in peacemaking. Miss Addams im-

50. Memorandum by Rosika Schwimmer and Chrystal Macmillan [August 2, 1915], SCPC. On Lansing see Robert Lansing, *War Memoirs of Robert Lansing, Secretary of State* (Indianapolis & New York, 1935), Chapter XIV, and Daniel M. Smith, *Robert Lansing and American Neutrality, 1914–1917* (" University of California Publications in History," Vol. LIV; Berkeley, 1958), p. 83. On House see Ernest R. May, *The World War and American Isolation, 1914–1917* (Cambridge, Mass., 1959), pp. 348 ff. For the various uncertainties between these two men and President Wilson see *ibid.*, pp. 73 ff. On House's lack of candor to the President and to Jane Addams about the Allies' position on a neutral conference, see Ray Stannard Baker, *Woodrow Wilson, Life and Letters* (Garden City, 1927–37), VI, 122–3.

mediately opposed the use of the " Oscar II." She told Ford that
his help was needed in organizing the conference, not in supplying
transportation. Ford made his announcement about getting the
boys out of the trenches by Christmas the next day; the sailing
of the " Oscar II " was set for December 4.[51]

The slogans and ballyhoo connected with Ford's enterprise soon
obscured the serious purpose behind the project. That purpose was
to establish a private conference of internationalists who would
circulate various proposals which might form the beginning basis
for peace negotiations. The flood of publicity generated by Ford
and Madame Schwimmer soon overwhelmed Jane Addams and
the Woman's Peace party. The more stable and responsible individuals whom Ford had originally invited, some of whom had
accepted, declined to involve themselves. Many of Miss Addams'
personal friends—Mary Smith, Lillian Wald, Louise DeK. Bowen
—tried to dissuade her from going, but Miss Addams said that
perhaps she could bring some stability to an enterprise for which
she had solicited so much publicity and for which she cherished
such hopes. On the first of December, however, Jane Addams
became seriously ill with a tubercular infection of the kidneys.
She was in a Chicago hospital when the " Oscar II " sailed.

All of Ford's publicity about the peace ship identified it with
the Woman's Peace party and with the organization in Europe
established by the women who attended The Hague congress
in 1915. From her hospital bed Miss Addams tried through
several press statements to distinguish between the two efforts.
" The Woman's Peace Party, as such, had nothing whatever to
do with the peace ship or with the slogans which became attached
to it." She tried to keep the excesses of the Ford venture from
wholly discrediting her organization. The New York *Times* quoted
her as saying on January 6, 1916: " I will not comment on the
wisdom or folly of the peace ship. But it was not related to our
own movement [the Woman's Peace party]. The women's plan
is to establish a clearing house for peace sentiment. . . . If there
was a clearing house through which the manifestoes of peace

51. On Ford's conversion to pacifism, see New York *Times*, August 23, 1915,
p. 3, col. 5. I have drawn on the Ford Peace Plan Papers, in the Library of
Congress; the American Neutral Conference Committee Papers at SCPC; Degen,
History of the Woman's Peace Party, pp. 429–52; and Louis P. Lochner, *Henry
Ford—America's Don Quixote* (New York, 1925).

groups, parties or even individuals might find publication, it would soon develop a sympathetic movement in all countries."

Partly through the coolness of this and other statements, partly through Rosika Schwimmer's deviousness and frailties as a leader, and partly for other reasons, Ford withdrew from the group on Christmas Eve, his promises to get the boys out of the trenches unfulfilled. With Ford and the publicity spotlight gone, the men and women Ford had taken to Europe reorganized themselves several times. Finally as the Neutral Conference for Continuous Mediation, based in Stockholm, the Ford group, augmented by several distinguished Europeans, did some useful work.[52]

Jane Addams and the Woman's Peace party continued to urge the President to appoint an official neutral commission, which would not " take place of a governmental [peace] conference but [would] prepare the way for it." Many activities had been pioneered by private experiment and sponsorship, she told party members in an effort to keep their spirits up, and when these " volunteer efforts have had a measure of success, the government has taken over the enterprise. . . ." Perhaps the Ford personnel could form the nucleus for an official neutral conference. In January, 1916, she still hoped that a conference of neutrals might " re-establish some sort of international understanding; that the men of Germany may know what Englishmen think and English-men may have some way of communicating with like-minded people in Germany from whom they are cut off, that international public opinion may again have the right of way. . . . No one," she said, expected a neutral conference to end the war. That could be done only by the accredited representatives of the warring nations. But a conference of neutral nations would make it impossible to end the war by secret diplomacy, and would prove valuable by " bringing open democratic discussion into interna-tional affairs." [53]

52. Jane Addams' address, in Woman's Peace Party, *Yearbook* (1916), p. 22. In April, 1916, the Conference circulated among the belligerents the peace program of the Union for Democratic Control. The Conference continued its agitation through 1916 and became especially active in December, 1916, when the German chancellor announced the willingness of the Central Powers to enter into peace negotiations. With American entry into the war in February, 1917, the efforts of the Conference came to an end. See Jane Addams, *Peace and Bread in Time of War*, pp. 41–6, for her account of these activities.

53. Jane Addams' speech, in Woman's Peace Party, *Yearbook*, pp. 21, 22, 23, 24.

Jane Addams continued to hope that Wilson would act, that he would be persuaded of the advantages of an official neutral conference. She wrote guardedly to Lillian Wald, a Democrat in good standing with the President, that she had heard an interesting suggestion. There was no doubt, she wrote, that

> if the country is at war before the November election Wilson will be re-elected on the general principle of not wishing to swap horses in the middle of the stream. But, of course, the same thing would be attained if we were in the midst of negotiations; while it could not be put so bluntly as that, and while it would be most unfortunate to have that presented as the motive, yet if it could be presented to someone near the throne, it might become a determining factor.[54]

Jane Addams combined this behind-the-scenes attempt to influence the President with organizational attempts to win a decision in favor of a neutral conference. The Woman's Peace party endorsed again in January, 1916, " the immediate calling [by the American government] of a Conference of Neutral Nations in the interests of a just and orderly peace." After midyear it seemed as if the ladies' pleas were having some effect, for by May, 1916, Wilson had rejected the position of Lansing and House that " Anglo-American cooperation [was] . . . a prerequisite for mediation. He had concluded that the Allies were no more eager than the Germans to make peace. He had come, moreover, to be almost as suspicious of Britain's future intentions as of Germany's." After May, 1916, Wilson turned toward the democratic strategy of public negotiations of peace terms suggested by Jane Addams. His series of speeches starting with the " League to Enforce Peace " speech in May, 1916, his request to the belligerents to state their peace terms in December, 1916, his " Peace Without Victory " speech of January, 1917, represented his new strategy. This approach, which she had advocated a year earlier when civilian control in the belligerent nations was immensely stronger, elicited a series of congratulatory messages from Jane Addams.[55]

54. Jane Addams to Lillian Wald, May 12, 1916, Wald Papers, New York Public Library.
55. May, *The World War and American Isolation*, p. 359. May also shows in detail the gradual erosion of Bethmann Hollwegg's and Grey's control, and the in-

During 1916 illness and convalescence reduced Jane Addams' vitality and her manifold activities.[56] She gradually felt a changing atmosphere in America which inhibited the expression of peace sentiment. Buoyed by Wilson's campaign and by his adoption of the diplomatic strategy she had urged, Miss Addams at the same time noted the diminishing public confidence in her activities. Her fears about America's involvement in the war became more and more vivid. She participated in the last frantic efforts to keep America neutral after Germany's resumption of unrestricted submarine warfare. In early February, 1917, the more radical peace societies, among them the Woman's Peace party, formed a second Emergency Peace Federation. This federation sponsored demonstrations at the White House and a campaign of personal visiting and letter writing to congressmen. The emergency campaign reached a climax in a personal call by Jane Addams and others on the President. He brushed aside Jane Addams' and her colleagues' suggestions of arbitration, or conciliation, or a war referendum, or a conference of neutrals. Wilson instead stressed his ability as a full belligerent to give effect to his democratic aims at the peace table, rather than—as a neutral—merely being able to "call through a crack in the door." The phrase, Miss Addams wrote later, was one she had heard only a short while before from the mouth of Colonel House. She realized then that Wilson had finally embraced House's scheme rather than the more democratic one she had so long advocated.[57]

Thus ended thirty months of strenuous activity for Jane Addams. Wilson repudiated her arguments and strategy for peace. What she had hoped would be a great opportunity to find " an adequate moral basis for a new relationship between nations " was lost.

---

creasing influence of what Miss Addams called the military party. Telegrams from Jane Addams and from other officers of the Woman's Peace party are in the party's files at SCPC. For instance, Jane Addams and Sophonisba P. Breckinridge thanked Wilson on January 23, 1917, for his "brilliant statement of the hopes of modern internationalists."

56. Organizations which Miss Addams helped to direct continued to oppose military preparedness and American military adventures in the Caribbean. See Degen, *History of the Woman's Peace Party*, pp. 471–4, and Lillian Wald, *Windows on Henry Street*, pp. 290–9, for the activities of the American Union against Militarism. On her growing sense of isolation and public opprobrium see Linn, *Jane Addams*, pp. 330–4.

57. The conversation with the President is recalled in *Peace and Bread in Time of War*, p. 64.

Her hopes that voluntary rather than official diplomatic efforts
might avert war were denied. Her belief that " reason and good
will can settle any difficulty between any set of men, whether
they be groups of men or groups of nations," was disappointed.[58]
Miss Addams' appeals to humanitarian convictions and the solidarity of women had proved unsuccessful against the hot passions
of war. After April, 1917, when America's privileged position
as a neutral was gone, Jane Addams tried to find other ways to
work for the goals that had inspired her efforts at mediation.

58. *Ibid.*, p. 50; Jane Addams' testimony in U.S. Congress, House, Committee
on Foreign Affairs, *United States and the Orient, Hearing on H. R. 16661* [*to
Provide a Commission of Relations between the U. S. and the Orient*], *12 December
1916*, 64th Cong., 2d Sess., 1916, p. 12.

CHAPTER VIII

THE WAR YEARS AND AFTER

*Was not war in the interest of democracy for the salvation
of civilization a contradiction in terms, whoever said it or
however often it was repeated?*

JANE ADDAMS, 1922

Jane Addams' attempts to help stop the war through the formation of a neutral mediation commission met no success. But
neither the events of these years nor Wilsonian rhetoric persuaded
her that American participation was necessary or desirable. In
April, 1917, as in August, 1914, she believed that fighting could
never resolve international disputes and that war destroyed the
only bases—reason and good will—that could solve such contro-
versies. Miss Addams did not make American entrance into the
war an opportunity to suspend or reverse her commitment to
democracy and culture. Although these were years of deep discouragement for her, she remained faithful to the full democratic
and humane ideals that undergirded so much reform effort before
1914.[1]

Jane Addams was a lonely figure in these war years. Most of
the other prewar Progressives supported the war. John Dewey,
for instance, embraced war because there seemed to be no alternative. In January, 1917, Dewey wrote that America should not
enter the war "until the Allies are fighting on our terms for
our democracy and civilization." In the next months he became
convinced that the war was unavoidable. By July he urged pacifists,
among whom he had recently counted himself, to stop opposing
the war and to use "their energies to form at a plastic juncture,
the conditions and objects" which would make the distasteful

---

1. Jane Addams wrote to Mrs. Robert Morss Lovett that just recalling the war
years in writing about them in *Second Twenty Years at Hull-House* made her
"shrink inside me as an Irishman would say." Jane Addams to Ida Lovett,
February 25, 1930, SCPC.

job worthwhile.[2]

This enlistment of humanitarians in the war did not go unchallenged. Randolph Bourne attacked Dewey by asking how pragmatic philosophers who found war too strong to prevent could imagine it weak enough to control and mold. Pragmatists who embraced war to further democratic ends had failed to realize, Bourne wrote, that war was as near an absolute coercive situation as it was possible to fall into; once accepted, war eliminated further choices. " The penalty the realist pays for accepting war is to see disappear one by one the justifications for accepting it." In addition, Bourne pointed to the vagueness of the war goals and war programs by which Dewey justified the war. Dewey and his disciples, Bourne said, had mastered the methods of organizing, ordering, and administering; but these techniques failed in any way to touch " the happiness of the individual, the vivifying of the personality, the comprehension of social forces, the flair of art—in other words, the quality of life." Bourne's ideals were as vague as Dewey's, but he bluntly described the poverty of pragmatism as a technique for framing social ideals and values, especially when pragmatists could imagine that war would advance peaceful cultural and democratic goals.[3]

Jane Addams had consistently concerned herself with the discovery and definition of social values and ideals. The development of methods and professional techniques had been of minor interest to her, and the administrative appeal that tempted many pragmatists to embrace the war failed to sway her. She wrote Randolph Bourne to praise the " masterly way " he had replied to the prowar liberals.[4] She remained convinced that war destroyed the social values of democracy and civilization. To believe that war provided a pragmatic instrumentality to strengthen these values was to believe a contradiction which was untrue.

In the spring of 1917 Jane Addams spoke several times on " Patriotism and Pacifists in Wartime." She insisted that rational discussion of peace terms and postwar arrangements were all the

2. Cited in Morton White, *Social Thought In America*, pp. 166, 168. See also Forcey, *Crossroads of Liberalism*, especially pp. 247 ff, for the shift toward war of the editors of the *New Republic*. Alice Hamilton wrote Jane Addams, June 13, 1917, SCPC, " I dined with the Croly's. . . . [They were] all what I should call pacifistically minded but under the obsession of the fatality of this war."
3. Bourne, *Untimely Papers*, pp. 99, 135.
4. Jane Addams to Randolph Bourne, June 30, 1917, Bourne Papers, Columbia University Library.

more pressing since America had declared war. Pacifists could no longer carry on their antiwar propaganda but surely Americans should be able to discuss " aspects of patriotism " which were as relevant in wartime as in time of peace. Miss Addams replied to charges that pacifists were cowards and slackers. Many pacifists, she said, individually and collectively " have long striven for social and political justice with a fervor perhaps equal to that employed by the advocates of force. . . ." And if the aim of the war was justice, as war's advocates insisted, then the experience of those who had worked for it before the war was relevant. War exhibited " some of the noblest qualities of the human spirit," Miss Addams admitted, but war was unable to solve international problems. War inevitably aroused the most barbaric antagonisms, and the spirit of fighting burned away all those impulses that fostered the will to justice. Men who maintained that war advanced justice were, Jane Addams said simply, wrong.[5]

These remarks provoked a strong public reaction. Chicago was a center of wartime hysteria and opposition to pacifism and pressures toward a monolithic, unitary patriotism were very strong there. With its large immigrant population and its wide extremes of class and living standards, the city was shaken by spasms of fear in 1917. Jane Addams explained this fearfulness by referring to the alleged " anarchist riots " of Chicago's history which had " left their traces upon the nervous system of the city somewhat as a nervous shock experienced in youth will long afterwards determine the action of a mature man under widely different circumstances." Another Chicagoan, Edgar Lee Masters, recalled that life in the city became a " purgatory."

> Like the other American cities, Chicago went through an orgy of hate and hyprocrisy, of cruelty and revenge. . . . Nothing like it had ever been seen before. . . . People died from nervous exhaustion and fear; and insanity of a definite character took the minds of nearly everyone. Scarcely a human being in the city was left untouched by mania, unless it was the magnates who profited by this slaughter in Europe; and, as to them, they suffered an accession of greed which might be called insanity.[6]

5. Jane Addams, " Patriotism and Pacifists in Wartime," pp. 184, 190, 186.
6. Jane Addams, *Peace and Bread in Time of War*, p. 144; Edgar Lee Masters, *The Tale of Chicago* (New York, 1933), pp. 302, 303.

The American Protective League was founded in Chicago and reflected this atmosphere of hysteria. In his authorized history, Emerson Hough explained that the founding of the league was like the response of an " astounded and anguished America " to a cry for help from God Himself. Hough explained how the league had to deal with Chicago's " Bolsheviki, socialists, incendiaries, I.W.W.'s, Lutheran treason-talkers, Russellites, Bergerites, all the other -ites, religious and social fanatics, third-sex agitators, long-haired visionaries and work haters from every race in the world. . . ." The league's major activity was filling reports on suspected traitors and slackers. Hough dignified this snooping by quoting Division Superintendent Clabough of the U.S. Department of Justice's Bureau of Investigation, who estimated that " the Chicago Division of the American Protective League did seventy-five percent of the Government investigating work during the war." [7]

The wartime Berger and I.W.W. trials took place in Chicago, and in the summer of 1919 the city was disgraced by terrible race riots. Chicago's foreign population seemed a special menace to American ideals for many patriots. The U.S. Attorney General, A. Mitchell Palmer, in planning his dragnet raid for the first of January, 1920, was disconcerted to discover that state agents in Illinois had already planned a round-up of foreign radicals for that day. Consequently, in Chicago there were two " Palmer raids ": the first conducted by state agents on New Year's Day, and the second by federal agents the following day.[8]

This kind of hysteria was the background for the rapid changes in public opinion which effectively isolated the advocates of peace once America entered the war. Miss Addams recalled that " early

7. Emerson Hough, *The Web, the Authorized History of the American Protective League* (Chicago, 1919), pp. 28, 180, 491. See also *ibid.*, p. 197: " On November 23, Fred I———, said to resemble the Crown Prince very much in his personal appearance, was fined five thousand dollars, whether for seditious utterances or for his resemblance to the Crown Prince does not appear, and is immaterial. Either would be enough. On November 26, nine men were given free transportation from Chicago to Fort Leavenworth. One of these was a Dunkard preacher who got ten years for saying, ' I'd kill a man rather than buy a Liberty bond.' He will have time to think that proposition over. These straws will show well which way the wind blew in Chicago for the last year or so."

8. Robert K. Murray, *Red Scare, a Study in National Hysteria, 1919–1920* (Minneapolis, 1955), pp. 216–7, 234–5. See also Zachariah Chaffee, *Freedom of Speech* (New York, 1920), pp. 191 ff, on Chicago.

in the war," she and her fellow members of peace organizations were convinced that "the country as a whole was for peace. . . ." They tried "again and again to discover a method for arousing and formulating the sentiment against war." In 1930 Miss Addams was still impressed with how strange it seemed "in the light of later experiences that [in 1915, 1916, and 1917] we so whole-heartedly believed . . . that if we could only get our position properly before the public, we would find an overwhelming response." She came to realize "only slowly" that, with the declaration of war, the group of people opposed to war shrank very rapidly.[9]

Jane Addams later described the uncertainties, the physical and moral strains, that resulted from this public opposition. She had, she wrote, experienced opposition before, but nothing like the wartime newspapers' "concerted and deliberate attempt" to misrepresent her views. Slowly she came to realize that this systematic attempt to malign and distort was part of the war technique itself, "an inevitable consequence of war. . . ." Instead of being able to move with mass opinion, she found herself in increasing opposition and felt the "destroying effect of ' aloneness.'"[10]

Jane Addams rehearsed the democratic arguments that had supported progressive reform: modern democratic theory relied on popular impulses and depended on their growth for its evolutionary development; mass judgment and instinctive mass enthusiasm had great value; a human emotion was enhanced when millions shared it. She described her doubts of the rightness of opposing an overwhelming majority. It seemed " impossible " to hold out against the majority and " at moments absolutely unnatural, and one secretly yearned to participate in ' the folly of all mankind.' " Had the individual " the right " to oppose millions of his countrymen, she asked? Even " if one were right a

9. Jane Addams, *Peace and Bread in Time of War*, pp. 144, 110; Jane Addams, *Second Twenty Years at Hull-House*, p. 134.

10. Jane Addams, *Peace and Bread in Time of War*, pp. 134, 135, 140. Miss Addams related this public opposition to her own health. She recalled that the war years were years of " semi-invalidism." " Suddenly to find every public utterance willfully misconstrued, every attempt at normal relationship repudiated, must react in a baffled suppression which is health-destroying. . . ." Social opprobrium and widespread misunderstanding had, during Miss Addams illness when the Ford peace ship sailed, " brought me very near to self pity, perhaps the lowest pit into which human nature can sink." See *ibid.*, pp. 148, 139.

thousand times over in conviction, was he not absolutely wrong"
in abstaining from the community's action? [11]

Then there was the practical objection that to criticize the war
mood surrendered "all possibility of future influence." Miss
Addams and her fellow pacifists knew "how feeble and futile"
their efforts were against not only mass opinion, but also against
"the coagulation of motives, the universal confusion of a world
at war." She also recalled the fear of fanaticism. Her commitment to pragmatism warned her against "preferring a consistency
of theory to the conscientious recognition of the social situation.
. . ." To keep out of the war, some suggested, was "pure quietism,
an acute failure to adjust . . . to the moral world." And as a
pragmatist Jane Addams also saw how pacifism in wartime could
not be realized in action. If a truth had to "vindicate itself in
practice," if a "sincere and mature opinion" had to be justified
in works, then pacifism in wartime was by the very nature of
things a cul-de-sac. [12]

Nevertheless Jane Addams denied that violence could advance
democracy, which depended, she insisted, upon inner consent. Her
realization that war sacrificed this democratic consent was "the
most poignant moment" of the whole war period. Hull House
was a registration station for the draft. Miss Addams knew many
of the men who came to register and knew that some of them had
come to America at least in part seeking freedom from military
service. The registration line presented, she wrote later, "the
final frontier of the hopes of their kind, the traditional belief in
America as a refuge had come to an end. . . . All that had been
told them of the American freedom, which they had hoped to
secure for themselves and their children, had turned to ashes."
One of the men who had been in a Hull House citizenship class to
which Jane Addams had spoken when they got their first papers
stopped in line and rebuked Miss Addams. Bitterly he thanked
her for his being sent to Europe to fight. "I went into the citizenship class in the first place because you asked me to. If I hadn't
my papers now I would be exempted." It seemed as if, Miss
Addams concluded, "the whole theory of [democratic] self-
government founded upon conscious participation and inner con-

11. *Ibid.*, p. 140.
12. *Ibid.*, pp. 142, 150.

sent, had fallen to the ground." " Social advance," she wrote, " depends as much upon the process through which it is secured as upon the result itself. . . ." Social change was insecure if it was justified only as a war measure.[13]

Jane Addams decided that it was no service to her country to continue the peace strategy she had pursued during the period of neutrality. Her neutral conference strategy had been based on a belief that there existed large numbers of people in every country opposed to the war. But public hysteria and the continued deliberate misrepresentation by the press finally convinced her that during wartime, it was " impossible for the pacifist to obtain an open hearing." After months of urging what she considered a " reasonable and vital alternative to war," she simply stopped talking about the effects of the war. " We gradually ceased to state our [pacifist] position as we became convinced that it served no practical purpose and, worse than that, often found that the immediate result was provocative." [14]

Thus in the fall and winter of 1917–8 Jane Addams searched for ways of affirming humanitarian and democratic ideals in an America increasingly intolerant of any talk of peace. Her opportunity came with the establishment of a federal Department of Food Administration. She was attracted by Herbert Hoover's first appeal to Americans about food: " the situation is more than war, it is a problem of humanity." [15] Work for Hoover's agency

13. Many Hull House residents did not follow Miss Addams in her pacifism, and, since one resident was head of the district draft board and the forms were difficult to fill out, Hull House was headquarters for the draft. *Ibid.*, pp. 133, 123, 117–8, 119.

14. *Ibid.*, pp. 109, 111, 110, 141. The Woman's Peace party adopted in October, 1917, a policy statement which read: " We have avoided all criticism of our Government as to the declaration of war, and all activities that could be considered as obstructive in respect to the conduct of the war, and this not as a counsel of prudence, but as a matter of principle." *Statement of the Executive Board of the National Woman's Peace Party*, issued October 25, 1917, SCPC. A perceptive interviewer wrote in the Boston *Herald*, June 14, 1926, p. 16, col. 3: " She believes herself to have rendered the country all the service in her power once we were at war and to have done nothing to impede the success of our arms." A student of this period has observed that " on the whole, then, in late 1917 the strength of the antiwar Socialists and pacifists was of little consequence." Arno J. Mayer, *Political Origins of the New Diplomacy, 1917–1918* (New Haven, 1959), p. 350.

15. The Department of Food Administration was created on August 10, 1917. For Jane Addams' reaction see her " World's Food Supply and Woman's Obligation," *Journal of Home Economics*, X (September, 1918), 389–90.

seemed to provide a chance to affirm civilized and humane ideals
and also to mitigate the war spirit in America. Miss Addams
spoke under the auspices of the Food Administration (and later
the Committee on Public Information) in many states.[16] She
urged American women to conserve food and to help increase food
production. She related the conservation and production of food
to her humanitarian and democratic beliefs, and especially to her
hopes for peace. Her speeches dealt with two related topics: the
special relationship of women to the war through their traditional
concern with food, and the relationship between food and the
organization and reconstruction of international life after the war.

Miss Addams tried to show how the beginnings of culture
involved women and food. She recalled later how she had read
" endlessly " in Frazer's *The Golden Bough*.[17] The food spirits
were " always feminine," she noted, perhaps from the natural
association with fecundity and growth. In one of her speeches for
the Food Administration, Jane Addams said that in primitive
societies—" back of history itself "—women " were the first agri-
culturists and were for a long time the only inventors and de-
velopers of its processes." The refusal of women to desert their
crops first broke the migratory pattern. " The desire to grow
food for her children led to a fixed abode and a real home from
which our democratic morality and customs are supposed to have
originated." [18]

Miss Addams urged wartime audiences to try to understand how
this traditional concern for food imposed a special duty on women
" to nurture the world." By understanding this primitive obligation American women could extend their sympathies and enlarge
their " conception of duty in such wise that the consciousness of
the world's [food] needs becomes the actual impulse " of their
daily activities. Such a sympathetic response afforded " an opportunity to lay over again the foundations for a wider morality, as

16. Linn, *Jane Addams*, p. 330 asserts that Miss Addams was " requested "
to serve by Hoover.

17. Jane Addams, *Peace and Bread in Time of War*, p. 77; J. G. Frazer, *The
Golden Bough. a Study in Magic and Religion* (London, 1911–5). See especially
Volume VII, Chapter 4, " Women's Part in Primitive Agriculture," and Chapter 5,
" The Corn-Mother and the Corn-Maiden in Northern Europe."

18. Jane Addams, " World's Food Supply and Woman's Obligation," pp. 396,
397, 398; Jane Addams, *The Long Road of Woman's Memory* (New York, 1916),
p. 127.

women's concern for feeding her children made the beginning of an orderly domestic life." By her food appeal Jane Addams hoped, she later recalled, to "break through into more primitive and compelling motives than those inducing so many women to increase the war spirit. There was something as primitive and real about feeding the helpless as there was about the fighting and in the race history the tribal feeding of children antedated mass fighting by perhaps a million years." [19]

War demanded a change in the nation's food habits, Miss Addams declared, if world famine was to be avoided. American women had to become aware of the needs of the whole world, and this awareness would be "in a sense but part of that long struggle from the blindness of individuality to the consciousness of common ends—almost an epitome of human progress itself." At the same time this change in food habits provided women with a long-sought opportunity. "From the time we were little children we have all of us, at moments at least, cherished overwhelming desires to be of use in the great world, to play a conscious part in its progress." These desires were frequently contradicted by household demands, or by the vague purposes of daily routine. But during the crisis of war, she said, usefulness to the world and household routine were "absolutely essential to each other." The great world purpose of feeding the starving could not be achieved without a conscious modification of women's domestic routine. This change was "probably the most compelling challenge which has been made upon women's constructive powers for centuries." [20]

In a similar way, according to Miss Addams, the international organization of the world's food supply was altering the aims and methods of international politics. War made the question of the production and distribution of the world's total food supply a matter of international concern and organization. The Allies established a joint food commission to collect and apportion food supplies on the basis of need, not profit. Thus, she said, the world's governments had been forced to assume the responsibility to see that food was apportioned fairly; commercial competition

19. Jane Addams, "World's Food Supply and Woman's Obligation," pp. 396, 398; Jane Addams, *Peace and Bread in Time of War*, p. 75.

20. Jane Addams, "World's Food Supply and Woman's Obligation," pp. 394, 395, 396.

" could not be trusted to feed the feeble and helpless." This new responsibility might unloose a " new and powerful force " in international relations, which had lacked the kind of humane modification that appeared in a nation's " internal politics by the increasing care of the poor, the concern for the man at the bottom. . . . In international affairs the nations have still dealt almost exclusively with political and commercial affairs considered as matters of " rights," consequently they have never been humanized in their relations to each other as they have been in their internal affairs." Wartime efforts to distribute food justly meant that each nation had to make " certain concessions to the common good that the threat of famine may be averted." Jane Addams labelled this development a revolution toward " a more reasonable world order . . . the war itself forming its matrix." [21]

The organization of the world's food supply provided a model for postwar international organization, Miss Addams said hopefully. The officers of the Woman's Peace party rejoiced that the United States and the Allies had acted in common regarding " the conservation and distribution of food supplies and other matters, quite outside the military field. . . ." Such international organization should be extended, the women said. " An interparliamentary conference thus developed might from [sic] the nucleus of a permanent international parliament. . . . Such an organization," the party's resolution read in words strongly suggesting Jane Addams' authorship, " arising in response to actual world needs, is in line with the genesis and growth of all permanent political institutions." [22]

Citing John Dewey, Miss Addams said that many discussions of international leagues and courts failed because they lacked a focus for more energies and moral ideals. This lack of focus was especially evident after war, which scattered and diffused moral energies. So often, she noted, enthusiasts for a new international order were reduced to the negative task of preventing war. They " had none of the positive incentive which arises from looking after social and economic needs." Various efforts to feed

21. *Ibid.*, pp. 399, 400; Jane Addams, in " World's Food and World's Politics," National Conference of Social Work, *Proceedings* (1918), p. 651.
22. *Statement of the Executive Board of the Woman's Peace Party*, issued October 25, 1917, SCPC.

the world might provide just this missing focus and incentive, she suggested. The attempt to feed the feeble and helpless was " constantly bringing into existence new obligations which may form the natural and normal foundations for a genuine international government." [23]

If energized pity for the hungry and dependent became the new motive in international affairs, Miss Addams hypothesized, some of the political causes of the war might be solved: the need for Russian wheat in western Europe might secure the internationalization of the Bosporus; the world's need for food from the Euphrates valley, rather than rival national ambitions, would determine the building and control of a Mesopotamian railroad; the need of every nation for a ready access to the sea might secure a railroad through a strip of international territory for landlocked nations like Serbia. " It is possible," Miss Addams said in hopeful summary,

> that the more sophisticated questions of national grouping and territorial control would gradually adjust themselves if the paramount human question of food for the hungry be fearlessly and drastically treated upon an international basis. The League of Nations, destined to end wars, . . . may be founded not upon broken bits of international law, but upon ministrations to primitive human needs. The League would then be organized *de facto* as all the really stable political institutions in the world have been.[24]

In these ways Jane Addams filled the war years with work for peace. She continued to believe that humanitarian ideals and reforms were the best way to displace the war spirit. She labored for the same ideals during the war that she had worked for before the war: the nurture of human life, the defense of the weak and helpless. These ideals provided what she called the matrix for new duties, for wider sympathy, and for an extended international ethic. The impulses and incentives and beliefs that justified her prewar humanitarian reforms also justified the peace and international order for which she worked during the war.

The spirit of war was not as easy to defeat as the Central Powers

23. Jane Addams, " World's Food and World's Politics," pp. 651–2.
24. *Ibid.*, p. 656.

had been. Long after November, 1918, the ghost of Caesar
haunted international life. Like many others, the women who
gathered at The Hague in 1915 had not expected any fundamental
transformation in European life. They assumed that the peace
conference following the war would be in a neutral country, and
they decided to convene again at the same time and place as the
peace conference. Prevented from doing this by the choice of Paris
as the site of the armistice negotiations, the women gathered at
Zurich on May 12, 1919 for their second congress. Jane Addams
noted that the date coincided with the enlargement of the Versailles Conference to include delegates from the Central Powers,
when "in a sense the official Peace Conference as such has
formally begun." [25] The women who assembled at Zurich had
discarded their assumption that peace would restore the old
Europe they had known before 1914. The delegates were conscious of meeting in a time of social and political revolution.
They met old friends so changed by war's privations that they
were scarcely recognizable. They were outraged at what the
civilized world had permitted itself to do, and to become. Indignation emboldened these women to pass a series of radical resolutions. "The events of the last four years have proved, that our
civilization has completely failed," the ladies resolved. "Our lives
have been dominated by a purely materialistic philosophy, by a
policy of sheer force and violence. . . . [We seek] to establish a
basis for a new human civilization." [26]

The first concern of the congress was the food problem, which
Jane Addams discussed in her presidential address. "Now that
the whole world has been brought to its knees by hunger," perhaps
the nations could approach each other on an older and surer basis.
Constitutions and resolutions had not seemed to work in preventing war. Perhaps, she said, the primitive desire to feed
hungry children—whether in Serbia, or Poland, or in Rumania,
for the life of one child was as valuable as that of any other—
was a strong enough bond to hold the race together. But the food
question also had darker potentialities, which the Allies exploited
with their food blockade. The delegates at Zurich quickly adopted

25. Jane Addams, *Peace and Bread in Time of War*, p. 154.
26. See *ibid.*, p. 159; International Congress of Women, Zurich, May 12–17,
1919, *Report* (Geneva, n. d. [1920]), p. 131.

a resolution, presented by Mrs. Pethick-Lawrence, which urged that the Allies immediately lift the blockade; it was a " disgrace to civilization." The ladies urged that all the resources of the world—food, raw material, money, and transport—be organized immediately for relief, and further, that all luxury trade be prohibited and food be rationed, until the necessaries of life were supplied to all. This resolution was telegraphed to President Wilson at Paris. He replied promptly that the message appealed " both to my head and to my heart," but that the outlook for such action was " extremely unpromising, because of infinite practical difficulties." [27]

The Zurich delegates soon discovered what Wilson meant by practical difficulties. They were in session when the terms of the Versailles Treaty were made public and were one of the first organizations to comment on them. The women deeply regretted, they said, that the Treaty " should so seriously violate the principles upon which alone a just and lasting peace can be secured, and which the democracies of the world had come to accept." The ladies passed a stinging indictment of the Treaty:

> By guaranteeing the fruits of the secret treaties to the conquerors, the terms of peace tacitly sanction secret diplomacy, deny the principles of self-determination, recognise the right of the victors to the spoils of war, and create all over Europe discords and animosities, which can only lead to future wars. By the demand for the disarmament of one set of belligerents only, the principle of justice is violated and the rule of force is continued. By the financial and economic proposals a hundred million people of this generation in the heart of Europe are condemned to poverty, disease and despair, which must result in the spread of hatred and anarchy within each nation.

The delegates urged amendments to bring the Treaty " into harmony with those principles first enumerated by President Wilson upon the faithful carrying out of which the honour of the Allied peoples depends." [28] The League Covenant was the most dis-

27. *Ibid.*, pp. 162, 195–6; Jane Addams, *Peace and Bread in Time of War*, pp. 167, 160.

28. International Congress of Women, Zurich, May 12–17, 1919, *Report*, pp. 242–3.

appointing part of the Treaty. The woman passed many detailed suggestions, some of which endorsed provisions of the Covenant, some of which suggested additions to strengthen the League, and some of which denounced omission from the Covenant of principles that the Fourteen Points asserted.[29]

The most important action of the congress was its insistence that civilization and a stable (and democratic) international order demanded an end to violence and coercion. An English delegate introduced a resolution which endorsed self-determination for Ireland by saying that " the test of the civilization of a State is the extent to which it relies upon moral appeal and consent rather than coercion. . . ." Socialist delegates to the Zurich meeting secured passage of resolutions recognizing " a fundamentally just demand underlying most of . . . [the] revolutionary movements " and declaring sympathy with the workers everywhere. But coupled with these sentiments the women at Zurich reasserted " their faith in methods of peace and believe[d] it [was] their special part in this revolutionary age to counsel against violence from any side." [30]

Jane Addams formulated this central idea of the congress in her closing speech. She believed, she told the delegates, that moral force could accomplish things that military force could not. She illustrated this point with a story from Herbert Hoover. Food destined for Russia had to be unloaded and transshipped by men whose families were desperately hungry. Only after a moral appeal was made to these dock and transport workers were they willing to let the food go through. The lesson was obvious: " We shall have to believe in spiritual power. We shall have to learn to use moral energy, to put a new sort of force into the world and believe that it is a vital thing—the only thing, in this moment of sorrow and death and destruction, that will heal the world. . . ." [31] But this new force was new only in scope. The moral appeal that had supported progressive domestic reform was now to be made international. All the disappointments of war, and the fresh disappointment in the peace designed at Versailles, did not destroy Jane Addams' faith in moral energy, in the possibility of civilized and just relations among nations.

29. *Ibid.*, pp. 168–71.
30. *Ibid.*, p. 259.
31. *Ibid.*, p. 237. Miss Addams was again made an envoy of the congress. She presented the congress resolutions to statesmen at the peace conference at Versailles. Her efforts had no effect.

In June, 1919, Jane Addams, accompanied by Alice Hamilton, returned to Germany. They investigated food and health conditions and distributed the first private relief in Germany for the American Friends' Service Committee. " In the midst of it all only the feeding of the hungry seemed to offer the tonic of beneficent activity," Miss Addams recalled. She saw at first hand the heart-rending effects of the Allied food blockade, continued through the seven months of armistice. " Our impressions," Miss Addams reported in the *Survey*, " crowded each other so fast that they merged into one, an impression of mass hunger as we had never imagined it, hunger of millions continued month after month for three years or more. . . ." Jane Addams and Alice Hamilton concentrated in their official report on the high incidence of tuberculosis, rickets, and acute nephritis, which they blamed on lack of food. They also described health and hospital conditions. Dr. Hamilton, perhaps, wrote the part of their report that described how doctors were easily able to diagnose ailments and then, for lack of medical equipment and medicine, had to watch their patients die. Medical men were reduced to a kind of horrible resignation and were almost glad that their patients had so little resistance, and died quickly.[32]

Jane Addams recalled later that it had been the plight of the children which had most affected her on this trip. The little emaciated bodies, stunted, listless, were " incredibly pathetic and unreal." On a playground in Leipzig the children were " utterly indifferent " to the playground director's announcements of prizes and activities. Only with the promise that perhaps they would get a little milk in their soup " day after tomorrow " did the children " break out into the most ridiculous, feeble little cheer ever heard." Challenged whether he could produce the milk, the director said he was not sure, but he had some prospect. And he said, in words which recalled Miss Addams' own words before the war and which must have touched her deeply, children had to have something to hope for, that was the prerogative of youth. Both women reported that they were constantly challenged to justify all of the Allies' actions, not only the terrible food blockade. Their discouraging report concluded that much remained " to be

---

32. Jane Addams, *Peace and Bread in Time of War*, p. 166; Jane Addams and Alice Hamilton, "After the Lean Years, Impressions of Food Conditions in Germany when Peace Was Signed," *Survey*, XLII (September 6, 1919), 793.

done in the way of interpretation and honest discussion before even a beginning of mutual understanding can be made." After her return to America, Miss Addams spoke on European relief during October, November, and December under the auspices of the American Friends' Service Committee.[33]

In these anxious months of late 1919 and early 1920, when the pacifists' worst prophesies of what war would destroy seemed to have come true, Jane Addams also returned to the cause of democratic and humanitarian reform. In her search for some connection with the overwhelming problems of reconstruction that she had just viewed at first hand, she returned to familiar, but now more urgent, efforts, as indicated in an address to the National Conference of Social Work in 1920.[34] Social workers had not been immune to wartime hysteria, and the conference was divided over questions of loyalty and patriotism. The Illinois section had withdrawn from the national conference to indicate its disapproval of the election of Owen Lovejoy as president. Lovejoy's offense was public praise of Eugene V. Debs. "The Atlantic City Conference [in 1919] was permeated with pacifism, socialism, parlor bolshevism," noted the editorial writer of the Illinois section's quarterly.[35]

Jane Addams took the occasion of the 1920 conference to emphasize again the need for social workers to advance humanitarian reform. The uncertainties and suspicions within the conference could be solved, she said, only by a return to the basic principles of social work and social reform. She described how war had interrupted and reversed the steady growth of the international effort to abolish hunger, poverty, and disease, to free childhood from danger, in sum, to enlarge life. The period of reconstruction was a challenge " so imperious and overwhelming that everything else must be put aside." Social workers who did

33. Jane Addams, *Peace and Bread in Time of War*, pp. 169–70, 171; " Report of Jane Addams and Dr. Hamilton to the American Friends' Service Committee on the Situation in Germany," American Friends' Service Committee, *Bulletin*, XXV (November, 1919), 17. For a brief description of Jane Addams' German trip see Mary Hoxie Jones, *Swords Into Ploughshares, an Account of the American Friends' Service Committee, 1917–1937* (New York, 1937), pp. 75 ff. The committee was formed in June, 1917.

34. In 1917 the National Conference of Charities and Correction became the National Conference of Social Work.

35. "Illinois Withdraws from the National Conference," Illinois Department of Public Welfare, *Institutional Quarterly*, X (September 30, 1919), 8.

not " take hold of this great world-situation " failed in an essential obligation; they betrayed the original purposes of social work. " After all, what is the spirit of social work? It was founded upon genuine, human pity, upon the desire to relieve suffering, to give food to the hungry and to shelter the homeless. . . ." Jane Addams urged her colleagues to " get back to that " because it underlay all the subdivisions and subtleties of social work activities. If social workers cut themselves off from these primitive human motives at the basis of social work, they would injure and cripple the spirit of social service for years to come.[36]

For Jane Addams, feeding Europe after the war was more basic than political ideology, and she joined all sorts of voluntary efforts to raise money in America for food and medicines.[37] In a newspaper interview in 1921 she is quoted as urging help for the starving in Austria and Russia without " so many ' ifs ' and ' ands ' about it. You can be as savagely anti-Bolshevik as you please, but you can't be or shouldn't be anti-human." Speaking to an audience of Kansas farmers, Miss Addams asserted that Americans had " no right to talk about a surplus crop of wheat or corn until [the underfed children of Austria and Armenia] are fed." Americans should bend all their energies to bring American surplus and European need together. Politics simply was not involved, Miss Addams asserted in her special appeal for relief for people in the Volga wheat region. Succoring the starving, restoring civilization in Europe, was above politics.[38]

The civilized and democratic values that impelled Miss Addams to advocate relief to both democrat and Bolshevik also persuaded her to become one of the seven members of the American Commission on Conditions in Ireland. The commission, sponsored by the *Nation*, provided an opportunity for American liberals to

36. Jane Addams, "The Spirit of Social Service," in National Conference of Social Work, *Proceedings* (1920), pp. 42, 41.

37. Letterheads at SCPC show Miss Addams as chairman in 1920 of American Relief for Russian Women and Children; honorary chairman of the American Welfare Association for German Children; honorary vice-president in 1921 of the American Committee for Relief in Ireland; a member of the board of directors of the Women's Emergency Committee for Near East Relief in 1922 and of the Russian Famine Fund in 1923. See Merle Curti, *American Philanthropy Abroad, a History* (New Brunswick, 1963), pp. 259–300.

38. "Jane Addams Pleads for the Starving," Cincinnati *Post*, September 29, 1921; Jane Addams, "The Threat of World Starvation," Kansas State Board of Agriculture, *Report*, XLI (January–March, 1922), 76.

express their sympathy for the Irish struggle for democratic self-government and to condemn the British for their cruel—uncivilized—military campaign. The commission members noted in their report that they were concerned only with aspects of the Irish situation which appealed to " the sympathy, conscience and sense of justice of mankind . . . [which] cannot be ignored if the traditions of civilization are to be the basis of human comity."

The commission elicited testimony that emphasized the use of passive resistance, women's participation in the democratic struggle, and the temperance of the Irish as opposed to the drunkenness of the British army men. Testimony also centered on the atrocities committed by the Black and Tans. British military actions were labeled " a relic of barbarism," almost without parallel in the practice of civilized nations.[39] British justice was discredited, Anglo-Saxon civilization was dishonored, the commission's report declared, and " decent folk, everywhere are shamed and scandalized that such things can still be in their day and generation." The remedy was democracy, these American progressives asserted. A majority of the Irish people had sanctioned the Irish Republic by ballot. They were giving their allegiance to it, paying its taxes, and respecting the decisions of its courts and civil officials. This democratic decision was the solution to the Irish problem.[40]

Miss Addams' renewed participation in voluntary organizations such as the Irish commission reflected discouragement over her inability to get official action in 1915 and 1916, and also discouragement with the Versailles settlement, and especially with the League of Nations. When she returned from Europe in 1919 she was torn between approval and opposition to the League. " I never said a word against it, but I could not go about advocating it." The unsatisfactory peace at Versailles, according to Jane Addams, was partly the President's fault. In the only bitter criticism she ever published, she attacked Wilson's

> whole theory of leadership. . . . I hotly and no doubt unfairly
> asked myself whether any man had the right to rate his

39. The American Commission on Conditions in Ireland, *Interim Report* (n.p. [New York], n.d. [1921]), pp. 7, 47, 52. The commission continually contrasted professed British war aims with British actions in Ireland.

40. *Ibid.*, p. 98. See also pp. 13–4.

moral leadership so high that he could consider the sacrifice of the lives of thousands of his young countrymen a necessity? . . . All the study of modern social science is but a revelation of the fallacy of such a point of view, a discrediting of the Carlyle contention that the people must be led into the ways of righteousness by the experience, acumen and virtues of a great man.[41]

American entrance into the war seemed only to have strengthened the hands of those demanding the harshest peace terms from a crushed Germany. Jane Addams asserted that Wilson had lost rather than gained influence by entering the war, because he went to Versailles only as a bargainer and not as a disinterested adjudicator. The world's hopes had centered on Wilson because of his antiwar utterances, she wrote. Had the President " stood firmly against participation in war [he] could have had his way with the common people in every country." Miss Addams softened her indictment of Wilson by blaming the debacle at Versailles not on him personally, but on war itself. It was not the men at Versailles, but " the human spirit itself which failed, . . . the human spirit under a temptation which an earlier peace might have diminished." [42]

Jane Addams believed that the most pressing problems at the end of the war were humanitarian, not, as the peacemakers thought, political. The politicians at Versailles had transformed the League of Nations from a great democratic instrument for peace into an antidemocratic force. The League's " very structure and functioning is pervaded by the war spirit, the victorious disciplining of the defeated, whereas the people had dreamed of a League of Peace lifting up all those who had been the victim of militarism." Miss Addams urged the League consciously to " focus shattered moral energies and . . . make effective moral ideas upon a more extended scale than that to which the time has become accustomed." [43] The great danger to the League, according to

41. *Ibid.*, pp. 64–5. For a description of Wilson's private doubts about a war for democracy see John L. Heaton, *Cobb of " The World," a Leader of Liberalism, Compiled from his Editorial Articles and Public Addresses* (New York, 1924), pp. 267–70.

42. Jane Addams, *Peace and Bread in Time of War*, pp. 67, 68.

43. Jane Addams, " Potential Advantages of the Mandate System," *Annals* XCVI (July, 1921), 73; Jane Addams, " Feed the World and Save the League," *New Republic*, XXIV (November 24, 1920), 325.

Miss Addams, was that its first work involved guaranteeing a purely political peace dependent on old political motives. The League should first perform some humanitarian act of which no other agency was capable. Once established on an humanitarian basis, she wrote, the League might turn to the political problems of peace and disarmament with a fund of sympathy, confidence, affection, and trust.[44]

Although she criticized the League of Nations as a defective instrument, Miss Addams became one of its active supporters in America. Her initial doubts were dispelled by the first meeting of the League Assembly in November, 1920, several sessions of which she observed in Geneva.

> I come back to America from Europe a reconvert [to the League of Nations]. When the League was formed I was for it. I campaigned for it. Later I had reactions. I began to wonder, to doubt. But after fresh contact with Europe, I no longer doubt. I once more believe strongly in the League of Nations and heartily wish our country might associate itself with the work the League alone can do. Put it to yourself this way: If you abolish the League, or if it dies, what is there to take its place? There is no answer.

Miss Addams described how the meeting of the League Assembly had cleared up all sorts of things. After the disappointments of Versailles, it was a relief to find that after all " the nations of the earth could get together and discuss openly and freely and also kindly, for the most part, and even unselfishly, the genuine concerns of the world. The meeting of the Assembly was like the beginning of a new era. . . ." Miss Addams singled out for particular praise the publicity about international affairs that the Assembly promoted. Publicity, Miss Addams wrote perhaps recalling her struggles for a democratic peace, was " all to the good "; and the Assembly fostered " publicity for the care of backward people, publicity for all treaties between nations which will in a specified time be invalid if they are not registered with the Secretariat at Geneva; publicity in international affairs, . . . most of all the free and open discussion. After December, 1920,

44. Jane Addams, " Feed the World and Save the League," pp. 325–6.

Miss Addams became an articulate advocate of co-operation with the League and with its specialized agencies.[45]

The Washington Naval Conference also revived Jane Addams' hopes for peace. The conference had " practical results " because it decreased naval power and construction. She was especially pleased with the conference because it seemed to show after the bitter experiences of the war years that public opinion could operate in international affairs in favor of peace. No international matter " ever received such an impact from public opinion as the conference for the limitations of armaments felt in Washington," she declared in 1922. " And there is no doubt but that the whole thing developed tremendously under the pressure of public opinion." The situation gave one " a fresh start—a de novo opening as it were, for this kind of public opinion." [46]

Public opposition during these trying years was not able to convince Jane Addams that the democratic and cultural ideals for which she had labored so long were false. During the war she discovered ways to reaffirm her belief in the nurture and up-building of human life. After the war the League of Nations seemed to offer an instrument for the reconstruction of those same cultural ideals. The democratic procedures in the League Assembly and the organization of public opinion in favor of peace which the naval conference showed seemed to promise a revival of democracy enfeebled by the war. For all her discouragement about mass opinion under the pressures of war, Jane Addams set to work in the 1920's to cultivate support for the ideals to which she had devoted her life. During the last fifteen years of her life, she explored new openings, new developments in international social and political experience, new motives that might strengthen men's will toward international peace. The years after sixty were, for Miss Addams, filled with the search for what she called international comity.

45. Miss Addams is quoted in the Cincinnati *Post*, September 29, 1921; Jane Addams, " Potential Advantages of the Mandate System," pp. 73, 74. Compare F. P. Walters, *History of the League of Nations* (London, 1952), I, 126–7: " It could not be doubted that the [1920] Assembly had revived the interest and the hopes which had illuminated the earlier versions of the League . . . the Assembly had begun the process of pulling the League away from the centripetal force of the Treaty of Versailles and all it stood for. . . ."

46. Jane Addams, " Opening Address," in Women's International League for Peace and Freedom, *Congress Report*, IV [1924], 1; Jane Addams, " What I Saw in Europe," *La Follette's Magazine*, XIII (February, 1922), 22.

CHAPTER IX

PACIFISM

I little dreamed what was ahead of me when I cast my lot with pacifism. . . . I see more clearly now than ever before how fundamental the problem of peace and war is. When I started on the work, I had little appreciation of how vitally it affects our whole social fabric. It interested me as a scientific problem of getting the world better organized, but I did not see then, as I see now, how the problem of slums, of unemployment, of capitalism, of the submerged portions of our populations is connected with the question of war. I thank God that my first field of activity was Chicago where I had the privilege of coming under the influence of Hull House and its great leader.

Louis Lochner to Jane Addams, 1917

The modern world is developing an almost mystic sense of the continuity and interdependence of mankind. . . . It lies with us who are here now to make this consciousness—as yet so fleeting and uncertain—the unique contribution of our time to that small handful of incentives which really motivates human conduct.

Jane Addams, 1929

The central concern of Jane Addams' life after the war was world peace. She believed that peace could exist only where justice existed, and she included the whole range of men's relations with each other in her demand for justice. All human experience, she wrote reflectively, was an "essential unity." Violence and coercion, which Jane Addams equated with injustice, destroyed this unity and balked the establishment of peace. The demand for peace based on measures to establish and extend economic and social justice filled her mature years.[1]

1. Jane Addams' statement in Ramananda Chatterjee (ed.), *The Golden Book of Tagore, a Homage to Rabindranath Tagore from India and the World in Celebration of His Seventieth Birthday* (Calcutta, 1931), p. 19.

The end of the war did not stop attacks on pacifists. During the Red Scare and all through the 1920's Jane Addams remained a prominent target. The American Legion, the Daughters of the American Revolution, self-styled patriots, and ephemeral but noisy patriotic organizations joined in the hue and cry against subversion and Jane Addams' suspect patriotism. During the fears and alarms of the decade following the war, her name led many lists of persons supposed to be subversive. She figured prominently in the Lusk report's attempt to identify pacifism and socialism, and to label both as parts of a foreign conspiracy to subvert American ideals and institutions. Archibald E. Stevenson, the author of most of the Lusk Committee's report, wrote a very colorful and exaggerated story of the peace efforts from 1914 to 1918 in which he attempted to show how these various pacifist activities were interrelated and were dominated by Socialists. Rosika Schwimmer's 1914 visit and the overlapping membership of peace organizations were adduced as conclusive evidence of a conspiracy led by foreigners.[2]

The spirit of the Lusk Committee's report was maintained and elaborated by the American Legion, which based its attacks on Miss Addams on her opposition to military training in the schools, opposition which she expressed only infrequently. The Legion's continuing public attacks nettled her because they consistently misquoted, misrepresented, or ignored what she had said and done. Members of the Legion perversely twisted every attempt to reply to their attacks until Miss Addams simply refused to make any public comment on the Legion's charges.[3] These attacks

2. New York, (State) Legislature, Joint Committee Investigating Seditious Activities, *Revolutionary Radicalism—Its History, Purpose and Tactics, with an Exposition and Discussion of the Steps Being Taken and Required to Curb It* (4 vols.; Albany, 1920). This report also inspired many small patriotic organizations. The most troublesome of these for Jane Addams was the unofficial "Military Intelligence Association of the Sixth Army Area" which was founded in 1923 in Chicago. Sydney L. Smith, an engineer employed by the Portland Cement Association, headed the association. He continually attacked Miss Addams as both an anarchist and Communist; he interpreted her opposition to military training in the schools as the advocating of a Bolshevik take-over of American government, and so on. See Norman Hapgood (ed.), *Professional Patriots* (New York, 1927), pp. 176–7.

3. Mrs. Sarah Schaar recalled how the American Legion on one occasion in the mid-twenties stoned the train on which Miss Addams was returning to Chicago (Personal interview, 1960). In 1923 the American Legion invited Mussolini to address its national convention. The national commander said then: "Do not

came to a climax on November 10, 1926, when Captain Ferre
Watkins, Commander of the Illinois Department of the American
Legion, spoke to the Illinois Federation of Women's Clubs. Captain Watkins branded Hull House "a hotbed of communism,
and charged that the Communist 'pinks' [at Hull House] were
trying to sell out America to international schemers for their own
personal advantage." The Captain quoted Jane Addams as saying
that through her White House influence she hoped to strip West
Point cadets of their uniforms, deprive all colleges of military
training, and leave America undefended.[4]

Sustained attacks on her patriotism were also launched by the
Daughters of the American Revolution. Jane Addams found these
less burdensome because more lunatic. "With his hand upon
his heart," Weber Linn wrote in 1937, "this biographer testifies
that to his knowledge the animosity of the D.A.R. against her
personally never gave Jane Addams anything but amusement."
Miss Addams explained that she had been the only woman on
a jury at the Paris Exhibition of 1900 where the Daughters of the
American Revolution exhibit won a gold medal. Subsequently
she was made an honorary member of the organization. "I supposed at the time that it had been for life, but it was apparently
only for good behavior. . . ." Members of the DAR circulated an
infamous chart that attempted to show the overlapping membership of a number of un-American and unpatriotic organizations.
Among the organizations was, as Jane Addams noted, the U.S.
Congress. Miss Addams refused to reply publicly to the DAR
charts, nor would she comment publicly on dossiers that the DAR
circulated.[5]

Miss Addams' friends, however, went to her defense and encouraged her to sue for libel. Mrs. Carrie Chapman Catt published
an open letter to the DAR in which she defended Jane Addams.

Miss Addams is not a Bolshevik.
She is not a Communist.

forget that the Fascists are to Italy what the American Legion is to the United
States." Cited in Hapgood (ed.), *Professional Patriots*, p. 62.

4. New York *Times*, November 11, 1926, p. 11, col. 3. Miss Addams' friends
countered this wild attack by tendering her a large civic banquet. Messages and
tributes, solicited and unsolicited, arrived from many prominent Americans, see
Linn, *Jane Addams*, pp. 369–73.

5. *Ibid.*, pp. 349–50; Jane Addams, *Second Twenty Years at Hull-House*, p. 180.

She is not a Revolutionist.
She is not a red.
She is not even a Socialist.

. . . . . .

The fact is that Miss Addams is one of the greatest women
this republic of ours has produced. . . . The literature distributed by you persuades the uninformed to believe what is
not true about an honorable citizen.[6]

Jane Addams was skeptical of any good coming from such efforts.
The DAR charges, she wrote Mrs. Catt, were " a very strange
mixture of truth and fiction. . . . I personally do not believe that
much can be done with the public in this state of mind." The
situation was so complicated, she observed, " that I think it would
be honestly better not to try to make it clear to the DAR's, but to
let me be ' thrown to the lions ' as it were." [7]
Like the strategy of progressive reform, Jane Addams' peace
strategy depended on an aroused public opinion. The last two
chapters described the origins and disappointments of this strategy
for peace and the revival of Miss Addams' hopes in democratic
opinion for peace after the first meeting of the League Assembly
and the Washington Naval Conference. Continuing attacks by
patriotic societies emphasized the urgency of winning over public
opinion. In the 1920's Jane Addams devoted special attention to
the propaganda and publicity that would create an " international
public " for peace. In devising her strategy she drew heavily on
John Dewey's *The Public and Its Problems*.[8]
Dewey conceived of a public as made up of those who realized
the " indirect, extensive, and serious consequences of conjoint and
interacting behavior " and who had " a common interest in con-
trolling these consequences." In her second autobiographical
volume in 1930 Miss Addams referred to Dewey's idea of a
public and pled for the formation of a peace public, a public
" stretched to world dimensions " to deal adequately with the
problems of international life. Dewey asserted that technology

6. Carrie Chapman Catt, " An Open Letter to the D.A.R.," *Woman Citizen*,
LXVI (July, 1927), 11–2.
7. Jane Addams to Carrie Chapman Catt, May 31, 1927, SCPC.
8. Jane Addams, *Peace and Bread in Time of War*, p. 11; John Dewey, *The
Public and Its Problems* (New York, 1927).

had enormously complicated and extended the indirect consequences of behavior until the public had become inchoate, diffuse,
and scattered. At the same time technology had increased the
means of communication and joint activity. Tools of communication existed as never before, but the thoughts and aspirations
congruous with such physical tools were not fully developed. In
order to organize the public, to permit it to identify itself and
hold itself together, symbols that could command men's attention
were needed. Symbols, Dewey asserted, controlled thought and
sentiment. Without adequate symbols, conjoint activity could
never become a community of interest and endeavor. Until aspiration and thought fit the techniques of communication, " the
public will remain shadowy and formless, seeking spasmodically
for itself, but seizing and holding its shadow rather than its
substance." [9]

Jane Addams tried to use Dewey's analysis to create a peace
public in America. In analyzing the problem, she, like Dewey,
emphasized the technical achievements in communication. She
asserted that peace workers had never before had " the possibility
of rapid and universal intercourse." These technical achievements
did not automatically support peace, but they did " make practicable a world organized for co-operation where war shall be
eliminated." Jane Addams thought she saw in the 1920's a
" widespread desire for peaceful solutions of difficulties, fair to
both sides, and a willingness patiently to endeavor to find such
solutions." These feelings were the aspirations that she hoped to
make appropriate to the techniques of world-wide, rapid communication.[10]

Like Dewey also, Miss Addams appreciated the importance of
language and symbols in the formation of public opinion. Before
the war she had noted how social workers were infusing new
words like prevention and social justice with vitality and warmth.
She quoted Simon Patten's remark that social workers had " coined
words that reshaped the sentiments " of Americans regarding

9. Dewey, *The Public and Its Problems*, pp. 126, 87; Jane Addams, *Second
Twenty Years at Hull-House*, p. 413. Compare Dewey's definition of a public
with his earlier definition of democracy in his *Democracy and Education*, p. 87,
" a mode of associated living, of conjoint communicated experience."
10. Jane Addams and Emily Greene Balch, " The Hopes We Inherit," in
Building International Goodwill (New York, 1927), pp. 15, 16.

social justice. In the years after the war, Miss Addams devoted a great deal of attention to forging adequate symbols to express the new feelings against war and to persuade men to act against war. " Facts never move people very much," she said in 1926. " People act when they have the sense of purpose, of impulse, of conviction. . . ." Men " had to be moved, persuaded, urged on by an appeal to their emotions rather than merely by an appeal . . . to a set of facts." [11] She strove to create emotive symbols— what she called motives and incentives—which would aid in forming a peace public. Much of Miss Addams' work for peace consisted of interpreting events, illustrating and illuminating the consequences of these events, defining the ideals of international life, and thus, she hoped, creating a language which would express and persuade men to adopt international ideals. By these imaginative means, she hoped to create a public committed to international peace.

For Miss Addams peace had to be based on justice. The identification of justice in all of man's relationships with peace was the climax of her mature thought. Around this idea she organized a complex group of beliefs. Her synthesis of peace ideals was sometimes diffuse and occasionally unclear. The wide range and radicalism of her pacifist beliefs were also their genius. As Francis Hackett observed, " Miss Addams' is an inclusive genius . . . hers is the great gift of synthesis, of bringing things to unity, by ' patience, subtlety and depth.' " She avoided the simplicity of much interwar pacifism. She believed in the League of Nations, disarmament, the outlawry of war, the codification of international law, free trade, and other peace proposals, because she believed that all these made men's relations more just. But she was never convinced that any single proposal exhausted or completed the necessary effort toward peace. No single reform, no single peace strategy was adequate for Jane Addams' identification of peace and justice.[12]

Jane Addams helped found, and led, a radical pacifist organiza-

11. Jane Addams, "Charity and Social Justice," in National Conference of Charities and Correction, *Proceedings* (1910), pp. 2–3; Jane Addams, *Second Twenty Years at Hull-House*, p. 26; Jane Addams, " The World Court," *Republican Woman*, III (February, 1926), 7.

12. Hackett, "Hull House—A Souvenir," p. 279; Jane Addams and Balch, " The Hopes We Inherit," p. 15.

tion that also identified peace with justice. The women who had gathered at The Hague in 1915 and at Zurich in 1919 organized permanently under the name of the Women's International League for Peace and Freedom (WILPF). Miss Addams served as president of the WILPF until 1929, and as honorary president thereafter until her death. It was she who had " the decisive voice " in the organization's affairs. There is hyperbole but also truth in a letter from one of the women who had been at The Hague and Zurich—Lida Gustava Heymann—which urged Jane Addams to reconsider her resignation as international president. " We here in Europe are of [the] opinion, that our W. I. L. is so deeply connected with your personality, that it is quite impossible that the League keep on without your name. Neither in America, nor in Europe exists another woman's name, who would give that flavour and that atmosphere to our League and work as your name does . . . do not leave your child and our League." [13]

Under Jane Addams' leadership the WILPF took an uncompromising, radical pacifist position. In 1915 at The Hague the ladies had insisted that they did not want peace " at any price." Mrs. Pethick-Lawrence wrote: " The peace demanded was the peace that is based on reason, on justice. . . ." The combination of peace and justice was " essential to the meaning of the Congress. . . ." Or again, " international relations must be determined not by force but by friendship and justice." The Hague congress demanded that " the peace which follows [the war] shall be permanent and therefore based on principles of justice. . . ." [14]

The members of the Women's International League for Peace

13. Mary Sheepshank to Jane Addams, February 4, 1929; Heymann to Jane Addams, March 1, 1929, both SCPC. A Hull House resident once wrote that the settlement " was not an institution over which Miss Addams presided, it was Miss Addams, around whom an institution insisted on clustering." See Hackett, " Hull House—A Souvenir," p. 277. In the same way the WILPF was in many respects an organization of women who insisted on clustering around Miss Addams. It remained a small organization under her leadership without many young members. David A. Swope, " The Women's International League for Peace and Freedom, United States Section, 1919–1941 " (unpublished Honor's thesis, Harvard University, 1963), p. 28, cites his interview with an American executive of the WILPF who said that Jane Addams consciously neglected organizational matters because she feared an expanded membership would dilute dedication to peace.

14. Emmeline Pethick-Lawrence, " Women's Crusade for Peace," *Socialist Review*, XII (August/September, 1915), 644; International Congress of Women at The Hague, 28th April–1st May 1915, *Report* (1915), pp. XLVI, 35, 36.

and Freedom wanted to embody pacifist ideals of peace and justice in actual experience rather than simply state them as abstractions and dogmas. One of the major purposes of WILPF congresses was "to receive the momentum and sense of vitality which results from encountering like-minded people from other countries and to tell each other how far we had been able to translate conviction into action." In opening the 1924 congress in Washington, the WILPF president asked the ladies "to speak from your hearts, from the depths of your own experiences. . . ." Jane Addams consistently appealed for peace in terms of experience rather than dogma. She reminded the delegates how abstractions had been used during the war, "how largely the war was kept going by abstract and theoretical slogans. . . ." These slogans had proved "an opiate to scruples as well as a stimulant to continued military activities," she said. Miss Addams believed that women's special concern for the nurture of living and growing things, the very opposite of abstract theory and mechanization, endowed women with their unique opportunity to establish peace. The uniqueness of a woman's pacifist organization was bringing humane impulses into international life and avoiding the abstract, mechanical, or dogmatic peace appeal.[15]

This opposition to dogmatic and abstract appeals effectively submerged religious pacifism in the WILPF. Although many Quakers belonged to the organization, especially to the United States section, the international congresses did not reflect religious ideas or religious formulations. One congress condemned the "passive assistance" of the churches in war, and Jane Addams wrote in 1927 that "the religious as well as the political organizations of our own time have been humbled and disgraced by the occurrence of the greatest war in history. The Church as well as the State stands indicted." When Miss Addams appealed for peace in religious language, she used the personal example of Jesus, rather than any dogmatic assertion. She never used religious belief to justify her own pacifism; she was probably an agnostic.[16]

15. Jane Addams, *Peace and Bread in Time of War*, p. 224; Jane Addams, "Opening Address," p. 3; Jane Addams, "Preface," Women's International League for Peace and Freedom, *Congress Report*, IV [1924], ix. See also Jane Addams, "Generous Impulses in Politics," *Pax International*, I (September, 1926), unpaged.

16. Women's International League for Peace and Freedom, *Congress Report*, IV [1924], 139; Jane Addams and Balch, "The Hopes We Inherit," p. 18.

The most straightforward appeal for peace in religious terms was a Christmas message in 1923 that Jane Addams drafted to members of the WILPF after a round-the-world trip. She held up the counsel and example of Jesus as a solution to the political disorganization of the world. " Be just and fear not" was His message to the frightened statesmen of Europe. " Lend, hoping for nothing again and your reward shall be great" was His message to Americans who distrusted and disliked " foreign entanglements." For Japan and China, newly enamored of military preparations, Jane Addams recalled Jesus' rebuke to Peter, " Put up thy sword . . . for all that draw the sword shall perish by the sword." In this uniquely religious statement, Miss Addams held up the example of Jesus to criticize and heal the nations.[17]

Much more characteristic and more important in understanding Miss Addams' pacifism was the rejection of violence by her and by other members of the WILPF. Occasionally their discussions of the evils of violence, and the necessity of rejecting force, were dogmatic. But Miss Addams always condemned violence because, she said, experience showed that force was a failure. The Women's International League for Peace and Freedom, she said once, was " made up of people who believe that we are not obliged to choose between violence and passive acceptance of unjust conditions for ourselves or others; who believe, on the contrary, that courage, determination, moral power, generous indignation, active goodwill can achieve their ends without violence."[18]

Marcet Haldeman-Julius, Jane Addams' niece, recorded a conversation with her aunt in the early 1930's, during which she asked Jane Addams if she were an agnostic. " Instead of giving me a direct answer, she replied: 'I seldom think about it.' Then she added: 'Intolerance in religion has been responsible for more suffering than any other cause.' 'True,' I agreed. 'But what I want to know is, what do you think. Do you believe in a God?' 'Not a personal one.' 'But do you believe in any God?' 'Part of the time I do and part of the time I don't.' 'I should think that you fulfilled perfectly the definition of an agnostic.'" Marcet Haldeman-Julius, " Jane Addams As I Knew Her," Reviewer's Library, VII (1936), 29. Miss Addams, by her title, insisted that forceful, active, devoted lives achieved immortality, Jane Addams, The Excellent Becomes the Permanent (New York, 1932).

17. Jane Addams, Christmas Message for 1923 (n.p., n.d.), unpaged. For her explanation of the circumstances surrounding this religious appeal, see Jane Addams, Second Twenty Years at Hull-House, pp. 169–70.

18. New York Times, April 27, 1924, Section IX, p. 6, col. 1. In 1919 and again in 1921 the WILPF demanded immediate, total, universal disarmament— land, sea, and air. This demand was a central one for the ladies. In 1932 the

Dorothy Detzer, the talented Washington lobbyist for the WILPF, recalled her first experience with Jane Addams' " flaming indignation." Finding a crying child huddled on the Hull House steps—this was around 1913—Miss Detzer coaxed the child to come in, eat something, and tell her story. The child revealed that she was illegally employed, along with thousands of others, after school in nut-shelling factories that ran until eleven at night. So sleepy that she had fallen asleep at work, the child had failed to bring home enough pay to her father who had beaten her until she had run away to Hull House. Miss Addams came in while the child was telling her story, and twenty years later Miss Detzer could

> even yet hear the curiously furious voice, burning with indignation that this should happen to a child. . . . I remember that night chiefly as a long continuous ride in police patrols . . . led by the little girl, I went with the officers who raided twenty-three secret nut-shelling factories which employed and exploited children. And as we swept through the streets of that great sprawling city, Miss Addams' anger rode with me . . . that driving emotion stirred by injustice—which can change a world.

Hers was a " moral indignation, utterly free from the spirit of violence, that yet contains a dynamic power giving substance and a robust quality to mere spiritual force." [19]

Jane Addams and other members of the WILPF searched for methods of nonviolent social change. Early in the 1920's they discovered Mahatma Gandhi's experiments with nonviolence, which permitted them to cite experience rather than dogma for their belief in this approach. The WILPF was one of the earliest organizations to discover and propagandize Gandhi's effort and his ideas of nonresistance. The 1921 congress was so enamored of his newly presented example that it resolved—in a vote that Jane Addams ruled was only an expression of personal opinion

international secretary reported that " the greater part of our resources and energy was employed during 1929, 1930 and 1931 in the *work for total and universal disarmament.* . . ." Women's International League for Peace and Freedom, *Congress Report*, VII [1932], 19.

19. Dorothy Detzer, " Memories of Jane Addams," *Fellowship*, IV (September, 1938), 5.

and purpose—to adopt the principle and practice of nonviolence under all circumstances. An English woman who had lived in India told how Gandhi and his followers used non-co-operation and passive resistance to overthrow the tyranny of English rule. Gandhi wanted to establish justice for men of every race in India and throughout the world, she explained. His rejection of Western culture was not mentioned, nor was his association of dietary and sumptuary prohibitions with nonviolence. An Indian woman connected Gandhi with previous leaders of nonviolence by describing him as a Tolstoy Christian. Members of the WILPF were told that Gandhi's power lay in his simple exemplification of his doctrine, the same appeal that Jane Addams had singled out in describing Tolstoy.[20]

Jane Addams talked about Gandhi throughout the decade of the twenties, but with decreasing enthusiasm. At the 1926 WILPF congress she emphasized the reactionary qualities of his movement. He stood " for an independent life outside western civilization. His teaching may be right or it may be wrong but it is not a mere sentimental thing. . . ." The real significance of Gandhi's movement was that the experiment of " running the world without violence " was actually being tried in India.[21]

Jane Addams and other members of the WILPF continued searching for ways to embody peace in the emotions and thinking and actions of large numbers of their fellow countrymen. Their conviction that men resorted to violence because there was no other way of remedying injustice spurred them to work for the widest kinds of social and economic reforms. Any proposal that promised to promote justice attracted their intelligent attention.

20. International Congress of Women, [Congress] Report, III [1921], 260, 95 ff. Jane Addams stressed the continuity between these two men in " Tolstoy and Gandhi," Christian Century, XLVIII (November 25, 1931), 1485–8. The WILPF newsletter carried articles by or about Gandhi in the issues of August and September, 1926, March, 1927, and January, 1932. In 1923 Miss Addams tried to see Gandhi and speak with him personally. But, she wrote, Gandhi received only two visitors every six months, and, since his wife was one of these, there was " no chance for the rank outsider." His spinning school and students suggested " a new holy man . . . founding his monastery." Jane Addams to Ida Lovett, February 7, 1923, SCPC.

21. Jane Addams, " New Methods of Procedure," Women's International League for Peace and Freedom, Congress Report, V (1926), 64, 65. Gandhi wrote Miss Addams on October 7, 1932, after she had been awarded the Nobel prize for peace, " Dear Sister, My inner being tells me that spiritual unity can only be attained by resisting with our whole soul the modern false life."

After initial doubts, Jane Addams came to believe that the League of Nations could help in making international life more just, and therefore might aid in securing peace. The Women's International League for Peace and Freedom was divided over the issue of the League, however. Their congress at Zurich in 1919 considered whether the "unsatisfactory and iniquitous" peace of which the League Covenant was a part condemned the whole League of Nations to failure. The congress was unable to arrive at any clear decision.[22] But after the first meeting of the Assembly in November, 1920, the WILPF began active co-operation with the League of Nations. Catherine Marshall, the WILPF international secretary, urged the 1921 congress to "resolve definitely that we will devote attention and energy to . . . following what the League of Nations had done, to answering the questions it brings up and getting questions on its programme, and do all the work necessary" to support our proposals. Then the "League will move in the way we want." Miss Marshall readily admitted that the League of Nations was a thoroughly defective instrument—especially the undemocratic League Council. But she was enthusiastic about the possible usefulness of the League. And it was, she reminded WILPF delegates, the only existing international group: "You have got to compare the League not with the one we would like but with the world as it would be without it." [23]

The WILPF lobbied at Geneva, with some small success. Between May, 1920, and July, 1920, it presented eight memorials to League bodies. These petitions dealt with matters as diverse as the white slave traffic, atrocities, marriage laws, mandates, and the representation of women in League organizations. Visible success came when a woman—Mrs. Anna Bugge-Wicksell of Stockholm—became a member of the Mandates Commission.

22. Jane Addams, "Presidential Address," International Congress of Women, [Congress] Report, III [1921], 2. Since the WILPF congresses could not agree on a unified position on co-operation with the League of Nations, each national section determined its own position. The American section was unable to adopt a single policy: several local branches of the United States section broke away so they could devote their full energy to advocating American entry into the League; other branches worked actively for reservations. These divisions were reported in ibid., p. 252.

23. See Miss Marshall's report in ibid., pp. 57, 68. Miss Marshall's recommendations were not passed, but were referred to the national sections for study; the international secretary was commended for her work and asked to continue it.

The WILPF was most interested in the activities of the specialized agencies of the League, such as the so-called Opium Committee, which League historian F. P. Walters noted became "the very advance guard of reform" under the secretariat leadership of Dame Rachel Crowdy. The Advisory Committee on the Traffic in Women and Children, the Refugees Organization, the Health Organization, and the International Labour Organization were all active in matters of economic and social reform, and these agencies attracted the women of the WILPF. Jane Addams noted proudly that the three American women connected with League commissions were all long-time Hull House residents. The WILPF never formally endorsed the League of Nations, however. Many of its members doubted that justice could be established by the threat of military sanctions, and they were discouraged by the failure of League efforts at disarmament.[24]

Jane Addams did not share all of these fears about the League of Nations. She was most vocal in advocating American support, co-operation, and participation in all sorts of international organizations, and especially co-operation with League agencies. Miss Addams identified the aims of these organizations with the reform goals of social justice for which progressive Americans had striven prior to World War I. In backing Robert M. La Follette for President in 1924, for instance, Miss Addams recalled his struggle to protect seamen in the years before America entered the war. But now, Jane Addams asserted, sailors' rights could only be secured through an international body—and the International Labor Organization of the League of Nations had already started to deliberate on the problem. Miss Addams believed that La Follette—and hopefully many of her fellow Americans—would find it natural and increasingly necessary to turn to international organizations, just as once Americans had discovered it natural and necessary to turn from state to federal agencies to achieve social justice. League activities provided new approaches toward justice in international life and therefore toward international peace; these activities embodied the same human approach that Progressives had called social justice.[25]

24. Walters, *History of the League of Nations*, I, 185; Jane Addams, *Second Twenty Years at Hull-House*, p. 216.
25. Jane Addams, "Why I Shall Vote for La Follette," *New Republic*, XL (September 10, 1924), 36; Jane Addams, *Second Twenty Years at Hull-House*, pp. 280–2.

Jane Addams endorsed American participation in the World Court for the same reasons. She reminded an audience of Republican women of America's happy experiences with arbitration at The Hague tribunal. The World Court was the same kind of institution. It allowed men " to get at life, away from our preconceptions, to envisage our international relations with some sort of moral standards such as we have long tried to apply to our relations within the nations. . . ." The Court would enable groups of men to use the newest kinds of knowledge about international relations and to apply the latest standards of international life. Perhaps, Miss Addams concluded the chapter devoted to the topic of justice in the *Second Twenty Years*, the World Court could unite " Latin logic, Slavic idealism, Asiatic quietude and Anglo-Saxon common sense into . . . a wider conception of justice than any one nation has as yet been able to obtain." [26]

Jane Addams supported the Kellogg-Briand Pact because she believed it embodied a new sense of justice in international life. Her support was also affected by the fact that the leading propagandist for the outlawry of war, S. O. Levinson, was a fellow Chicagoan who contributed to the WILPF and participated in a WILPF summer school following the 1924 congress held in America. Miss Addams was not convinced that the Kellogg-Briand agreement would bring peace. She was not active in the movement for outlawry, but she did endorse the pact as a " great advance toward an organized and peaceful world," and called it the " most significant event since [the] promulgation of the League of Nations covenant." [27] The special feature of the Kellogg-Briand Pact that Miss Addams singled out for praise was its reliance on world public opinion rather than military measures for enforcement. The pact, she wrote, showed the transformation from dependence on military security to dependence on political security rooted in a sense of civilized justice.[28]

26. Jane Addams, "The World Court," p. 7; Jane Addams, *Second Twenty Years at Hull-House*, p. 342.

27. Jane Addams, "How To Build a Peace Program," *Survey*, LXVII (November 1, 1932), 441; Jane Addams' telegram to *Christian Science Monitor*, August 20 [1928], SCPC. Robert H. Ferrell has described the various motives and aims which brought about the Kellogg-Briand Pact in his *Peace in Their Time, the Origins of the Kellogg-Briand Pact* (New Haven, 1952); see also John E. Stoner, *S. O. Levinson and the Pact of Paris; a Study in the Techniques of Influence* (Chicago, 1942).

28. Jane Addams, *Second Twenty Years at Hull House*, p. 219.

Jane Addams believed that world public opinion could establish, and also sustain, peace. Whenever international mediation or conciliation commissions had been tried, she noted, they had been " uniformly successful. No nation has ever gone back upon their findings, enforced only by the invisible power of public opinion." She urged the substitution of the power of public opinion for the military sanctions mentioned in the League of Nations Covenant. To associate military power with the purposes of the League was " an anachronism." As the League grew older and more experienced, " it is less and less probable that military sanctions will be used." In fact, she continued, " the use of military force is possible to the League of Nations only under such very remote and exceptional circumstances that it may never be invoked, as it never has been. The League would have been a thousand times stronger if the possibility were removed. . . ." [29] Miss Addams found confirmation for her belief that peace could best be guaranteed by public opinion in Secretary of State Henry L. Stimson's handling of the Manchurian crisis. She pointed with satisfaction to Stimson's note to Japan which refused to recognize conquests in Manchuria and insisted that armies would be useless when the organized opinion of the world stood ready to demand justice and to deny the fruits of aggression to the aggressor, as Secretary Stimson had done to Japan. " I firmly believe that nothing else will prevail but this gradual moralization of our international relations." [30]

In the 1920's Jane Addams continued to work through voluntary organizations for domestic reform. These domestic reform efforts elaborated the concern for justice that underlay her pacifism. She became a member of a symposium on the prevention and cure of crime that William Randolph Hearst sponsored in Chicago in 1927. In discussing the growth of crime Miss Addams criticized both policy and judges. Law enforcement was " inefficient," she

29. Jane Addams, " What Is Security? . . ." *Conference on the Cause and Cure of War*, VI (1930), 38; Jane Addams, " How To Build a Peace Program," p. 550.

30. Jane Addams, " How To Build a Peace Program," p. 551. For an interesting discussion of Miss Addams' ideas on international relations by John Dewey, Arthur O. Lovejoy, T. V. Smith, Joseph P. Chamberlain, William Ernest Hocking, E. A. Burtt, Glenn R. Murrow, Sidney Hook, and Jerome Nathanson, see " Discussion of the Theory of International Relations," *Journal of Philosophy*, XLII (August 30, 1945), 477–97.

said. "In a very real sense," she complained, "the people who represent the administration of the law are often as much a part of the criminal situation as the so-called criminals themselves." Speaking frankly to the lawyers and judges who dominated the symposium membership she wondered

> why, in the minds of many good, simple people, you are believed to give your energies to the purely legalistic aspect of the case rather than to finding out the equity and justice involved. I am confident that this widespread belief brings a certain lack of respect for the courts, a certain willingness to get out of trouble in any way that is possible, by political pull and even by bribing because the whole thing is a legal game and acquittal for any reason is a victory.[31]

Miss Addams also spoke about the dual philosophy of punishment: whether it was better to punish the crime or the criminal. She applauded "the growing tendency to individualize punishments, to find out what the criminal needs to deter him from further crimes or to ' reform ' him, . . . to try to fit the punishment to his needs." But she also noted a growing proclivity for harsher punishment, which Miss Addams called " a grave mistake." " Human punishment after all is usually such a stupid, un-understanding ineffectual sort of thing. It remedies so few situations. It solves so few problems. And it multiplies so many tragedies." The fact that there were many repeaters in jails indicated to her that the judicial system was not working as well as it might. The central problem, she charged, was " too much violence. If we could only disarm everybody we could do away with much crime and much incentive to crime. Disarm the criminals first, but eventually also disarm the police." [32]

In addition to this effort to change judicial and legal attitudes, Jane Addams continued to work for reforms that she believed would promote economic and social justice among Americans. She tried to arouse those who had championed reform before the war

---

31. Jane Addams, " Problem of Crime Unsolved, Let Us Start Anew," in American Crime Study Commission, *The Prevention and Cure of Crime* (n. p., 1927), pp. 26, 28.

32. *Ibid.*, p. 27; Jane Addams, " Rosa Stable," a National Education Association Service syndicated story appearing in various newspapers, e.g., New York *Telegraph*, March 31, 1927.

and criticized those whose reform fervor had become inhibited. In 1926 she complained directly to the National Conference of Social Work that by shying away from reform, social workers ignored the ethical side of their jobs. By failing to make clear to the public their " special human experience, the reactions which come to him who is brought close to ignorance, poverty, disease and crime," social workers failed to develop the ethical resources of the community. They were " living on accumulated capital in spiritual and ethical affairs." [33]

For Jane Addams, growing professionalization among social workers was the villain. Professionalization sapped the emotional drive of the early settlement movement. Social workers of a later generation were more scholarly, more detached and scientific in approach, and might be better social workers, she admitted. But the nonprofessional approach, she said frankly, had her sympathy. Specialization deflected an individual from his natural generous impulses and imposed a professional sense of duty on him which " befogged and deadened " human relationships. A specialized and limited sense of duty " excludes the penetrating sense of the fundamental unity and interdependence of society." The specialist, Miss Addams told the guild, lost " the challenge to a wider and more human relationship—the lure of a fuller fellowship." Jane Addams used the newest and most exciting of these specialized techniques—psychiatric social work—as an example of the ill effects of specialization. She urged psychiatric social workers to go beyond *individual* to *social* psychiatric work. " We now ask them to get back a little from a purely individual study into something which considers the many," something that might provide the community with a creative and inventive program of social reform.[34]

Even without the united support of old reform allies, Jane

33. Jane Addams, "How Much Social Work Can a Community Afford?" *Survey*, LVII (November 15, 1926), 199, 200.
34. Jane Addams, *Second Twenty Years at Hull-House*, p. 155; Jane Addams, "How Much Social Work Can a Community Afford?", p. 200. See also Jane Addams to Eva Whiting White, November 22, 1928: "I am a little distressed at some of the new schools of social service which pay so little attention to the group . . . ," in White Papers, Radcliffe Women's Archives. A fine description of the social work guild and reform between the wars is Clarke A. Chambers, *Seedtime of Reform, American Social Service and Social Action, 1918–1933* (Minneapolis, 1963), especially relevant here are pp. 89–97.

Addams tried to create an American public opinion that understood the basis of peace in social reform. She attempted to explain
to Americans how their domestic policies disrupted efforts toward
world peace. She confronted Americans with the consequences—
indirect, extensive, enduring, and serious in Dewey's terminology
—of American policy. The most incisive of her criticisms was
her identification of a peculiar self-righteousness that characterized
American policies after the war. This American self-righteousness
was " responsible for the most subtle forms of lawlessness " and
injustice and was " the essence of immorality " because it persuaded Americans to make an exception of America in international life. In all of this Miss Addams tried to create the
symbols and aspirations to peace that would create a peace public
in America.[35]

American policy toward the League of Nations had consequences that delayed and disrupted international life, Miss Addams
said. After deciding not to join the League, America protested
against the League's handling of the Assyrian and Mesopotamian
mandates. When the League postponed action and invited the
United States to join the negotiations, the American government
refused to respond, thus delaying and complicating this important
business. The disarmament plans and activities of the League
were disrupted by a large American naval construction program.[36]
Miss Addams asserted that the attitude of the war years had
become reversed: " While the United States went into the war
asking no rewards and taking full responsibilities, in regard to
the international organization since [the war], she takes no responsibilities but does ask for the reward. . . ."[37] American action
vis-à-vis the Kellogg-Briand Pact provided another illustration of
American self-righteousness, the consequences of which disrupted
international life. Jane Addams pointed out that after outlawing
war the United States had acted almost immediately in direct

35. Jane Addams, *Second Twenty Years at Hull-House*, p. 336; Jane Addams,
" The Process of Social Transformation," in Charles A. Beard (ed.), *A Century
of Progress* (New York, 1932), p. 249.

36. Denna Frank Fleming, *The United States and World Organization, 1920–
1933* (New York, 1938), records America's attempts to ignore or subvert the
League. Fleming describes the confusion and obstruction which Secretaries Hughes
and Kellogg produced at Geneva, see especially Chaps. IV and IX.

37. Jane Addams, *Christmas Message for 1923*, unpaged; Jane Addams, " What
I Saw in Europe," p. 21.

contradiction to the spirit of the pact. " Other nations . . . could
not in the least understand how Congress was able to ratify the
Kellogg Pact and only a few weeks later make an astounding
appropriation for increasing the United States navy." [38]

Miss Addams interpreted the Sacco-Vanzetti trial as another
example of American sanctimoniousness which delayed newer
standards of international life. While she was abroad in 1926,
Miss Addams discovered that people all over the world had
become aroused over the trial. It was one of those cases that
occurred " from time to time and take[s] shape in men's minds
as an epitome of the problem of justice itself." Sacco and Vanzetti
came " to embody a sudden warning that the universal sense of
justice was imperiled." Miss Addams related that she had a
" sinister foreboding " about the trial since it was held in a " New
England court where, ever since the days of Anne Hutchinson, the
bog of self-righteousness has so often mired fast the feet of good
men." She appealed to Governor Alvan T. Fuller for commu-
tation of the death sentences on the grounds that execution would
bring American justice into disrepute all over the world, and she
asked Senator William E. Borah, the chairman of the Senate
Foreign Relations Committee, to join this appeal because so many
foreign nations had protested the courts' decisions. Borah rebuffed
her efforts as unconstitutional meddling. His reply, Miss Addams
wrote, was " so confident that our national judgement was supreme
. . . [he] unhappily assumes that one's own country is always
in the right and the other countries uniformly in the wrong—a
sort of national self-righteousness." [39]

The outcome of the trial persuaded her that a unique opportunity had been discarded for " demonstrating that we are here
attaining a conception of justice broad and fundamental enough
to span the reach of our population and their kinsfolk throughout
the world." Americans could not be content with a narrow
national justice. " The demands of a new world consciousness . . .
[permit] no other conception of justice than that which is world-
wide." Such justice promised security and stability, Miss Addams
concluded, because it approached a " universal type." [40]

38. Jane Addams, " A Needed Implement in Social Reform," *Christian Leader*,
XXXIV (June 20, 1931), 780.
39. Jane Addams, *Second Twenty Years at Hull-House*, pp. 334–5, 337, 336,
338.
40. *Ibid.*, pp. 339, 343.

The reparations question was another area in which American self-righteousness frustrated the development of international peace. Jane Addams wrote in 1923 that America had failed to treat her war loans as part of her international responsibility. After 1929 this failure became more obvious. "If it had been taken for granted from the beginning that the United States sent supplies in the same spirit that it sent its soldiers, the public would not have gotten into this attitude of a righteous creditor claiming his own, irrespective of the debtor's ability to pay or the consequences to the creditor himself in case he did pay." The most handsome offer concerning reparations had been made by Senator Borah, Miss Addams said. The Senator suggested that America cancel the debts of those nations that would consent to reduce their armaments. Borah's proposition was flawed, Miss Addams said, only by the self-righteous failure of the United States to offer to disarm. This failure was "doubtless due to the fact that we are so sure that our own intentions are beneficent, that our army is small, and that no one could suspect us of unworthy ambitions." But such sanctimony might make the whole offer unacceptable to those nations. Miss Addams never suggested that the war debts simply be cancelled, but she insisted that generosity rather than self-righteousness was the way to overwhelm the suspicion and distrust that characterized international life. "A statement by the United States that the war debts were being considered generously and impartially . . . might go far toward dispelling that sense of depression with which most of the world is surrounded," she wrote.[41]

Through her analysis and interpretation of American attitudes toward the League of Nations, the Kellogg-Briand Pact, the Sacco-Vanzetti case, and the reparations question, Jane Addams hoped to cultivate new impulses and incentives in international affairs. These issues provided her the opportunity to discuss new conceptions of justice and to try to establish new motives for the conduct of America's foreign relations. She hoped for an American public committed to peace, for a public that would understand how America's self-righteousness ignored the increasingly obvious

41. Jane Addams, *Christmas Message for 1923*; Jane Addams, "How To Build a Peace Program," p. 553; Jane Addams, "Social Deterrent of Our National Self-Righteousness; With Correctives Suggested by the Courageous Life of William Penn," *Friends' Intelligencer*, LXXXIX (Eleventh month 5, 1932), 890.

fact " that the welfare of all nations is interdependent." America's search for national advantage, if need be at the expense of others, conflicted with " the newer principle of [international] social welfare and the zeal for practical justice in our human affairs." American self-righteousness denied " the great political experiment of these later centuries, the supreme contemporary effort to make international relations more rational and human." [42]

Miss Addams remained confident that men could establish peace and the justice upon which it had to be based. America was still, she is quoted as saying in 1928, " in the war period, from an intellectual point of view." Wartime passions had been modified, but " the moral power which directs the energies of the war" had not been applied to the problems of international life. The strengthening of the spirit of co-operation in international life " needs only that men have faith in one another and in their common purposes. . . . But," Miss Addams noted unhappily in 1934, " because faith in mankind and the resulting good will are exactly what war has always destroyed we must wait for the subsidence of the war psychology for the vigorous prosecution " of international tasks.[43] But this discouraging estimate was more than balanced by subdued confidence. Man had a " natural tendency . . . to come into friendly relationship with ever larger and larger groups and to live in constantly higher and more extended life," she wrote in 1921. Indeed, she continued, this progressive tendency for man " to widen the circle of his interest and sympathy . . . has been largely responsible for his development." It was as practicable " to abolish war as it was to abolish the institution of chattel slavery which also was based on human desires and greeds. These are still with us, but slavery has joined cannibalism, human sacrifice, and other once sacred human habits, as one of the shameful and happily abandoned institutions of the past. . . . A great Kingdom of Peace," she continued, " lies close to hand, ready to come into being if we would but turn toward it." [44]

42. Jane Addams, " Exaggerated Nationalism and International Comity," *Survey Graphic*, XXIII (April, 1934), 168; Jane Addams, " Social Deterrent of Our National Self-Righteousness," pp. 895, 894.

43. Herbert M. Davidson, " Life Means Opportunity to Work for Humanity to Jane Addams," New York *World*, July 22, 1928, Section E, p. 1; Jane Addams, " Because Wars Interfere with the Normal Growth of Civilization," in Rose Young (ed.), *Why Wars Must Cease* (New York, 1935), p. 138.

44. Jane Addams, " The Attack on War," *Christian Century*, XXXVIII (October

After 1929, when the economies of America and the rest of the world were plunged into depression, the " consciousness of the continuity and interdependence of mankind " which Jane Addams had tried to express and upon which she built her peace strategy became increasingly obvious. The last years before her death in 1935 were filled with awards, recognitions, and honors. In 1931 the Norwegian parliament awarded her the Nobel prize for peace. Named with Miss Addams to share the prize was Nicholas Murray Butler. In congratulating Miss Addams, Gilbert Murray wrote that " you, at any rate, have worked all your life for Peace— which can not be said of many of the Nobel Prizemen." [45] Miss Addams was praised in Oslo at the formal ceremonies as the American symbol of woman's protest against war. " In Jane Addams there are assembled all the best womanly attributes which shall help us establish peace in the world. . . . She was the right spokesman for all the peace-loving women of the world." This speaker at the Nobel ceremony called attention to the continuity between Miss Addams' earlier advocacy of progressive legislation based on women's special concern for the nurture of human life and the extension of this ideal to international life. [46]

Miss Addams endorsed Herbert Hoover's candidacy for re-election in 1932, but she enthusiastically supported most of the New Deal reforms. In 1932 she became chairman of the Illinois Committee for Old Age Security, and between 1933 and 1935 she was an active member of the Chicago Advisory Board on Housing under the Public Works Administration. She hoped that New Deal policies, like other reforms she advocated, would eventually aid the establishment of peace. In praise of President Franklin D. Roosevelt, she wrote that no one

---

13, 1921), 12; Jane Addams and Balch, " The Hopes We Inherit," pp. 17, 16, 18.

45. Jane Addams, " After Sixty-Five," *Survey*, LXII (June 1, 1929), 303; Gilbert Murray to Jane Addams, December 16, 1931, SCPC. The Nobel award climaxed eight years of letter writing by Miss Addams' friends on her behalf. Julia Lathrop seems to have initiated this campaign. See copies of her letters at SCPC in 1923. Jane Addams never publicly commented on being coupled with Nicholas Murray Butler. In *Peace and Bread*, however, nine years before they were named to share the Nobel award, she had noted with emphasis that " everyone knew he [Butler] was for the war! " (see p. 128). The *Christian Century*, XLVIII (December 23, 1931), 1612, commented with some acerbity that the reasons for Dr. Butler's sharing the award were " perhaps more discernible to the eyes of the Norwegian parliament than at a nearer view. . . ."

46. Cited in Linn, *Jane Addams*, p. 390.

on the face of the earth is doing more in the direction of sane readjustment at the present moment than the President of the United States and the group about him. Conscious, as thinking men are everywhere, that the power of the human mind to make rapid reorganizations is tremendously strained, they still insist that it should be possible to continue the long effort made through the centuries for a well-ordered world. . . .

New Deal efforts " to meet the requirements for food and shelter of the unemployed within the nation . . . may change the very conception of Nationalism. . . . Under this interpretation of governmental obligation, human needs may in time become the basis for a sounder Internationalism. . . ." [47]

In May, 1935, the twentieth anniversary congress of the Women's International League for Peace and Freedom, meeting in Washington, turned into a personal tribute to Jane Addams. Eleanor Roosevelt entertained the women at the White House, and spoke at one of the banquets. " When the day comes when difficulties are faced and settled without resorting to [war], . . . we shall look back in this country upon the leadership you have given us, Miss Addams, and be grateful for having had you living with us." In a radio broadcast with speakers in London, Tokyo, Moscow, Paris, and Washington, Miss Addams was also acclaimed and honored. One of the American speakers was deeply stirred by " this unparalleled tribute to a rare human being and leader. . . ." [48]

In his history of American peace movements, published the year after Jane Addams' death, Merle Curti emphasized the economic causes of war but also warned that " unless pacific means are found for securing a greater degree of justice in all categories of human relationships—racial, national, and economic . . . the struggle against war in America, in the world, probably will not end." In addition to endorsing this central idea in Jane Addams' pacifism, Professor Curti singled out for special praise

47. Chambers, *Seedtime of Reform*, Chap. VI and VII, emphasizes how housing reform and security against old age dependency connect progressive reform before the war and the New Deal. Reformers, especially social workers, hammered out a consensus in favor of these reforms during the 1920's. Jane Addams, " Exaggerated Nationalism and International Comity," p. 170.

48. Cited in Linn, *Jane Addams*, pp. 415, 417.

those who had maintained a " complete and unequivocal opposition to all war, in wartime as in peacetime. . . ." These pacifists
had preserved " the virtues so necessary for the successful waging
of peace." [49]

Jane Addams was one of those who remained faithful to her
convictions about peace. When both her courage and conscience
were tested, she refused to reject her beliefs in peace. And she
was able to infuse these beliefs with passionate conviction. She
insisted that men of " courage, determination, moral power, generous indignation, [and] active goodwill" were able to achieve
positive ends without violence. Unlike many pacifists, she strove
to understand those who supported war. It would be easy to
discover evil motives in those who endorsed the World War,
easy, she told Hull House residents during 1917, " to shirk the
discussion of current issues under the plea of remaining impartial.
It is a temptation to become a silent coward and think oneself
a tolerant spectator . . . he alone can be impartial who has the
courage of his convictions." A niece of Miss Addams, writing
in the year following her aunt's death, told how " she maintained
a relative appreciation of the value of her own feelings and the
feelings and actions of the rest of the world." Jane Addams'
ability to see differing sides of an issue and to appreciate the
reasons why partisans differed from her enabled her to invigorate
her intellectual analysis of peace and justice with a passionate
emotional quality. For her the intellectual response was in the
best sense an emotional one.[50]

In the years after World War I, Jane Addams was one of
America's most vital and impressive pacifists. Many other peace
efforts were negative; other pacifists believed they could abolish
or outlaw war and bring in a final changeless condition of peace.
Miss Addams' identification of peace with justice and her commitment to reform in order to make justice more real made her
pacifism dynamic and creative. Other pacifists in the 1920's
labored to persuade individuals to pledge themselves to pacifism.
Jane Addams looked beyond the conversion of individuals. She

49. Merle Curti, *Peace or War: the American Struggle, 1636–1936* (New York,
1936), pp. 309, 307.

50. New York *Times*, April 27, 1924, Section IX, p. 6, col. 1. Miss Addams
is quoted by Detzer in her " Memories of Jane Addams," p. 5; Haldeman-Julius,
" Jane Addams as I Knew Her," p. 22.

tried to create social institutions and methods that embodied equivalents to war in actual experience. The humane reform ideals which Jane Addams meant by culture and democracy were the creative sources and bases for peace.

Jane Addams' identification of peace with justice and her ability to infuse this intellectual perception with compelling emotional qualities helped to rescue pacifism from the aftermath of a second world war. Revived hopes for peace in this generation center on a renewed concern for justice as the source and basis for peace. This generation affirms what Jane Addams wrote in 1907: the most modern, fundamental, and trenchant ideal of peace " founded the cause of peace upon the cause of righteousness "—righteousness in politics and economics and in all men's relations.[51] This identification of peace with justice, set down in terms both passionate and disinterested, is Jane Addams' intellectual legacy to this generation's search for peace.

51. Jane Addams, *Newer Ideals of Peace* (New York, 1907), p. 237. Miss Addams cited the prophet Isaiah (32:17) in identifying peace and righteousness: " And the effect of righteousness will be peace; and the result of righteousness, quietness and trust forever."

BIBLIOGRAPHY

THE ADDAMS MANUSCRIPTS

The major resource for this study has been Miss Addams' published writings. Her papers are part of the Swarthmore College Peace Collection (SCPC). For a description of this collection see Ellen Starr Brinton and Hiram Doty (comps.), *Guide to the Swarthmore College Peace Collection, a Memorial to Jane Addams* ("Swarthmore College Library, Peace Collection Publication," No. 1, Swarthmore, Pa., 1947). For Miss Addams' papers see Marjorie Edwards, "Jane Addams Papers—a Brief Description," *Social Service Review*, XXXVI (June, 1962), 231–2. The papers are fully described in "Check List of the Jane Addams Papers" ("Swarthmore College Peace Collection," mimeographed, undated). This collection originated in a deposit by Miss Addams of material having to do with her work for peace. After her death the rest of her papers were added to this original deposit. The papers are fragmentary, for Jane Addams was not systematic about such matters. Always fearful that the settlement movement would become institutionalized and that settlement workers would become diverted into administration, Miss Addams was most informal in handling "the unmitigable mail of the morning" (Dorothea Moore, "A Day at Hull House," *American Journal of Sociology*, II [March, 1897], 635). Miss Addams did not have a regular secretary until after 1920, and she did not use a typewriter. She habitually discarded much of the incoming correspondence. Her papers at Swarthmore contain only a few of her replies to the scattered letters she preserved, and some of these are almost indecipherable. When I interviewed Dr. Alice Hamilton in 1961, she recalled the standing joke among Hull House residents that someone might publish a life of Miss Addams but no one would ever publish her life and letters.

The most revealing personal letters in the collection are a long series between Jane Addams and Mary Rozet Smith, her most intimate friend. According to Alice Hamilton, Mary Smith was the "one supremely lovely figure . . . the most universally beloved person" she had ever known (*Exploring the Dangerous Trades, the Autobiography of Alice Hamilton, M.D.* [Boston, 1943], p. 67). A letter from Ellen Gates Starr to Jane Addams indicates the nature of the relationship between Miss Addams and Mary Rozet Smith: "I think I have always—at any rate for a good many years—been thankful that Mary Smith came to supply what you needed. At all events I thank God that I was never envious of her in any vulgar or ignoble way. I couldn't be of any one so noble and generous and in every way fairminded as she, so humble: really self-depreciating" (Ellen Starr to Jane Addams, April 12, 1935, SCPC). The correspondence at Swarthmore was particularly useful for describing the various preliminaries to the founding of Hull House.

In addition to correspondence, Jane Addams' papers contain about 110,000 newspaper clippings, dated between 1892 and 1935. Unhappily Miss Addams gave many clippings away and used them for various other purposes. The collection, therefore, like her letters, is fragmentary. Miss Addams divided her personal library between Swarthmore and Rockford College. The five hundred books at Swarthmore relate mostly to peace. These few books hardly reflect the enormous amount of reading which Miss Addams did during her lifetime.

The Ellen Gates Starr Papers are in the Sophia Smith Collection at Smith College.

217

Letters between Jane Addams and Miss Starr between 1879 and 1889 are particularly revealing and suggest why these two young ladies were attracted to each other. The letters contain much immature religious searching and fill in many gaps in the correspondence at Swarthmore. Jane Addams' letters to Ellen Starr from Europe and from Baltimore are especially interesting. Letters in 1889 and 1890 help illuminate the founding and early activities at Hull House.

The Stephenson County Historical Museum in Freeport, Illinois, has a most interesting collection of material. Many of the family books from the Addams homestead are in the museum. There is also a library catalogue and some of the books of the Union Library Company, Cedar Creek Mills, which had its headquarters in the Addams household. The museum also has some very interesting letters from Jane Addams to members of her family in the years before 1890. Miss Addams' cash books for the years she was at the seminary are in the museum, along with some other material connected with her stay at Rockford. The hilarious minutes of the Addams family phrenological society, dated from August 21, 1876, to June 11, 1877, and a chart of Jane Addams' personality based on phrenological analysis—she scored very high in firmness and cautiousness, and average in combativeness and spirituality—complete the museum's holdings.

The Rockford College Archives include much memorabilia of the years when Jane Addams attended the institution. The major source of information is a scrapbook started in the early years of the seminary by Miss Sill. All sorts of programs, invitations, schedules, and miscellany are mounted in the scrapbook. Numerous newspaper accounts (mostly undated) of activities, exercises, and speeches at the seminary are included. There are complete files of the seminary catalogue and the *Rockford Seminary Magazine*. The Frank A. White Papers contain an occasional letter to or from Jane Addams and several reminiscences that mention Miss Addams. A transcript of her academic work and some of her classroom notebooks are also in the archives. Julia Lathrop's papers are deposited in the archives, but they contained little of interest.

RELATED COLLECTIONS

The Henry Demarest Lloyd Papers at the Wisconsin Historical Society include a good deal of correspondence from the women at Hull House—Jane Addams, Ellen Gates Starr, Florence Kelley. Most of the letters deal with local affairs in Chicago. The letters establish the close relationship between Lloyd and Jane Addams and show her dependence on him for advice, money, encouragement, and an occasional speech at Hull House.

Lillian Wald's papers are in the New York Public Library. There were frequent letters between these two settlement leaders, who shared in many projects and wrote frankly to each other. The letters are forthright and lively; the salutations are extremely formal: "Dear Lady"; "Dear Madam"; "My Dear Miss Wald"; "Beloved Lady." Miss Wald finally asked Jane Addams to address her more informally in a letter dated August 14, 1917. There is considerable helpful information in these letters concerning the Progressive party, the American Union against Militarism, and the attempts to influence Wilson in 1915, 1916, and early 1917.

Manuscript collections in two large depositories failed to yield much helpful information for this study. In addition to the Lloyd Papers, I checked other collections at the Wisconsin Historical Society. The Ada James Papers contain nothing of substance. The Louis P. Lochner Papers have an occasionally useful letter during the years between 1915 and 1917. The Edward A. Ross, Zona Gale, and Albion Small collections were of little aid. The Raymond Robbins Papers are disorganized and difficult to use. I have not worked through them. There are several interesting items concerning Jane Addams in the Richard T. Ely Papers. Jane Addams material in the Julia Grace Wales Papers deals exclusively with the development and refinement of plans for neutral mediation by Miss Wales in the period 1915-7. Mrs. Emmons Blaine's papers are a part of the McCormick Collection at Wisconsin. The numerous letters, and later records of phone calls, deal almost entirely with financial contributions and other gifts by Mrs. Blaine to Hull House.

The Library of Congress holds a number of collections that were tangentially useful for this study. The widow of Ben B. Lindsey has deposited a large collection of correspondence. Included is an index which is not altogether accurate. There are many letters between Miss Addams and Judge Lindsey, but most of them are routine acknowledgments and arrangements about travel and speeches. The Ray Stannard Baker Papers, especially for the early years when Baker was a Chicago newspaper reporter, provided diverting background information. The Louis F. Post, Clarence Darrow, and Jacob A. Riis Papers were disappointing. All three collections are small. None contained aid for my purposes. Papers deposited in the names of Mary Church Terrell and Sophonisba P. Breckinridge were also outside the focus of this study, although both contain Jane Addams material. I searched the appropriate parts of the papers of Albert J. Beveridge, William Allen White, Booker T. Washington, and Newton D. Baker for insights into the Progressive campaign of 1912. The Ford Peace Plan Papers describe that venture and contain various appeals and greetings to Miss Addams. The Oscar S. Straus Papers contain several letters of no relevance to this study. I have not investigated the deposits of the League of Women Voters of the United States, the National Women's Trade Union League of America, the National Consumer's League, nor the National Child Labor Committee, in all of which Jane Addams was an active participant.

The files of the Survey Associates have recently been deposited at the University of Minnesota. The strategy and personnel of many progressive reform movements in the years after 1909 will be illuminated by this material, but I have not consulted it. The National Federation of Settlements and Neighborhood Centers permitted me to use their correspondence archives. There are many letters to and from Miss Addams, but most of them deal with organizational matters not germane to this study.

Some of the manuscript collections in the Radcliffe College Women's Archives contain material about Jane Addams, but very little of relevance to this study. Alice Hamilton's papers focus on her medical career. There are none of her sharp, wonderfully descriptive letters to match those at Swarthmore. There are some Jane Addams letters in the Anna Howard Shaw, the Leonora O'Reilly, the Harriet Burton Laidlaw, the Eva Whiting White, and Fannie Fern Andrews collections.

Manuscript collections in the Chicago area have some Jane Addams letters, but do not contain any very revealing or interesting material. At the Chicago Historical Society I have consulted the Anne Morgan, Mrs. Potter Palmer, Lorado Taft, and Agnes Nestor collections without finding important data. The Graham Taylor Papers are in the Newberry Library. There is little useful material about Miss Addams in this collection. Included in the manuscript division of the William Rainey Harper Library at the University of Chicago there are some interesting items concerning Miss Addams in the Presidents' Papers. The Marion Talbot and Robert Herrick collections were less helpful. There are no archives at Hull House. When I visited the settlement in 1960, the only items of historical significance were a double-entry ledger of expenses, a list of donors dated 1890 to 1897, and a minute book of residents' meetings for 1893-5 and 1896. The file of residents who had lived at Hull House was incomplete. There was no file of the irregular *Hull-House Bulletin*, Vol. 1–7 (1895–1905/1906), or its successor, the *Hull-House*

Yearbook (1906/1907 +). The best source of information on Hull House is the *Bibliography of College, Social, University and Church Settlements.* This bibliography was compiled variously by: M. Katherine Jones, 1st and 2nd editions (Philadelphia, 1893, 1895), John Palmer Gavit, 3rd edition (Cambridge, Mass., 1897), and Carolina Wilson Montgomery, 4th and 5th editions (New York, 1900, and Chicago, 1905).

No indexed manuscript collection at Harvard contains Jane Addams material except the Oswald Garrison Villard Papers, and the letters in it were not important for this study. The William Kent Papers at Yale had several interesting items relating to Miss Addams. The Kent collection is the only relevant one at Yale. At the Columbia University Library, there is material referring to Jane Addams in the Randolph Bourne Papers, the Allan Nevins Papers, and the Lincoln Steffens Papers, but the letters did not prove helpful for this study. Miss Addams is mentioned in interviews in the Columbia Oral History Project by Louis H. Pink, Henry Bruere, William Wilson Cumberland, Stanley Isaacs, Ralph Albertson, and William Prendergast, but none of these recollections were particularly helpful or suggestive. Beside the Lillian Wald Papers, there are other collections with occasional material about Jane Addams in the New York Public Library. I have investigated the A. W. Anthony collection, the Annie Russell collection and the Elizabeth Jordan Papers. The Lola Maverick Lloyd and Rosika Schwimmer Papers are restricted.

The compilation by the Library of Congress of a *National Union Catalog of Manuscript Collections, 1959–1961* (Ann Arbor, 1962), and a second volume for 1962 (Hamden, Conn., 1964), has made the location of manuscript material immensely easier. Jane Addams material located in the Gilbert Tracy collection in the New Jersey Historical Society and in the William Channing Gannett Papers at the University of Rochester was not relevant to my work. The Richard Henry Edwards and the James Ernest Boyle collections, both in the Cornell University Library Collection of Regional History and University Archives, contained nothing useful for this study.

The Emily Greene Balch Papers and the papers and files of the Woman's Peace party, the Women's International League for Peace and Freedom, and the United States Section of the Women's International League for Peace and Freedom are in the Swarthmore College Peace Collection. I have consulted them in order to understand how Miss Addams organized and led various reform groups. Among the interesting items in the Balch Papers are the minutes of the meetings at the Henry Street Settlement in 1914 and 1915.

Dr. Alice Hamilton permitted me to visit and talk with her for an afternoon. She very graciously answered my questions and enlightened me on several topics. Jessie Binford, who went to live at Hull House in 1906, also talked with me. I am in her debt for much Hull House lore. Miss Lea Taylor told me about Miss Addams from the vantage of another Chicago settlement. Mrs. Sarah Schaar shared her recollections of Hull House with me and was most cordial and kind. Jordan Cavan, who lived at Hull House during and after World War I, also shared his memories with me. Albert J. Kennedy provided me with his lively interpretation of Miss Addams and recalled her attitudes from his vantage in the 1920's as secretary of the National Federation of Settlements. Mrs. John Allen, James Weber Linn's daughter, was most patient and helpful with all sorts of research questions.

PUBLISHED WRITINGS BY MISS ADDAMS

Jane Addams revealed her ideas most fully in her public writings. After her visit to Tolstoy she resolved to live on the earnings from her speaking and writing, rather than on the income from farmland she had inherited from her father. Miss Addams found wide opportunities for speaking and publishing. Many magazines requested articles from her. The Macmillan Company was anxious to publish books from her pen. Miss Addams devoted much time and effort to writing, for she was anxious to inform as wide a public as possible about her interests. As a result, she frequently reworked similar material for various occasions, and there is a good deal of repetition in the things she published. The curators at Swarthmore have compiled an incomplete bibliography of Miss Addams' writings based on the material in the Jane Addams Papers. A larger effort is M. Helen Perkins, *A Preliminary Checklist for a Bibliography on Jane Addams* (Rockford, Ill., 1960). Miss Perkins arranged her bibliography into awkward categories (addresses, then articles, then books) and alphabetized within these categories. In the following bibliography I have tried to list Jane Addams' published writings in chronological order. I have included verbatim transcripts of speeches and addresses, but have excluded newspaper articles which she wrote, even though some of the material in these newspaper articles was not used elsewhere. I have noted duplication where the texts are the same, but this annotation is not exhaustive.

1. " Plated Ware," *Rockford Seminary Magazine*, VI (April, 1878), 60–2.
2. " The Element of Hopefulness in Human Nature," *ibid.*, VII (May, 1879), 120–2.
3. " Summary of ' Marks,' " a Play, *ibid.*, p. 130.
4. " One Office of Nature," *ibid.*, VII (June, 1879), 154–6.
5. " Home Items," *ibid.*, VII (July, 1879), 199–202.
6. Speech to the Vesperian Society, October 3, 1879, *ibid.*, VII (November, 1879), 242.
7. " The Girl Who Had Too Much To Do," *ibid.*, pp. 235–7. The article was co-authored by Sarah F. Anderson.
8. " The Macbeth of Shakespeare," *ibid.*, VIII (January, 1880), 13–6.
9. " Bread Givers," Rockford *Daily Register*, April 21, 1880.
10. " Self Tradition," *Rockford Seminary Magazine*, IX (April, 1881), 97–101.
11. " Valedictory," *ibid.*, IX (July, 1881), 219–22.
12. " Three Days on the Mediterranean Subjectively Related," *ibid.*, XIV (January, 1886), 11–7.
13. " Rockford Seminary Endowment," in *Memorials of Anna Peck Sill, First Principal of Rockford Female Seminary, 1849–1889* (Rockford, Ill., 1889), pp. 70–5.
14. " How Would You Uplift the Masses? " *Sunset Club [of Chicago] Yearbook* (1891/1892), pp. 118–21.
15. " With the Masses," *Advance* (Chicago), XXV (February 18, 1892), 133. This is a revision of number 14.
16. " Hull House, Chicago: an Effort toward Social Democracy," *Forum*, XIV (October, 1892), 226–41.
17. " A New Impulse to an Old Gospel," *ibid.*, XIV (November, 1892), 345–58.
18. " The Subjective Necessity for Social Settlements," in Henry C. Adams (ed.), *Philanthropy and Social Progress, Seven Essays by Miss Jane Addams, Robert A. Woods, Father J. O. S. Huntington, Professor Franklin H. Giddings and Bernard Bosanquet Delivered before the School of Applied Ethics at Plymouth, Mass., during the Session of 1892* (New York, 1893), pp. 1–26. This is the same as number 17.
19. " Objective Value of a Social Settlement," in *ibid.*, pp. 27–56. This is the same as number 16.

20. "What Shall We Do for Our Unemployed?" *Sunset Club* [*of Chicago*] *Yearbook* (1893/1894), pp. 81–2.

21. "Domestic Service and the Family Claim," in May Wright Sewall (ed.), *A Historical Resume for Popular Circulation of the World Congress of Representative Women, Convened in Chicago on May 15, and Adjourned on May 22, 1893, under the Auspices of the Woman's Branch of the World's Congress Auxiliary* (Chicago & New York, 1894), II, 626–31.

22. Address at Western Reserve College for Women, *College Folio*, II (June, 1894), 129–31.

23. "Art-Work Done by Hull-House," *Forum*, XIX (July, 1895), 614–7.

24. "Prefatory Note," *Hull-House Maps and Papers, by Residents of Hull-House, A Social Settlement, a Presentation of Nationalities and Wages in a Congested District of Chicago, Together with Comments and Essays on Problems Growing out of the Social Conditions* (New York, 1895), pp. vii–viii.

25. "The Settlement as a Factor in the Labor Movement," *ibid.*, pp. 183–204.

26. "The Settlement," in Illinois State Conference of Charities and Correction, *Proceedings*, I (1896), 54–8.

27. "A Belated Industry," *American Journal of Sociology*, I (March, 1896), 536–50. This is a revision with additions of number 21.

28. "The Objects of Social Settlements," *Union Signal*, XXII (March 5, 1896), 148–9.

29. "The Problem of Domestic Servants Viewed Scientifically," *Review of Reviews*, XII (May, 1896), pp. 604–5. This is excerpted from number 27.

30. "Foreign-Born Children in the Primary Grades," in National Education Association, *Journal of Proceedings and Addresses* (1897), pp. 104–12.

31. "Social Settlements," in National Conference of Charities and Correction, *Proceedings* (1897), pp. 338–46.

32. Discussion of after-care of convalescent and recovered insane patients, in *ibid.*, pp. 464–6.

33. Discussion of social settlements, in *ibid.*, pp. 472–6.

34. "Growth of Corporate Consciousness," in Illinois State Conference of Charities and Correction, *Proceedings*, II (1897), 40–2.

35. *Study of the Milk Supply of Chicago.* ("Illinois Agricultural Experiment Station Circular," No. 13.) Urbana, 1898. Pp. 1–8. The circular was co-authored by H. S. Grindley.

36. "Ethical Survivals in Municipal Corruption," *International Journal of Ethics*, VIII (April, 1898), 273–91.

37. "Why the Ward Boss Rules," *Outlook*, LVIII (April 2, 1898), 879–82. This is excerpted from number 36.

38. "A Study in Municipal Politics," *Review of Reviews*, XVII (May, 1898), 605–6. This is excerpted from number 36.

39. "The College Woman and the Family Claim," *The Commons*, III (September, 1898), 3–7.

40. "The Significance of Organized Labor," *Machinist's Monthly Journal*, X (September, 1898), 551–2.

41. "Woman's Work for Chicago," *Municipal Affairs*, II (September, 1898), 502–8.

42. "Christmas Fellowship," *Unity*, XLII (December 22, 1898), 308–9.

43. "Democracy or Militarism," in Central Anti-Imperialist League of Chicago, *Liberty Tract*, I (1899), 35–9.

44. "Trade Unions and Public Duty," *American Journal of Sociology*, IV (January, 1899), 448–62.

45. "The Subtle Problems of Charity," *Atlantic Monthly*, LXXXIII (February, 1899), 163–78.
46. "The Charity Visitor's Perplexities," *Outlook*, LXI (March 11, 1899), 598–600. This is excerpted from number 45.
47. "A Function of the Social Settlement," *Annals*, XIII (May, 1899), 323–45.
48. "What Peace Means," *Unity*, XLIII (May 4, 1899), 178. This is a reprinting of number 43.
49. "Social Settlement and University Extension," *Review of Reviews*, XX (July, 1899), 93. This is excerpted from number 47.
50. "Trade Unions and Public Duty," *Railroad Trainman's Journal*, XVI (December, 1899), 1070–86. This is a reprinting of number 44.
51. "Social Education of the Industrial Democracy," *The Commons*, V (June 30, 1900), 17–20.
52. "The Hull-House Labor Museum," *Current Literature*, XXIX (October, 1900), 423–4. This is excerpted from number 51.
53. "What Is the Greatest Menace to Twentieth Century Progress?" *Sunset Club [of Chicago] Yearbook* (1899/1901), pp. 338–41.
54. *The Greatest Menace to Progress.* Chicago, 1901. This is a separate publication of number 53.
55. "Respect for Law," *Independent*, LIII (January 3, 1901), 18–20.
56. "One Menace to the Century's Progress," *Unity*, XLVII (April 4, 1901), 71–2. This is a reprinting of number 53.
57. "College Women and Christianity," *Independent*, LIII (August 8, 1901), 1852–5.
58. *First Report of the Labor Museum at Hull-House, Chicago, 1901/1902.* Chicago, 1902. This pamphlet is unsigned, but it was reprinted under Miss Addams' signature. See number 61.
59. Speech, in University Settlement Association of New York, *Annual Report*, XVI (1902), 51–6.
60. *Democracy and Social Ethics.* New York, 1902. Chapter II is a revision, with additions, of number 45. Chapter III includes excerpts from number 39. Chapter IV is a revision, with additions, of number 27. Chapter V contains some sections originally published in number 44. Chapter VI is a revision of number 30. Chapter VII is a revision, with additions, of number 36.
61. "First Report of the Labor Museum at Hull House, Chicago, 1901–1902," *Unity*, XLIX (March 13, 1902), 20–23.
62. "What the Theatre at Hull-House Has Done for the Neighborhood People," *Charities*, VIII (March 29, 1902), 284–6.
63. "The Housing Problem in Chicago," and discussion, *Annals*, XX (July, 1902), 99–107.
64. "Newer Ideals of Peace," *Chautauqua Assembly Herald*, XXVII (July 8, 1902), 5.
65. "Arts and Crafts and the Settlement," *ibid.*, XXVII (July 9, 1902), 2.
66. "The Newer Ideals of Peace," *ibid.*, XXVII (July 10, 1902), 6.
67. "Count Tolstoy," *ibid.*, XXVII (July 11, 1902), 5.
68. "Tolstoy's Theory of Life," *ibid.*, XXVII (July 14, 1902), 2–3.
69. "Child Labor and Pauperism," in National Conference of Charities and Correction, *Proceedings* (1903), pp. 114–21.
70. Discussion and summary on child labor, in *ibid.*, pp. 546–8.
71. "Address of Miss Jane Addams," in Chicago Union League Club, *Exercises in Commemoration of the Birthday of Washington, 23 February 1903* (Chicago, 1903), pp. 6–9.
72. "The Friendship of Settlement Work," *Charities*, X (March 28, 1903), 315–6. This is excerpted from number 59.

73. "Women's Clubs *versus* Child Labor," *The Commons*, VIII (July, 1903), 1–2. This letter is co-signed by Florence Kelley and Caroline D. G. Granger. It is included in Mrs. A. O. Granger, "The Work of the General Federation of Women's Clubs against Child Labor," *Annals*, XXV (May, 1905), 516–7.

74. "The Servant Problem," *Good Housekeeping*, XXXVII (September, 1903), 233–40.

75. "Child Labor and Pauperism," *Charities*, XI (October 3, 1903), 300–4. This is a reprinting of number 69.

76. "Henry Demarest Lloyd, His Passion for a Better Social Order," *The Commons*, VIII (December, 1903), 1–3.

77. "The Responsibilities and Duties of Women toward the Peace Movement," in Universal Peace Congress, *Official Report*, XIII (1904), 120–2.

78. "The Interests of Labor in International Peace," in *ibid.*, pp. 145–7.

79. Address, in *ibid.*, pp. 261–2.

80. "Neighborhood Improvement," in National Conference of Charities and Correction, *Proceedings* (1904), pp. 456–8, and repeated at pp. 560–2.

81. Remarks as chairman of discussion, in *ibid.*, pp. 608–17.

82. Address, in *Dedication of the Hull-House Organ Given in Memory of Sarah Rozet Smith, Sunday, March 27, 1904* (n.p., n.d. [1904]), unpaged.

83. "Henry Demarest Lloyd, His Passion for a Better Social Order," *The Commons*, IX (January, 1904), 20–2. This is a reprinting of number 76.

84. "Henry Demarest Lloyd, His Passion for a Better Social Order," in Chicago Teachers' Federation, *Bulletin*, III (January 29, 1904), 1–3. This is a reprinting of number 76.

85. "Educational Methods as They Relate to Labor Unions," *ibid.*, III (March 25, 1904), pp. 1–2. This is excerpted from Chapter VI of number 60.

86. "Humanizing Tendency of Industrial Education," *Chautauquan*, XXXIX (May, 1904), 266–72.

87. "Hull-House and Its Neighbors," *Charities*, XII (May 7, 1904), 450–1.

88. "Larger Social Groupings," *ibid.*, XII (June 25, 1904), 675. This is a brief summary of number 80.

89. "The Present Crisis in Trades-Union Morals," *North American Review*, CLXXIX (August, 1904), 178–93.

90. "Woman's Peace Meeting—Jane Addams's Address," *Woman's Journal*, XXXV (October 22, 1904), 337, 340–1.

91. "Child Labor Legislation: a Requisite for Industrial Efficiency," in National Child Labor Committee, New York, *Child Labor, the Proceedings of the First Annual Conference, New York City, February 14–16, 1905* (New York, 1905), pp. 128–36.

92. "Child Labor Legislation: a Requisite for Industrial Efficiency," in National Child Labor Committee," New York, *Pamphlet*, XIII (1905). This is a reprinting of number 91.

93. "Speech at the Hull House Memorial Meeting, Chicago, January 21, 1905," in *Jessie Bross Lloyd, September 27, 1844–December 29, 1904* (n.p. [Chicago], n.d. [1905]), pp. 41–3.

94. "Speech at the Winnetka Memorial Meeting, February 12, 1905," in *ibid.*, pp. 57–62.

95. "Immigrants and American Charities," in Illinois Conference of Charities and Correction, *Proceedings* (1905), 11–8.

96. "Problems of Municipal Administration," *American Journal of Sociology*, X (January, 1905), 425–44.

97. "Recent Immigration, a Field Neglected by the Scholar," *University [of Chicago] Record*, IX (January, 1905), 274–84.

98. "Recent Immigration, a Field Neglected by the Scholar," *The Commons*, X (January, 1905), 9–19. This is a reprinting of number 97.

99. "Recent Immigration, a Field Neglected by the Scholar," *Unity*, LIV (January 19, 1905), pp. 328–33. This is a reprinting of number 97.

100. "Recent Immigration," *Education Review*, XXIX (March, 1905), 245–63. This is a reprinting of number 97.

101. "Child Labor," *Journal of Education*, LXI (March 16, 1905), 289.

102. "A House Stands on a Busy Street," *Unity*, LV (March 30, 1905), p. 85.

103. "The Subjective Necessity of Social Settlements," *Social Service*, XI (April, 1905), 38–47. This is excerpted from number 17.

104. "A House Stands on a Busy Street," *The Commons*, X (April, 1905), 225. This is a reprinting of number 101.

105. "Child Labor Legislation: a Requisite for Industrial Efficiency," *Annals*, XXV (May, 1905), 542–50. This is a reprinting of number 91.

106. Speech at the civic dedication of the Abraham Lincoln Center, *Unity*, LV (May 27, 1905), 364–5.

107. "Work and Play as Factors in Education," *Chautauquan*, XLII (November, 1905), 251–5.

108. "Day Nurseries—Do They Foster Parental Irresponsibility?" *Charities and The Commons*, XV (December 30, 1905), 411–2.

109. Ed. of, Henry Demarest Lloyd. *Man, the Social Creator*. New York, 1906. Anne Withington edited this book with Miss Addams.

110. "The Modern City and the Municipal Franchise for Women," in National American Woman Suffrage Association, *Woman Suffrage, Arguments and Results* (n.p., n.d. [1906?]), variously paged.

111. "Operation of the Illinois Child Labor Law," in National Child Labor Committee, New York, *Child Labor, a Menace to Industry, Education and Good Citizenship, the Proceedings of the Second Annual Conference, Washington, December 8–10, 1905* (New York, 1906), pp. 69–72.

112. "Operation of the Illinois Child Labor Law," in National Child Labor Committee, New York, *Pamphlet*, XXIX (1906). This is a reprinting of number 111.

113. Letter to the Speaker of the United States House of Representatives, June 11, 1906, U. S. *Congressional Record*. 59th Cong., 1st Sess., 1906, XL, Part 9, p. 8515.

114. "Social Settlements in Illinois," Transactions of the Seventh Annual Meeting of the Illinois State Historical Society, in Illinois State Historical Library, *Publication*, XI (1906), 162–71.

115. "Child Labor and Other Dangers of Childhood," in American Humane Association, *Report of the Proceedings of the Annual Convention* (1906), pp. 28–30.

116. "On Behalf of the Community," *Unity*, LVI (January 18, 1906), 366–7.

117. "Jane Addams on Judge Tuley," *Woman's Journal*, XXXVII (January 27, 1906), 14. This is excerpted from number 116.

118. "Jane Addams' Own Story of Her Work: Fifteen Years at Hull House," *Ladies' Home Journal*, XXIII (March, 1906), 13–4.

119. "Operation of the Illinois Child Labor Law," *Annals*, XXVII (March, 1906), 327–30. This is a reprinting of number 111.

120. "Some Childhood Experiences of Jane Addams," *Unity*, LVII (March 1, 1906), 11. This is excerpted from number 118.

121. "Judge Tuley," *Charities and The Commons*, XV (March 3, 1906), 752–3. This is a reprinting of number 116.

122. "Probation Work under Civil Service," *ibid.*, XV (March 17, 1906), 881.

123. " Jane Addams' Own Story of Her Work: the First Five Years at Hull House," *Ladies' Home Journal*, XXIII (April, 1906), 11–2.
124. " The Modern City and the Municipal Franchise for Women," *Woman's Journal*, XXXVII (April 7, 1906), 53–5. This is a reprinting of number 110.
125. " Woman's Relations to Civic Housekeeping," *Public*, IX (April 28, 1906), 86–7. This is excerpted from number 110.
126. " Jane Addams' Own Story of Her Work: How the Work at Hull House Has Grown," *Ladies' Home Journal*, XXIII (May, 1906), 11–2.
127. Statement concerning Judge Ben B. Lindsey, *Public*, IX (October 20, 1906), 691–2.
128. *Newer Ideals of Peace*. New York, 1907. Chapters II and III are revisions, with additions, of number 96 and 97. Chapter V includes material originally published in number 89. Chapter VII is a revision, with additions, of number 110. Chapter VIII includes material originally used in numbers 43 and 97.
129. Address, in *A Living Memorial to John A. Davis, Colonel 46th Illinois Volunteer Infantry* (Chicago, 1907), pp. 15–18.
130. " New Ideals of Peace," in National Arbitration and Peace Congress, *Proceedings* [I] (1907), pp. 106–10.
131. " New Internationalism," in *ibid.*, pp. 213–6.
132. " National Protection for Children," in National Child Labor Committee, New York, *Child Labor and the Republic, the Proceedings of the Third Annual Conference, Cincinnati, Ohio, 13–15 December 1906* (New York, 1907), pp. 57–60.
133. " National Protection for Children," in National Child Labor Committee, New York, *Pamphlet*, XLVII (1907). This is a reprinting of number 132.
134. " Problems of Municipal Administration," in Howard J. Rogers (ed.), *International Congress of Arts and Science, Universal Exposition, St. Louis, 1904* (Boston & New York, 1905–7), VII, 434–50. This is a revision of number 96.
135. " An Interpretation of the Chicago Industrial Exhibit," in *Handbook of the Chicago Industrial Exhibition, Brooke's Casino, March 11–17, 1907* (Chicago, 1907), pp. 20–3.
136. " Class Conflict in America," in American Sociological Society, *Papers and Proceedings*, II (1907), pp. 152–5.
137. " National Protection for Children," *Annals*, XXIX (January, 1907), 57–60. This is a reprinting of number 132.
138. Address, in National Society for the Promotion of Industrial Education, *Bulletin*, I (January, 1907), 37–44.
139. " Newer Ideals of Peace," *Charities and The Commons*, XVII (January 5, 1907), 599–606. This is a reprinting of Chapter I, number 128.
140. " National Program," *ibid.*, pp. 641–2. This is excerpted from number 132.
141. " How Shall We Approach Industrial Education? " Educational *Bi-Monthly*, I (February, 1907), 183–90. This is a reprinting of number 138.
142. Memorial address for John A. Davis, *Unity*, LIX (May 30, 1907), 201. This is a reprinting of number 129.
143. " Public Recreation and Social Morality," *Charities and The Commons*, XVIII (August 3, 1907), 492–4.
144. " Why Girls Go Wrong," *Ladies' Home Journal*, XXIV (September, 1907), pp. 13–4.
145. " Do We Want Rifle Practice in the Public Schools? " in Peace Association of Friends, *Do We Want Rifle Practice in the Public Schools* (Philadelphia, 1908), pp. 5–6.
146. " Hull House," in William D. P. Bliss (ed.), *New Encyclopedia of Social Reform* (New York, 1908), pp. 587–90.

147. "The Public School and the Immigrant Child," in National Education Association, *Journal of Proceedings and Addresses* (1908), pp. 99–102.

148. "The Home and the Special Child," in *ibid.*, pp. 1127–31.

149. "Woman's Conscience and Social Amelioration," in Charles Stelzle *et al.*, *Social Application of Religion* ("Merrick Lectures, Ohio Wesleyan University, Delaware, Ohio," 1907–1908, Cincinnati, 1908), pp. 41–60.

150. "Child Labor and Education," in National Conference of Charities and Correction, *Proceedings* (1908), pp. 364–9.

151. "The Relation of 'Settlements' and Religion; or, the place of Religion as It May Be Experienced in the Settlement," *Unity*, LX (January 9, 16, 1908), 295–7, 311–3. Jane Addams presided at this discussion which included addresses by Mary Kingsbury Simkhovitch and Mary E. McDowell.

152. Address, *Journal of Education*, LXVII (February 13, 1908), 175–6. This is inaccurately excerpted from number 157.

153. "The Relation of Women to Industry and Social Relations," *Woman's Journal*, XXXIX (March 28, 1908), p. 42.

154. "Working Women and the Ballot," *Woman's Home Companion*, XXXV (April, 1908), 19.

155. Address, *Playground*, II (April, 1908), 25–8.

156. Address at Smith College, *Woman's Journal*, XXXIX (April 4, 1908), 56.

157. Discussion, in National Society for the Promotion of Industrial Education, *Bulletin*, VI, Part 2 (May, 1908), 92–7.

158. "The Chicago Settlements and Social Unrest," *Charities and The Commons*, XX (May 2, 1908), 155–66.

159. "Advantages and Disadvantages of a Broken Inheritance," *Atlanta University Bulletin*, CLXXXIII (June, 1908), 1–2.

160. Speech at the Abraham Lincoln Center, *Unity*, LXI (July 2, 1908), 280.

161. "The 'Piece-Work' System as a Factor in The Tuberculosis of Wage-Workers," in International Congress on Tuberculosis, *Proceedings*, VI, Section 5 (September, 1908), 139–40. Dr. Alice Hamilton co-authored this article.

162. "Some Reflections on the Failure of the Modern City to Provide Recreation for Young Girls," *Charities and The Commons*, XXI (December 5, 1908), 365–8. This is a reprinting of number 155.

163. *Hull House, 1889–1909*. Chicago, n.d. [1909].

164. *The Spirit of Youth and the City Streets*. New York, 1909. Chapter 1 used material which was originally published as number 155. Chapter III includes number 144.

165. "Modern Devices for Minimizing Dependencies," in U.S. Senate, *Proceedings of the Conference on the Care of Dependent Children, Washington, 25–26 January 1909*, Senate Document 721, 60th Cong., 2nd Sess., 1909, pp. 99–101.

166. "Report of the Committee on Immigrants," in National Conference of Charities and Correction, *Proceedings* (1909), pp. 213–5.

167. "The Federal Children's Bureau—a Symposium," in National Child Labor Committee, New York, *Child Workers of the Nation, the Proceedings of the 5th Annual Conference, Chicago, Illinois, January 21–23, 1909* (New York, 1909), pp. 28–30.

168. "Street Trading," in *ibid.*, pp. 237–8.

169. "The Federal Children's Bureau—a Symposium," in National Child Labor Committee, New York, *Pamphlet*, CI (1909), 8–10. This is a reprinting of number 167.

170. "Street Trading," in *ibid.*, CXIV (1909), 8–9. This is a reprinting of number 168.

171. " Woman's Special Training for Peacemaking," in American [National Arbitration and] Peace Congress, *Proceedings*, II (1909), 252–4.
172. " The Federal Children's Bureau—a Symposium," *Annals*, XXXIII, Supplement (March, 1909), 28–30. This is a reprinting of number 167.
173. " Street Trading," *ibid.*, pp. 232–3. This is a reprinting of number 168.
174. " The Reaction of Modern Life upon Religious Education," *Religious Education*, IV (April, 1909), 23–9.
175. " Reaction of Moral Instruction upon Social Reform," *Survey*, XXII (April 3, 1909), 17–9. This is a shorter version, partially rewritten, of number 174.
176. " Immigrants," *ibid.*, XXII (June 26, 1909), 453–4. This is a reprinting of number 166.
177. " Bad Boy of the Streets," *Ladies' Home Journal*, XXVI (October, 1909), 17. This is excerpted from Chapter III of number 164.
178. " When Youth Seeks a Mate," *ibid.*, XXVI (November, 1909), 22. This is excerpted from Chapter II of number 164.
179. " Foreword," in Immigrants' Protective League, Chicago, *Annual Report* (1909/1910), p. 4.
180. *Twenty Years at Hull-House with Autobiographical Notes.* New York, 1910.
181. " Charity and Social Justice," in National Conference of Charities and Correction, *Proceedings* (1910), pp. 1–18.
182. " Woman Suffrage and the Protection of the Home," *Ladies' Home Journal*, XXVII (January, 1910), 21.
183. " Gospel of Recreation," *Northwestern Christian Advocate*, LVIII (January 5, 1910), 9–10. This is excerpted from Chapter I of number 164.
184. " Autobiographical Notes upon Twenty Years at Hull-House. A Wartime Childhood," *American Magazine*, LXIX (April, 1910), 723–34. This is a reprinting of Chapters I and II of number 180.
185. " Autobiographical Notes upon Twenty Years at Hull-House. Early Undertakings at Hull House," *ibid.*, LXX (June, 1910), 192–202. This is a reprinting of Chapter VII of number 180.
186. " Charity and Social Justice," *Survey*, XXIV (June 11, 1910), 441–9. This is a reprinting of number 181.
187. " Charity and Social Justice," *North American Review*, CXCII (July, 1910), 68–81. This is a reprinting of number 181.
188. " Autobiographical Notes upon Twenty Years at Hull House. Problems of Poverty," *American Magazine*, LXX (July, 1910), 338–48. This is a reprinting of Chapter VIII of number 180.
189. " Autobiographical Notes upon Twenty Years at Hull-House. Resources of Immigrants," *ibid.*, LXX (August, 1910), 494–505. This is excerpted from Chapters XI and XV of number 180.
190. " Autobiographical Notes upon Twenty Years at Hull-House. Echoes of the Russian Revolution," *ibid.*, LXX (September, 1910), 638–46. This is a reprinting of Chapter XVII of number 180.
191. " Stage Children," *Survey*, XXV (December 3, 1910), pp. 342–3.
192. " Child Labor on the Stage," in National Child Labor Committee, New York, *Uniform Child Labor Laws, the Proceedings of the 7th Annual Conference of the National Child Labor Committee, Birmingham, Alabama, 9–12 March 1911* (New York, 1911), pp. 60–5.
193. " Ten Years' Experience in Child Labor Legislation in Illinois," in *ibid.*, pp. 144–8.
194. " What Does Child Labor Reform Cost the Community? " in National Child Labor Committee, New York, *Pamphlet*, CLV (1911). This is a reprinting of number 193.

195. "Symposium—Child Labor on the Stage," in *ibid.*, CLXV (1911). This is a reprinting of number 192.
196. "Recreation as a Public Function in Urban Communities," in *American Sociological Society, Publications*, VI (1911), 35–9.
197. "Opening of the Exhibit," in Chicago Child Welfare Exhibit, 1911, *The Child in the City, a Handbook of the Child Welfare Exhibit, 11–25 May 1911, Chicago Coliseum* (Chicago, 1911), pp. 4–5.
198. "The Child Welfare Exhibit—a Foreword in Explanation," in *ibid.*, p. 5.
199. "The Hull House Labor Museum," in *ibid.*, pp. 410–4.
200. Address, in University Settlement Society of New York, *Annual Report*, XXV (1911), 21–4.
201. "Standards of Education for Industrial Life," in National Conference of Charities and Correction, *Proceedings* (1911), pp. 162–4.
202. "The Call of the Social Field," in *ibid.*, pp. 370–2.
203. "Social Control," *Crisis, a Record of the Darker Races*, I (January, 1911), 22–3.
204. "A Visit to Tolstoy," *McClure's Magazine*, XXXVI (January, 1911), 295–302. This is a reprinting of Chapter XII of number 180.
205. "The Ballot for Health and Beauty," *Woman's Journal*, XLII (February 11, 1911), 48.
206. "The Social Situation: Religious Education and Contemporary Social Conditions," *Religious Education*, VI (June, 1911), 145–52.
207. Speech, *Woman's Journal*, XLII (June 17, 1911), 185–6.
208. "Child Labor on the Stage," *Annals*, XXXVIII, Supplement (July, 1911), 60–5. This is a reprinting of number 192.
209. "Ten Years Experience in Child Labor Legislation in Illinois," *ibid.*, pp. 144–8. This is a reprinting of number 193.
210. "Why Women Should Vote," *Woman's Journal*, XLII (October 28, 1911), 337.
211. "A New Conscience and an Ancient Evil, Chapter I," *McClure's Magazine*, XXXVIII (November, 1911), 2–13.
212. "A New Conscience and an Ancient Evil, Chapter II: Economic Pressure and Its Inevitable Results," *ibid.*, XXXVIII (December, 1911), pp. 232–40.
213. "The Church and the Social Evil," in *Men and Religion Forward Movement: Messages of the Men and Religion Movement* (New York, 1912), II, 130–41.
214. "Child at the Point of Greatest Pressure," in National Conference of Charities and Correction, *Proceedings* (1912), pp. 26–30.
215. "Remarks," in U.S. House of Representatives, Committee on the Judiciary, *Hearings on Woman Suffrage, 13 March 1912*, Serial 2, 62nd Cong., 2nd Sess., 1912, pp. 7–8.
216. Speech seconding Theodore Roosevelt's nomination for President at the Progressive convention, in U.S. *Congressional Record*, XLVIII, Part 12, Appendix, 62nd Cong., 2nd Sess., 1912, pp. 564–5.
217. *A New Conscience and an Ancient Evil*. New York, 1912. Chapter I is a reprinting of number 211. Chapter III is a reprinting of number 212.
218. "A New Conscience and an Ancient Evil, Chapter III: Lack of Moral Education and Its Dangers," *McClure's Magazine*, XXXVIII (January, 1912), 338–44. This is a reprinting of Chapter IV of number 217.
219. "Mrs. J. T. Bowen," *American Magazine*, LXXIII (January, 1912), 292–6.
220. "A New Conscience and an Ancient Evil, Chapter IV: Tragedies of Lonely and Unprotected Girls," *McClure's Magazine*, XXXVIII (February, 1912), 471–8. This is a reprinting of Chapter V of number 217.
221. "Recreation as a Public Function in Urban Communities," *American Journal*

of Sociology, XVII (March, 1912), 615–9. This is a reprinting of number 196.

222. "A New Conscience and an Ancient Evil, Chapter V: Social Control," *McClure's Magazine*, XXXVIII (March, 1912), 592–8. This is a reprinting of Chapter VI of number 217.

223. "A New Conscience and an Ancient Evil," *Woman's Journal*, XLIII (March 16, 1912), 82. This is excerpted from Chapter VI of number 217.

224. "Humanitarian Value of Civil Service," *Survey*, XXVIII (April 6, 1912), 14–6.

225. "The Church and the Social Evil," *Vigilance*, XXV (May, 1912), 1–6. This is a reprinting of number 213.

226. "A Challenge to the Contemporary Church," *Survey*, XXVIII (May 4, 1912), 195–8. This is a reprinting of number 213.

227. Speech, in *City Club [of Chicago] Bulletin*, V (May 27, 1912), 212–3.

228. "The Civic Value of Higher Education for Women," *Bryn Mawr Alumnae Quarterly*, VI (June, 1912), 59–67.

229. "Votes for Women and Other Votes," *Survey*, XXVIII (June 1, 1912), 367–8.

230. "Votes for Women and Other Votes," *Woman's Journal*, XLIII (June 15, 1912), 191. This is excerpted from number 229.

231. "Why I Seconded Roosevelt's Nomination," *ibid.*, XLIII (August 17, 1912), 257.

232. "The Church and the Social Evil; Christian Responsibility for a Terrible Modern Scourge," *Methodist Quarterly Review*, LXI (October, 1912), 665–72. This in a reprinting of number 213.

233. "Pragmatism in Politics," *Survey*, XXIX (October 5, 1912), 11–2.

234. "Woman in Politics," *Progress, a Progressive Monthly Review, Political Social, Economic*, I (November, 1912), 37–40. I have been unable to verify this article.

235. "The Progressive Party and the Negro," *Crisis; a Record of the Darker Races*, V (November, 1912), 30–1.

236. "My Experiences as a Progressive Delegate," *McClure's Magazine*, XL (November, 1912), 12–4.

237. "The Progressive's Dilemma—the New Party," *American Magazine*, LXXV (November, 1912), 12–4.

238. "A Modern Lear," *Survey*, XXIX (November 2, 1912), 131–7.

239. "Indirect Influence," *Woman's Journal*, XLIII (November 23, 1912), 373.

240. "Lessons of the Election," *City Club [of Chicago] Bulletin*, V (November 27, 1912), 361–4.

241. "Communion of the Ballot," *Woman's Journal*, XLIII (December 14, 1912), 397.

242. *Plea for More Play, More Pay and More Education for Our Factory Boys and Girls, from the Writings of Jane Addams.* N.p. [Chicago], n.d. [1913]. An editorial note in *Survey*, XXX (August 30, 1913), p. 671 identifies this pamphlet.

243. Introduction, in Graham Taylor, *Religion in Social Action* (New York, 1913), pp. xi–xxxv.

244. "Why Women Should Vote," in Frances Maule (ed.), *Woman Suffrage, History, Arguments and Results* (New York, 1913), pp. 139–58. This is a reprinting of number 182.

245. Foreword, in Robert A. Woods and Albert J. Kennedy (eds.), *Young Working Girls* (Boston & New York, 1913), pp. xi–xiii.

246. "Struggle for Life above the Poverty Line," National Federation of Settlements, *Conference*, III (1913), 16–9.

247. Jane Addams' page, *Ladies' Home Journal*, XXX (January, 1913), 25.
248. "Pen and Book as Tests of Character," *Survey*, XXIX (January 4, 1913), 419–20.
249. Jane Addams' page, *Ladies' Home Journal*, XXX (February, 1913), 23.
250. "Has the Emancipation Act Been Nullified by National Indifference?" *Survey*, XXIX (February 1, 1913), 565–6.
251. Jane Addams' page, *Ladies' Home Journal*, XXX (March, 1913), 27.
252. Jane Addams' page, *ibid.*, XXX (April, 1913), 27.
253. Jane Addams' page, *ibid.*, XXX (May, 1913), 27.
254. Jane Addams' page, *ibid.*, XXX (June, 1913), 21.
255. Jane Addams' page, *ibid.*, XXX (July, 1913), 19.
256. Jane Addams' page, *ibid.*, XXX (August, 1913), 19.
257. "Solving the Problem of the Unemployed," *ibid.*, XXX (September, 1913), 23.
258. "The ' Juvenile-Adult' Offender," *ibid.*, XXX (October, 1913), 24.
259. "The Sheltered Woman and the Magdalen," *ibid.*, XXX (November, 1913), 25. This is a revision with additions of number 213.
260. "Should the Chicago Aldermanic Elections Next Spring Be Non-Partisan?" *City Club [of Chicago] Bulletin*, VI (November 7, 1913), 302–4.
261. "Peace on Earth," *Ladies' Home Journal*, XXX (December, 1913), 27.
262. "Why Women Are Concerned with the Larger Citizenship," in Shailer Mathews (ed.), *Woman Citizen's Library* (Chicago, 1913–4), IX, 2123–42.
263. "Women's Clubs and Public Policies," in General Federation of Women's Clubs, *Biennial Convention*, XII (1914), 24–30.
264. "The Immigrant Woman as She Adjusts Herself to American Life," *ibid.*, 370–4.
265. "Humanitarian Aspects of the Merit System," in National Civil Service Reform League, *Proceedings at the Annual Meeting* (1914), pp. 108–13.
266. Testimony, in U.S. House of Representatives, [Sub-] Committee on Woman Suffrage of the Committee on Rules, *Hearing on Resolution Establishing a Committee on Woman Suffrage*, House Document 754, 63rd Cong., 2nd Sess., 1914, pp. 13–8.
267. "Democracy and Social Ethics," in Andrew C. McLaughlin and Albert Bushnell Hart (eds.), *Cyclopedia of American Government* (New York, 1914), I, 563–4.
268. Preface, in Louise DeK. Bowen, *Safeguards for City Youth at Work and at Play* (New York, 1914), pp. vii–xiii.
269. "Social Justice through National Action," in *Speeches Delivered at the Second Annual Lincoln Day Dinner of the Progressive Party, Hotel Astor, New York City, 12 February 1914* (New York, 1914), pp. 6–9.
270. "Unexpected Reactions of a Traveler in Egypt," *Atlantic Monthly*, CXIII (February, 1914), 178–86.
271. Telegram on woman suffrage, *Outlook*, CVI (March 7, 1914), 511.
272. Telegram, *Independent*, LXXVII (March 16, 1914), 366. This is excerpted from number 271.
273. "The Girl Problem—Its Community Aspects," *American Youth*, III (April, 1914), 81–5.
274. "The Need of a Constructive Appeal," *Child Labor Bulletin*, III (May, 1914), 11–3.
275. "A Modern Devil Baby," *American Journal of Sociology*, XX (July, 1914), 117–8.
276. "Passing of the War Virtues," *Craftsman*, XXVII (October, 1914), 79–80. This is excerpted from number 128.

277. "Need a Woman over Fifty Feel Old?" *Ladies' Home Journal*, XXXI (October, 1914), 7.

278. "Is the Peace Movement a Failure?" *ibid.*, XXXI (November, 1914), 5.

279. "Larger Aspects of the Woman's Movement," *Annals*, LVI (November, 1914), 1–8. This is a reprinting with slight changes of number 229.

280. "A Memory (Caroline M. Severance)," *California Outlook*, XVII (December 12, 1914), 9.

281. Introduction, in Eleanor Smith, *Hull-House Songs* (Chicago, n.d. [1915]), p. 2.

282. "A Modern Lear, a Parenthetical Chapter," in Graham Romeyn Taylor, *Satellite Cities, a Study of Industrial Suburbs* (New York & London, 1915), pp. 68–90. This is a reprinting of number 238.

283. "Presidential Address," in International Congress of Women at The Hague, 28th April–1st May, 1915, *Report* (1915), pp. 18–22.

284. "Women and War," in Lucia Ames Mead (ed.), *The Overthrow of the War System* (Boston, 1915), pp. 1–9. This is a reprinting of number 283.

285. Address, in *Report of the International Congress of Women at The Hague . . . President's Address, Resolutions Adopted, Report of Committees Visiting European Capitols* (Chicago, 1915), pp. 6–9. This is a reprinting of number 283.

286. "Filial Relations," in John Milton Berdan *et al.* (eds.), *Modern Essays* (New York, 1915), pp. 369–86. This is a reprinting of Chapter III of number 60.

287. "Why Women Should Vote," in Frances M. Bjorkman and Anne G. Porritt (eds.), *Woman Suffrage, History, Arguments and Results* (New York, 1915), pp. 131–50. This is a reprinting of number 182.

288. *Women at The Hague, the International Congress of Women and Its Results.* New York, 1915. This was co-authored by Emily G. Balch and Alice Hamilton. Miss Addams contributed Chapter III, "The Revolt against War," Chapter IV, "Factors in Continuing the War," and Chapter VII, "Women and Internationalism."

289. "Address," in Woman's Peace Party, *Addresses Given at the Organization Conference of the Woman's Peace Party, Washington, D.C., January 10, 1915* (Chicago, n.d. [1915]), pp. 10–2.

290. "The Unemployment Question," *City Club [of Chicago] Bulletin*, VIII (February 24, 1915), pp. 63–6.

291. "What War Is Destroying," *Advocate of Peace*, LXXVII (March, 1915), 64–5. This is a reprinting of number 289.

292. "Songs for the Hull House Quarter Century," *Survey*, XXXIII (March 6, 1915), 597. This is a reprinting of number 281.

293. Foreword to "War and Social Reconstruction," *ibid.*, p. 603.

294. "Towards the Peace That Shall Last," *ibid.*, Part II, unpaged. This statement is signed also by seventeen others.

295. "Towards the Peace That Shall Last," *Unity*, LXXV (March 25, 1915), 54–7. This is a reprinting with minor changes of number 294.

296. "The President's Address," *Jus Suffragii*, IX (June 1, 1915), 303–4. This is a reprinting of number 283.

297. "The Revolt against War," *Survey*, XXXIV (July 17, 1915), 355–9. This includes excerpts from Chapter III, Chapter IV, and Chapter VII of number 288.

298. "Address of Miss Jane Addams, Delivered at Carnegie Hall, Friday, July 9, 1915," *Christian Work*, XCIX (July 31, 1915), 145–8. This is a reprinting of number 297.

299. "Women, War, and Babies," *Harper's Weekly*, LXI (July 31, 1915), 101.
300. "As I See Women," *Ladies' Home Journal*, XXXII (August, 1915), 11.
301. "The Revolt against War," *Unity*, LXXV (August 5, 1915), 358–63. This is a reprinting of number 297.
302. "Europe Would Welcome Peace," *Christian Herald*, XXXVIII (August 11, 1915), 218–19. This is excerpted from number 297.
303. "Jane Addams and World Peace," *Congregationalist and Christian World*, C (August 12, 1915), 218–9. This is extracted from number 297.
304. "Peace and the Press," *Independent*, LXXXIV (October 11, 1915), 55–6. This is excerpted from Chapter IV of number 288.
305. "Woman Suffrage," *Survey*, XXXV (October 23, 1915), 85.
306. Letter to President Wilson, *Commoner*, XV (November, 1915), 6. The letter was also signed by Lucia Ames Mead, Anna Garlin Spencer, Alice Thatcher Post, and S. P. Breckinridge.
307. "Women, War and Suffrage," *Survey*, XXXV (November 6, 1915), 148–50. This is excerpted from Chapter VII of number 288.
308. "The Food of War," *Independent*, LXXXIV (December 13, 1915), 430–1. This is excerpted from Chapter IV of number 288.
309. "Towards Internationalism," in U.S., Second Pan American Scientific Congress, *Report on Women's Auxiliary Conference held in Washington in Connection with 2nd Pan American Scientific Congress, December 28, 1915–January 7, 1916*, prepared by Mrs. Glen Levin Swiggert (Washington, 1916), pp. 59–60. This also appeared in a Spanish edition.
310. *The Long Road of Women's Memory*. New York, 1916. Chapter VI is a shortened version of number 270.
311. Address, in Woman's Peace Party, *Yearbook* (1916), pp. 21–4.
312. Testimony, in U.S. House of Representatives, Committee on Military Affairs, *To Increase Efficiency of the Military Establishment of the United States* (*Hearings on National Defense*) (13 January 1916), 64th Cong., 1st Sess., 1916, pp. 201–13.
313. Testimony, in U.S. House of Representatives, Committee on Foreign Affairs, *United States and the Orient, Hearing on H. R. 16661* (*to Provide for a Commission on Relations between the U.S. and the Orient*) 12 December 1916, 64th Cong., 2nd Sess., 1916, pp. 10–2.
314. Testimony, in U.S. House of Representatives, Committee on Foreign Affairs, *Commission for Enduring Peace* (*Hearings on H. R. 6921 and H. J. Resolution 32*) (11 January 1916), 64th Cong., 1st Sess., 1916, pp. 3–17.
315. "Towards the Peace That Shall Last," in Randolph Bourne (ed.), *Towards an Enduring Peace, a Symposium of Peace Proposals and Programs, 1914–1916* (New York, n.d. [1916]), pp. 230–9. This is co-signed by Lillian Wald and Paul U. Kellogg. This is a reprinting of number 294.
316. "Conference of Neutrals," *Survey*, XXXV (January 22, 1916), 495.
317. "Reaction of Simple Women to Trade Union Propaganda," *ibid.*, XXXVI (July 1, 1916), 364–6. This is excerpted from Chapter IV of number 310.
318. "War Times Challenging Woman's Traditions," *ibid.*, XXXVI (August 5, 1916), 475–8. This is excerpted from Chapter V of number 310.
319. "The Devil Baby at Hull House," *Atlantic*, CXVIII (October, 1916), 441–51. Material included in this article appeared as Chapters I and II of number 310.
320. "Disturbing Conventions," *Survey*, XXXVII (October 7, 1916), 1–5. This is a reprinting of Chapter III of number 310.
321. "Why Women Should Vote," in Frances M. Bjorkman and Anna G. Porritt (eds.), *Woman Suffrage, History, Arguments and Results* (New York, 1917),

pp. 110–29. This is another edition of number 287, and a reprinting of number 182.

322. Testimony, in U.S. House of Representatives, Committee on the Judiciary, *Espionage and Interference with Neutrality, Hearings on H. R. 291, April 9 and 12, 1917,* Serial LIII, Part 2, 65th Cong., 1st Sess., 1917, pp. 50–52.

323. Statement, in U.S. House of Representatives, Committee on Military Affairs, *Volunteer and Conscription System,* 65th Cong., 1st Sess., 1917, pp. 20–2.

324. Statement, in U.S. House of Representatives, Committee on Military Affairs, *Selective-Service Act, Hearings on the Bill Authorizing the President to Increase Temporarily the Military Establishment of the United States,* 65th Cong., 1st Sess., 1917, pp. 238–40. This is a reprinting of number 323.

325. "What Jane Addams Learned from the Devil Baby," *Current Opinion,* LXII (January, 1917), 44–5. This is excerpted from number 319.

326. "Patriotism and Pacifists in Wartime," *City Club* [*of Chicago*] *Bulletin,* X (June 18, 1917), 184–90.

327. "Labor as a Factor in the Newer Conception of International Relationships," in Academy of Political Science, *Proceedings,* VII (July, 1917), 282–8.

328. "Are Pacifists Cowards?" *Unity,* LXXIX (July 19, 1917), 331. This is excerpted from number 326.

329. "Tolstoy and the Russian Soldiers," *New Republic,* XII (September 29, 1917), 240–2.

330. "Devil Baby at Hull House," in *Atlantic Classics, Second Series* (Boston, 1918), pp. 52–77. This is a reprinting of number 319.

331. "World's Food and World's Politics," in National Conference of Social Work, *Proceedings* (1918), pp. 650–6.

332. Discussion of state child care, *ibid.,* pp. 395–6.

333. "World's Food and World's Politics," in National Conference of Social Work, *Pamphlet,* CCXVIII (1918). This is a reprinting of number 331.

334. "Lest We Forget Toynbee Hall and Canon Barnett," in National Federation of Settlements, *Conference Report,* VIII (1918), 4–5.

335. "World's Food Supply and Woman's Obligation," in General Federation of Women's Clubs, *Biennial Convention,* XIV (1918), 251–63.

336. "World's Food Supply and Woman's Obligation," in National Education Association, *Journal of Addresses and Proceedings* (1918), pp. 108–13. This is a reprinting of number 335.

337. "Tolstoy and the Russian Soldiers," *Friends' Intelligencer,* LXXV (19th First Month 1918), 35–6. This is a reprinting of number 329.

338. "Tolstoy and the Russian Soldiers," *Unity,* LXXX (January 31, 1918), pp. 344–6. This is a reprinting of number 329.

339. "World's Food Supply and Woman's Obligation," *General Federation Magazine,* XVII (July, 1918), 11–5. This is a reprinting of number 335.

340. "World's Food Supply and Woman's Obligation," *Journal of Home Economics,* X (September, 1918), 389–400. This is a reprinting of number 335.

341. "The Corn Mother," *World Tomorrow,* I (November, 1918), 277–80. This is excerpted from number 335.

342. Memorial address for Jenkins Lloyd Jones, *Unity,* LXXXII (November 28, 1918), 148–9.

343. "Newer Ideals of Peace," in H. Stanley Redgrove and Jeanne Heloise Rowbottom, *An Indictment of War* (London, 1919), pp. 24–6. This is excerpted from number 128.

344. "Americanization," in American Sociological Society, *Publications,* XIV (1919), 206–14.

345. "A Tribute to Mary H. Wilmarth," in *Funeral Services for Mary Hawes*

Wilmarth at Hubbard Woods, Illinois, August 30, 1919 (n.p. [Chicago], n.d. [1919]), unpaged.

346. "Theodore Roosevelt—a Social Worker," *Survey*, XLI (January 18, 1919), 523.

347. Message, *Towards Peace and Freedom* (August, 1919), p. 1. This is excerpted from number 180.

348. "A Belated Industry," *Journal of Home Economics*, XI (August, 1919), 355–64. This is excerpted from number 27.

349. "After the Lean Years, Impressions of Food Conditions in Germany when Peace Was Signed," *Survey*, XLII (September 6, 1919), 793–97. The article was co-authored by Dr. Alice Hamilton.

350. "A Tribute (in Memory of Mary H. Wilmarth)," in Chicago Women's Club, *Bulletin*, III (October, 1919), 5–7. This is a revision of number 345.

351. "Report of Jane Addams and Dr. Hamilton to the American Friends' Service Committee on the Situation in Germany," in American Friends' Service Committee, *Bulletin*, XXV (November, 1919). This is a revision of number 349.

352. "Where the Christmas Spirit Will Wane," *Life Boat* (Hinsdale, Ill.), XXII (December, 1919), 353–6. This is excerpted from number 351.

353. Presidential address, International Congress of Women, Zurich, May 12–17, 1919, *Report*, 1920, pp. 1–3.

354. Speech, *ibid.*, pp. 195–8.

355. Closing address, *ibid.*, pp. 235–7.

356. "Immigration: a Field Neglected by the Scholar," in Philip Davis and Bertha Swartz (comps.), *Immigration and Americanization* (Boston, 1920), pp. 3–22. This is a reprinting of number 97.

357. "The Spirit of Social Service," in National Conference of Social Work, *Proceedings* (1920), pp. 41–3.

358. "The Immigrant and Social Unrest," in *ibid.*, pp. 59–62.

359. "Nationalism—a Dogma?" *Survey*, XLIII (February 7, 1920), 524–6. This is a reprinting of number 344.

360. Speech dedicating the Jenkins Lloyd Jones Chair of English Literature, *Unity*, LXXXV (May 13, 1920), 170–1.

361. "A Pioneer Settlement," *ibid.*, LXXXV (June 10, 1920), 233–7.

362. "A Pioneer Philanthropist," Review of *Canon Barnett*, by S. A. [*sic*] Barnett, *Yale Review*, n.s. IX (July, 1920), 867–72.

363. Memorial address for Judge Merritt W. Pinckney, *Unity*, LXXXV (July 1, 1920), 281.

364. "German Women Appeal from the Way of Violence," *World Tomorrow*, III (August, 1920), 251.

365. "Feed the World and Save the League," *New Republic*, XXIV (November 24, 1920), 325–7.

366. "Madeline McDowell Breckenridge," *Survey*, XLV (December 25, 1920), 469.

367. Testimony, in U.S. Senate, Committee on Banking and Currency, *Rehabilitation and Provisions for European Countries* (*Hearings Relative to Need of Assistance in Exporting our Goods and Rendering Financial Aid Generally in Rehabilitating European Countries*), 66th Cong., 3rd Sess., 1921.

368. "Some Phases of the Disarmament Conference," in Illinois Conference on Public Welfare, *Proceedings* (1921), pp. 11–4.

369. "Some Phases of the Disarmament Conference," in Illinois Department of Public Welfare, *Institutional Quarterly*, XII–XIII (September 30, 1921/June 30, 1922), 88–91. This is a reprinting of number 368.

370. The American Commission on Conditions in Ireland, *Interim Report* (n.p. [New York], n.d. [1921]). This is also signed by Frederic C. Howe, James G. Maurer, Oliver P. Newman, George W. Norris, Norman Thomas, and L. Hollingsworth Wood.

371. Presidential address, in International Congress of Women, *Report*, III [1921], 1–3.

372. Testimony, in *Evidence on Conditions in Ireland: Comprising the Complete Testimony, Affidavits and Exhibits Presented before the American Commission on Conditions in Ireland, Transcribed and Annotated by Albert Coyle, Official Report to the Commission* (Washington, n.d. [1921]).

373. "What is the Practical Ideal of Protection and Care for Children Born Out of Wedlock?" in U.S., Children's Bureau, *Bureau Publications*, LXXVII (1921), 35–7.

374. "Chicago's School of Social Service Administration," *Survey*, XLVI (May 21, 1921), 220–21.

375. "Potential Advantages of the Mandate System," *Annals*, XCVI (July, 1921), 70–4.

376. "Disarmament and Life," *Church Militant* (October, 1921, Supplement), pp. lv–lvi. This is a reprinting of number 368.

377. "Disarmament and Life," in National Peace Council, Joint Disarmament Committee, *Disarmament Pamphlet*, II (October, 1921). This is a reprinting of number 368.

378. "The Attack on War," *Christian Century*, XXXVIII (October 13, 1921), 10–12. This is a reprinting of number 368.

379. "Peace and Bread, I. A Speculation on Bread-Labor and War Slogans," *Survey*, XLVII (December 31, 1921), 527–30.

380. *Peace and Bread in Time of War.* New York, 1922. Chapter V, includes material published in number 379.

381. "Aftermath of the War," *Christian Century*, XXXIX (January 5, 1922), 10–2. Excerpted from number 380, Chapter IX.

382. "Why the League Limps," *ibid.*, XXXIX (January 19, 1922), 71–4. This is excerpted from number 380, Chapter X.

383. "Peace and Bread, II. President Wilson's Policies, III. Personal Reactions during the War," *Survey*, XLVII (January 28, 1922), 659–63. This is excerpted from number 380, Chapters III and IV.

384. "What I Saw in Europe," *La Follette's Magazine*, XIII (February, 1922), 20–1.

385. "Peace and Bread, IV. Witness Borne by Women," *Survey*, XLVII (February 25, 1922), 842–4. This is excerpted from Chapter IV of number 380.

386. "The Threat of World Starvation," in Kansas State Board of Agriculture, *Report*, XLI (January–March, 1922), pp. 75–9.

387. "Washington's Birthday," in Ashley H. Thorndike (ed.), *Modern Eloquence* (New York, 1923), I, 16–9. This is a reprinting of number 71.

388. "Seconding the Nomination of Roosevelt for President, 1912," in *ibid.*, VIII, 1–2. This is a reprinting of number 216.

389. "In Memory of Henry Lloyd," in *ibid.*, IX, 1–5. This is a reprinting of number 76. Subsequent revised editions of *Modern Eloquence* published in 1928, 1936, and 1941 contain numbers 387, 388, and 389 with the same volume and page numberings.

390. *Christmas Message for 1923* (n.p., n.d.).

391. Speech, *City Club [of Chicago] Bulletin*, XVI (October 22, 1923), 117–8.

392. "A New Political Method Emerging in the Orient," in Illinois League of Women Voters, *Bulletin*, III (December, 1923), 11.

393. "International Co-operation for Social Welfare," in National Conference of Social Work, *Proceedings* (1924), pp. 107–13.

394. *Opening Address as President of the Women's International League for Peace and Freedom, at the Fourth Biennial Congress, Washington, May 1–8, 1924* (Geneva, n.d. [1924]).

395. Preface, Women's International League for Peace and Freedom, *Congress Report*, IV [1924], vii–xi.

396. "Opening Address," *ibid.*, pp. 1–3. This is a reprinting of number 394.

397. "Whoso Liveth to Himself," *Survey*, LI (January 15, 1924), 373. This is a reprinting of number 390.

398. "Intimate Glimpses," *City Club of [Chicago] Bulletin*, XVII (February 11, 1924), 22–3.

399. "Is Woman Suffrage Failing?" *Woman Citizen*, VIII (April 19, 1924), 15–6.

400. "Why I Shall Vote for La Follette," *New Republic*, XL (September 10, 1924), 36–7.

401. Introduction, in *The Child, the Clinic and the Court, a Group of Papers* (New York, 1925), pp. 1–2.

402. "Impressions of Mexico," in Women's International League for Peace and Freedom, United States Section, *Bulletin*, XIV (April/May 1925), unpaged.

403. "How Much Social Work Can a Community Afford?" in National Conference of Social Work, *Proceedings* (1926), pp. 108–13.

404. "New Methods of Procedure," Women's International League for Peace and Freedom, *Congress Report*, V (1926), 63–5.

405. Foreword, in Winthrop D. Lane, *Military Training in Schools and Colleges in the United States, the Facts and an Interpretation* (n.p. [New York], n.d. [1926]), pp. 3–4. The foreword is co-signed by fifty-seven other people.

406. "The World Court," *Republican Woman*, III (February, 1926), 7–8.

407. "My Greetings to the Youth's Companion," *Youth's Companion*, C (February 4, 1926), 90.

408. Letter to the editor, *Pax International*, I (June, 1926), unpaged.

409. "New Methods of Procedure," *ibid.*, I (August, 1926), unpaged. This is a reprinting of number 404.

410. "Generous Impulses in Politics," *ibid.*, I (September, 1926), unpaged.

411. "New Methods of Procedure," *Unity*, XCVIII (September 6, 1926), 15. This is a reprinting of number 404.

412. "How Much Social Work Can a Community Afford?" *Survey*, LVII (November 15, 1926), pp. 199–201. This is a reprinting with minor deletions of number 403.

413. "Problem of Crime Unsolved, Let Us Start Anew," in American Crime Study Commission, *The Prevention and Cure of Crime* (n.p., 1927), pp. 26–8.

414. "The Hopes We Inherit," in *Building International Goodwill* (New York, 1927), 3–18. This is co-authored by E. G. Balch.

415. "Social Consequences of the Immigration Law," in National Conference of Social Work, *Proceedings* (1927), pp. 102–6.

416. "A Book that Changed My Life," *Christian Century*, XLIV (October 13, 1927), 1196–8.

417. "Chicago's Mayor Turns Censor," *Woman Citizen*, XII (December, 1927), 15, 39.

418. Introduction, in Abraham Epstein, *The Challenge of the Aged* (New York, 1928), pp. xi–xiii.

419. Statement, in *Liber Amicorum Romain Rolland* (n.p. [Zurich], n.d. [1928]), pp. 9–10.

420. Foreword, in Howard E. Wilson, *Mary McDowell, Neighbor* (Chicago, 1928), pp. ix–xi.
421. Preface, in Giovanni Ermenegildo Schiavo, *Italians in Chicago, a Study of Americanization* (Chicago, 1928), p. [5].
422. "Social Attitudes and Character," in *Building Character: Proceedings of the Mid-West Conference on Parent Education, February 1928* (Chicago, 1928), pp. 291–5.
423. Presidential address, in Pan-Pacific Woman's Conference, Honolulu, *Women of the Pacific, Proceedings of the Pan-Pacific Woman's Conference*, I (1928), 13–4.
424. "Sailing Orders," *Neighborhood*, I (January, 1928), 3.
425. "The Importance to America of the Josephine Butler Centenary," *Social Service Review*, II (March, 1928), 10–23.
426. "Pioneers in Sociology," *Neighborhood*, I (July, 1928), 6–11.
427. "What to Do Then," *Russian Student*, V (September, 1928), 19–22. This is a revision of number 416.
428. "Tolstoy, Prophet of Righteousness," *Unity*, CII (September 10, 1928), 11–2. This is a reprinting of number 427.
429. "Address to the Pan-Pacific Women's Conference, *Pax International*, III (October, 1928), unpaged. This is a reprinting of number 423.
430. "The Opening of a Women's Congress," *Mid-Pacific*, XXVI (October, 1928), 303–6.
431. "Graham Taylor—Pioneer in Sociology," *Chicago Theological Seminary Register*, XVIII (November, 1928), 17–28. This includes number 426.
432. President's Address, in Women's International League for Peace and Freedom, *Congress Report*, VI (1929), 13–5.
433. "Women and War," in F. C. Hicks (ed.), Famous Speeches by *Eminent American Statesmen* (St. Paul, 1929), pp. 439–43. This is a reprinting of number 283.
434. Statement, in Anna Morgan (comp. and ed.), *Tribute to Henry B., from Friends in Whose Minds and Hearts He Will Live Always* (n.p., 1929), p. 129.
435. Address, in Illinois Conference on Public Welfare, *Proceedings* (1929), 10–1.
436. "Law—Not War," review of *Law or War*, by Lucia Ames Mead, *World Tomorrow*, XII (April, 1929), 183.
437. "After Sixty-Five," *Survey*, LXII (June 1, 1929), 303.
438. "The Settlement as a Way of Life," *Neighborhood*, II (July, 1929), 139–46.
439. "The Pageant of Emancipation," *Woman's Press*, XXIII (August, 1929), 525–8.
440. "Opening Speech at Prague Congress," *Pax International*, IV (September, 1929), unpaged. This is a reprinting of number 432.
441. "Decade of Prohibition," *Survey*, LXIII (October 1, 1929), 5–10.
442. "Prohibition as Seen from Hull House," *Literary Digest*, CIII (October 19, 1929), 22–3. This is excerpted from number 441.
443. "Safety in the Home," in National Broadcasting Company, *Second Universal Safety Series* (October 23, [1929]), unpaged.
444. "Immigrants under the Quota," *Survey*, LXIII (November 1, 1929), 135–9.
445. "Toast to John Dewey," *ibid.*, LXIII (November 15, 1929), 203–4.
446. "Safety in the Home," *American Labor Legislation Review*, XIX (December, 1929), 409–10. This is excerpted from number 443.
447. "Immigrants under the Quota," *Review of Reviews*, LXXX (December, 1929), 94–5. This is excerpted from number 444.

448. "Appreciation of A. S. B. [Alice Stone Blackwell]," *Woman's Journal*, n.s. XIV (December, 1929), 10.
449. "Efforts to Humanize Justice," *Survey*, LXIII (December 1, 1929), 275–8.
450. Memorial address, in *Helen Castle Mead* (n.p., n.d. [1930]), pp. 19–23.
451. "Jane Addams," in Helen J. Ferris (ed.), *When I Was a Girl; the Stories of Five Famous Women as Told by Themselves* (New York, 1930), pp. 167–222. This is excerpted from number 180.
452. "Reflections on the First Pan-Pacific Women's Conference," in Pan-Pacific Women's Conference, Honolulu, *Record of Proceedings*, II (1930), ix–x.
453. "Social Workers and the Other Professions," in National Conference of Social Work, *Proceedings* (1930), pp. 50–4.
454. "John Dewey and Social Welfare," in Henry W. Holmes (ed.), *John Dewey: the Man and His Philosophy* (Cambridge, Mass., 1930), pp. 140–52. This is a reprinting of number 445.
455. *The Second Twenty Years at Hull-House, September 1909 to September 1929, with a Record of a Growing World Consciousness.* New York, 1930. Chapter IV includes a reprinting of number 452. Chapter VI includes a reprinting of number 390. Chapter VIII includes a reprinting of number 441. Chapter IX includes a reprinting of number 444. Chapter X includes a reprinting of number 449.
456. "What Is Security? How Does Each Naval Power, Including Germany, Define Security; and What Agreements or Armaments Does Each Believe Necessary to Maintain Peace? How Far Does Each Country Depend upon Political Agreement; How Far upon Armaments Held in Readiness for War?" *Conference on the Cause and Cure of War*, VI (1930), 33–40.
457. "Widening the Circle of Enlightenment, Hull House and Adult Education," *Journal of Adult Education*, II (June, 1930), 276–9.
458. "Aspects of the Woman's Movement," *Survey*, LXIV (August 1, 1930), 384–7. This is a reprinting of Chapter IV of number 455.
459. "Education by the Current Event," *ibid.*, LXIV (September 1, 1930), 461–4. This is a reprinting of Chapter XII of number 455.
460. "Contrasts in a Post-War Generation," *ibid.*, LXV (October 1, 1930), 21–5. This is a reprinting of Chapter VII of number 455.
461. "The Post-War Generation," *Pax International*, VI (November, 1930), unpaged. This is excerpted from Chapter VII of number 455.
462. "The Play Instinct and the Arts," *Religious Education*, XXV (November, 1930), 808–19. This is a reprinting of Chapter XI of number 455.
463. Statement, in Ramananda Chatterjee (ed.), *The Golden Book of Tagore, a Homage to Rabindranath Tagore from India and the World in Celebration of His Seventieth Birthday* (Calcutta, 1931), p. 19.
464. Introduction, in Victor Lefebure, *Scientific Disarmament* (New York, 1931), p. 8.
465. "Tribute," in Sydney D. Strong (ed.), *What I Owe to My Father* (New York, 1931), pp. 1–8. This is an excerpt from number 180.
466. *Social Consequences of Business Depressions.* Chicago, 1931.
467. "Twenty Years at Hull House," in Clara L. Myers (ed.), *Readings in Biography* (New York, 1931), pp. 277–92. This is excerpts from number 180.
468. "Casting Out Fear," *Pax International*, VI (February, 1931), unpaged.
469. "Reply," *Bryn Mawr Alumnae Bulletin*, IX (June, 1931), 5.
470. "A Needed Implement to Social Reform," *Unitarian Register and News-letter,* CX (June 4, 1931), 464–5.
471. "A Needed Implement in Social Reform," *Christian Leader*, XXXIV (June 20, 1931), 778–80. This includes the material in number 470.

472. "Through Disarmament Nations Will Substitute Political for Military Arrangements," *International Disarmament Notes*, IV (August 17, 1931), [1].

473. "Not Afraid of Unpopular Causes," *Progressive*, II (November 7, 1931), 3.

474. "Tolstoy and Gandhi," *Christian Century*, XLVIII (November 25, 1931), 1485-8.

475. "The Process of Social Transformation," in Charles A. Beard (ed.), *A Century of Progress* (New York, 1932), pp. 234-52. A revised edition which was published in 1933 retained the same pagination.

476. *The Excellent Becomes the Permanent*. New York, 1932. The memorial to Sarah Rozet Smith is a reprinting of number 82. The memorial to Henry Demarest Lloyd is a reprinting with a small deletion of number 76. The memorial to Judge Murray F. Tuley is a reprinting with slight changes of number 116. The memorial to Mary Hawes Wilmarth is an excerpt with many revisions of number 345. The memorial to Canon Samuel A. Barnett uses excerpts from numbers 334 and 362. Chapter XII is a reprinting of number 270.

477. "Social Consequences of Business Depressions," in Felix Morley (ed.) *Aspects of the Depression* (Chicago, 1932), pp. 12-21. This is a reprinting of number 466.

478. "The Friend and Guide of Social Workers," in *Ernest Freund, 1864-1932* (n.p., n.d. [1932]), pp. 43-5.

479. "Social Consequences of the Depression," *Survey*, LXVII (January 1, 1932), 370-1. This is a reprinting of number 466.

480. "Disarm and Have Peace, a Pacifist Plea to End War," *Liberty*, IX (March 12, 1932), 25.

481. "The Excellent Becomes the Permanent," *Illinois Voter*, XII (June, 1932), 3.

482. "A Great Public Servant, Julia C. Lathrop," *Social Service Review*, VI (June, 1932), 280-5. This is an expanded version of number 481.

483. "How to Build a Peace Program," *Survey*, LXVIII (November 1, 1932), 550-3.

484. "Social Deterrent of Our National Self-Righteousness; with Correctives Suggested by the Courageous Life of William Penn," *Friends' Intelligencer*, LXXXIX (Eleventh month 5, 1932), 890-5.

485. "The Education of Negroes," *Opportunity*, X (December, 1932), 370-1.

486. Introduction, in Leo Tolstoy, *What Then Must We Do?* trans. Alymer Maude (Oxford, 1933), pp. vii-xiii. This is a revision with additions of number 416.

487. "The Philosophy of a New Day," in *Our Common Cause—Civilization, Report to the International Congress of Women, Chicago, 1933, Including the Series of Round Tables, 16-22 July 1933* (New York, 1933), pp. 65-8.

488. "Introduction to the Forum," "Response," and remarks, in *ibid.*, pp. 185, 203, 204, 210, 213, 216, 218, 242-3.

489. Discussion, in Thomas H. Reed (ed.), *Legislatures and Legislative Problems* (Chicago, 1933), pp. 1-9.

490. "The Rise in Negro Education," *School Life*, XVIII (January, 1933), 98. This is excerpted from number 485.

491. "Friend and Guide of Social Workers—Ernest Freund," *University [of Chicago] Record*, XIX (January, 1933), 43-5. This is a reprinting of number 478.

492. "The Social Deterrent of our National Self-Righteousness with Correctives Suggested by the Courageous Life of William Penn," *Survey Graphic*, XXII (February, 1933), 98-101. This is a reprinting with a few deletions of number 484.

493. "Our National Self-Righteousness," *University [of Chicago] Magazine*, XXVI (November, 1933), 8–10. This is a reprinting with several deletions of number 484.

494. "Pioneering in Social Work," *Federation News*, I (November, 1933), 1–2.

495. "Exaggerated Nationalism and International Comity," in William H. Cordell (ed.), *Molders of American Thought, 1933–1934* (New York, 1934), pp. 43–51.

496. "Is a United Peace Front Desirable?" *Survey Graphic*, XXIII (February, 1934), 60. This is co-authored by Emily Greene Balch.

497. "A Feminist Physician Speaks: a Review of Rachelle S. Yarros' *Modern Woman and Sex*," *Survey*, LXX (February, 1934), 59.

498. "Exaggerated Nationalism and International Comity," *Survey Graphic*, XXIII (April, 1934), 168–70. This is a reprinting of number 495.

499. "Letters of Julia Lathrop," *Survey*, LXX (May, 1934), 174. This is co-signed by Grace Abbott.

500. "Because Wars Interfere with the Normal Growth of Civilization," in Rose Young (ed.), *Why Wars Must Cease* (New York, 1935), 129–39. Much of this material is reprinted from number 495.

501. Statement, in Herman Bernstein, *Can We Abolish War?* (New York, 1935), pp. 30–1. This is excerpted from number 414.

502. "Opening the First Session, June 18, 1933," in Charles Frederick Weller (ed.), *World Fellowship, Addresses and Messages by Leading Spokesmen of All Faiths, Races, and Countries* (New York, 1935), pp. 11–2.

503. *My Friend, Julia Lathrop*. New York, 1935. Material originally published in numbers 481 and 482 is included in this book.

504. "Julia Lathrop and Outdoor Relief in Chicago, 1893–1894," *Social Service Review*, IX (March, 1935), 24–33. This is a reprinting of Chapter V, number 503.

505. "Child Labor Amendment—Yes," *Rotarian*, XLVI (March, 1935), 12–5.

506. "Old Age Security," *Booklist*, XXXI (March, 1935), 215.

507. "In Memoriam," *National Parent Teacher*, XXIX (May, 1935), 24.

508. "Julia Lathrop's Services to the State of Illinois," *Social Service Review*, IX (June, 1935), 191–211. This is a reprinting of number 503, Chapter VII.

509. "There Is a River," *Advance*, CXXVII (June 6, 1935), 444.

510. "The Home," *Unity*, CXV (July 15, 1935), 186.

511. "Julia Lathrop at Hull House," *Survey Graphic*, XXIV (August, 1935), 373–7. This is excerpted from number 503.

512. "Julia Lathrop at Hull House. II Women and the Art of Government," *ibid.*, XXIV (September, 1935), 434–8. This is excerpted from number 503.

513. "Julia Lathrop at Hull House, III Young People and Old Laws," *ibid.*, XXIV (October, 1935), 488–92. This is excerpted from number 503.

514. "The Profession of Social Service," in Earl G. Lockhart (comp.), *My Vocation, by Eminent Americans: or What Eminent Americans Think of Their Callings* (New York, 1938), pp. 311–23. This is co-authored by Edith A. Abbott.

WRITINGS ABOUT JANE ADDAMS: GENERAL

I have already noted my dependence on James Weber Linn, *Jane Addams, a Biography* (New York & London, 1937), for much of the personal detail which informed this study. No other source approaches Linn's in completeness and thoroughness. Linn self-consciously tried to suppress family pride in his aunt's accomplishments. He decided, perhaps wisely, not to try to estimate Miss Addams' place in American history, but did the job for which he was best qualified: he described her personality. Jane Addams' niece has left a shorter biography; Marcet Haldeman-Julius, " Jane Addams As I Knew Her," *Reviewer's Library*, VII [1936], 1–29, is full of sharp insights into Jane Addams' personality. Mrs. Haldeman-Julius was a perceptive and independent author who criticized her aunt's beliefs from her own position as a socialist. In her introduction to the John Harvard library edition of Jane Addams, *Democracy and Social Ethics* (Cambridge, Mass., 1964), pp. vii–lxxv, Anne Firor Scott emphasizes Jane Addams' life as an example of the changing role of women in America. Mrs. Scott singles out as key elements in Jane Addams' thought " Darwinism, ' experience,' pragmatism, and personal value " (p. xlv). Less valuable than Mrs. Scott's able introduction is Margaret Tims, *Jane Addams of Hull House, 1860–1935, a Centenary Study* (London, 1961). Mrs. Tims, a leader in the British section of the Women's International League for Peace and Freedom, did not consult manuscript collections in America. She depended too heavily on Miss Addams' two autobiographical accounts. This dependence limits her study to a kind of summary of Miss Addams' own reflections on her life, supplemented by Linn's biography.

Merle Curti, " Jane Addams on Human Nature," *Journal of the History of Ideas*, XXII (April–June 1961), 240–53, is a most useful summary of Miss Addams' place in American intellectual history. Of similar interest, although less extensive, is Jill Conway, " Jane Addams: an American Heroine," *Daedalus*, XCIII (Spring, 1964), 761–80. Two other general treatments deserve mention as informing my study: Robert M. Hutchins, " ' The Nurture of Human Life,' " in Center for the Study of Democratic Institutions, *Bulletin*, X (March, 1961), 1–7, and Archibald MacLeish, " Jane Addams and the Future," *Social Service Review*, XXXV (March, 1961), 1–5. Mr. MacLeish, whose mother was the first president of Rockford College, appropriately emphasizes the Rockford heritage of duty, Jane Addams' commitment to *do* something. Donald Meiklejohn, " Jane Addams and American Democracy," *ibid.*, XXIV (September, 1960), 253–64, emphasized and interpreted this sense of duty. An interesting interpretation of Jane Addams' life appeared in Herbert M. Davidson, " Life Means Opportunity to Work for Humanity," New York *World*, July 22, 1928, editorial section, p. 1. On the more restricted topic of the radical quality of Jane Addams' thought, see Staughton Lynd, " Jane Addams and the Radical Impulse," *Commentary*, XXXII (July, 1961), 54–9, and Daniel Levine, " Jane Addams: Romantic Radical, 1889–1912," *Mid-America*, XLIV (October, 1962), 195–210. Margaret Carol Dunne, " Jane Addams as a Political Leader " (unpublished Master's essay, University of Chicago, 1926), was of little value. The title of a strange little book set me thinking about the large problem in Miss Addams' thought. Charles Kuhlman, *Pacifism as the Unifying Thesis of All Social Reform* (Boston, 1922), excoriates reformers and all their works. Kuhlman's arguments are like Herbert Spencer's and William Graham Sumner's. Much of his book is vituperation of the least interesting kind, but his title first provoked my efforts to analyze the relation between Miss Addams' reform thought and her pacifism.

I have used several accounts of American progressive reform. Two contemporary books remain valuable. William English Walling, *Progressivism—and after* (New York, 1914), and Benjamin P. DeWitt, *The Progressive Movement, a Non-Partisan, Comprehensive Discussion of Current Tendencies in American Politics* (New York, 1915), are both perceptive and useful statements. For excitement and enthusiasm, Eric F. Goldman's *Rendezvous with Destiny, a History of Modern American Reform* (New York, 1952) is difficult to match. Charles A. Madison, *Critics and Crusaders, a Century of American Protest* (New York, 1959), is tame and predictable by comparison. Madison's treatment of Randolph Bourne is better than many other sections of his book; I have drawn on it. Daniel Aaron, *Men of Good Hope, a Story of American Progressives* (New York, 1951), is a generally helpful, well-written treatment. Henry Steele Commager, *The American Mind, an Interpretation of American Thought and Character since the 1880's* (New Haven, 1950), includes progressive reform among other broader considerations, for which Professor Commager provides a full bibliography. Two other books were of general use in acquainting me with this period. Henry F. May, *The End of American Innocence, a Study of the First Years of Our Own Time, 1912–1917* (New York, 1959), although cumbered by obtuse categories, contains many valuable insights. Blake McKelvey, *The Urbanization of America, 1860–1915* (New Brunswick, 1963), is a comprehensive and concise account. Lloyd R. Morris tells his story in a lively and imaginative way in *Postscript to Yesterday, America: The Last Fifty Years* (New York, 1947).

More specialized and important for this study were: Richard Hofstadter, *Social Darwinism in American Thought* (Philadelphia, 1944), and Morton White, *Social Thought in America, the Revolt against Formalism* (Boston [1947] 1957). Both studies concentrate on the intellectual bases of progressive reform, as does Charles Forcey's fine book, *The Crossroads of Liberalism; Croly, Weyl, Lippmann, and the Progressive Era, 1900–1925* (New York, 1961). David W. Noble supplements White and Hofstadter in his sophisticated *Paradox of Progressive Thought* (Minneapolis, 1958). I have relied on Professor Noble's useful discussion of these reformers, especially Henry Demarest Lloyd and Thornstein Veblen. Arthur Mann, " British Social Thought and American Reformers of the Progressive Era," *Mississippi Valley Historical Review*, XLII (March, 1956), 672–92, is also relevant.

For a more general background on the period of this study I have consulted Ida M. Tarbell, *The Nationalizing of Business, 1878–1898*, Vol. IX in the " History of American Life Series," edited by Arthur M. Schlesinger and Dixon Ryan Fox (New York, 1936), which remains a dependable narrative of political and economic events. Mathew Josephson, *The Politicos* (New York, 1938) and *The Robber Barons, the Great American Capitalists, 1861–1901* (New York, 1934) are also useful, if dated, accounts of these same events. Harold U. Faulkner, *The Quest for Social Justice, 1898–1914*, Vol. XI in the " History of American Life Series " (New York, 1931) has been superceded by the vast amount of recent study and writing on the progressives. This scholarship has failed to persuade Faulkner to change his ideas about the period in any substantial way and his *Politics, Reform and Expansion, 1890–1900*, " New American Nation Series," edited by Henry Stele Commager and Richard B. Morris (New York, 1959), repeats many of his older formulations. Among those most responsible for new insights and understanding of progressivism is Richard Hofstadter, *American Political Tradition and the Men Who Made It* (New York, 1949) and *The Age of Reform: from Bryan to F. D. R.* (New York, 1955). Hofstadter works out in convincing detail the argument of Frank T. Carlton, " Humanitarianism, Past and Present," *International Journal of Ethics*, XVII (October, 1906), 48–55, that a class losing its hold upon " social and political influence," upon " social and economic supremacy invariably produces humanitarian (reform) leaders " (p. 52). Much of this argument is irrelevant to an understanding of the motivation of women reformers in the progressive era. Unenfranchised, their personal political influence was not striking. Their economic independence was improving, their social supremacy secure. For a wonderfully extravagant account of these matters see Chapter I, " The Titaness," in Thomas Beer, *The Mauve Decade, American Life at the End of the 19th Century* (New York [1926] 1961). George E. Mowry, *Theodore Roosevelt and the Progressive Movement* (Madison, 1946), and *Era of Theodore Roosevelt and the Birth of Modern America, 1900–1912*, " New American Nation

Series " (New York, 1958), are most helpful. I have depended on both volumes in specific detail and in matters of interpretation of progressivism. My ideas about progressivism have also been broadened by Arthur S. Link, *Woodrow Wilson and Progressive Era, 1910–1917*, "New American Nation Series" (New York, 1954), and the volumes of his uncompleted *Wilson* (Princeton, 1947—). The two volumes in a "Chicago History of American Civilization," Samuel P. Hays, *Response to Industrialism 1885–1914* (Chicago, 1957), and William E. Leuchtenburg, *The Perils of Prosperity, 1914–1932* (Chicago, 1958), are nicely handled summaries. Leuchtenburg's study gains luster by the pedestrian quality of John D. Hicks's treatment of the same material in his *The Republican Ascendency 1921–1933*, "New American Nation Series" (New York, 1960). Arthur Schlesinger, Jr., has made many interesting suggestions about progressivism in the first volume of his *Age of Roosevelt, The Crisis of the Old Order, 1919–1933* (Boston, 1957). Schlesinger suggests how the continuity between two reform impulses of 1912 and 1933 was especially the work of social workers, a theme argued in convincing detail by Clarke A. Chambers, *Seedtime of Reform, American Social Service and Social Action, 1918–1933* (Minneapolis, 1963). Finally Arthur Mann, *Yankee Reformers in an Urban Age* (Cambridge, Mass., 1954), was useful in several ways. His sympathetic account of Vida D. Scudder's career suggested interesting parallels with that of Ellen G. Starr, and his treatment of Robert A. Woods made me realize how different the settlement houses in Boston were from those in Chicago.

These secondary accounts need to be supplemented with the autobiographies of leading progressives. Jane Addams' two autobiographic volumes, the first a classic, are only part of a much larger literature which reveals a great deal about its authors. *The Autobiography of Lincoln Steffens* (New York, 1913); Theodore Roosevelt, *An Autobiography* (New York, 1913); *The Autobiography of William Allen White* (New York, 1946); Brand Whitlock, *Forty Years of It* (New York, 1914); and *LaFollette's Autobiography, a personal narrative of political experiences* (Madison [1913] 1960); all are of this genre. The autobiographies of settlement workers, while not as famous as these, were of great use to this study. See Vida Dutton Scudder, *On Journey* (New York, 1937); Lillian D. Wald, *Windows on Henry Street* (Boston, 1936); and two wonderful accounts by Alice Hamilton, *Exploring the Dangerous Trades*, and *The Autobiography of Alice Hamilton, M.D.* (Boston, 1943). Florence Kelley started an autobiography which appeared as " My Philadelphia," *Survey*, LVII (October 1, 1926), 7–11, 50–7; " When Co-Education Was Young," *ibid.*, LVII (February 1, 1927), 557–61, 600–2; " My Monitor," *ibid.*, LVIII (April 1, 1927), 31–5; " I Go to Work," *ibid.*, LVIII (June 1, 1927), 271–4, 301. These fragments should be supplemented by Josephine Goldmark, *Impatient Crusader: Florence Kelley's Life Story* (Urbana, 1953). Eleanor H. Woods' memoir of her husband, *Robert A. Woods, Champion of Democracy* (Boston & New York, 1929), imitates its subject by being stuffy and is most valuable for the letters it includes, many of which are now lost. Mary Heaton Vorse, *A Footnote to Folly, Reminiscences of Mary Heaton Vorse* (New York, 1935), also contained some useful information. There is a great richness of printed source material for understanding how progressives imagined themselves as reformers.

CHAPTER I: INTRODUCTION

I have not exhausted the available resources on the situation in Chicago. But I have tried to place Jane Addams in the local context at Halstead and Polk Streets and to describe local events when they were appropriate to the story I wanted to tell. I have not tried to write a history of Hull House or Hull House activities. The materials for a history of Chicago are enormously complex, especially for a historian interested in the interaction of immigrant and midwestern cultures. Bessie Louise Pierce has published three volumes in her *History of Chicago* (New York, 1937–57), which bring her narrative to 1893. Miss Pierce has delayed dealing with Hull House until her next volume, but her third volume, subtitled *The Rise of a Modern City, 1871–1893*, describes the background in a broad and reliable fashion. I have depended on her book heavily. Chester M. Destler, *American Radicalism, 1865–1900, Essays and Documents*, "Connecticut College Monographs," No. 3 (New London, 1946), contains several helpful chapters on the Chicago situation in the 1890's. Bernard Duffy, *The Chicago Renaissance in American Letters* (East Lansing, 1954), describes Chicago's genteel culture and the ferment and excitement of the city's cultural life in the late 1890's and early years of this century. For treatments of Jane Addams as a Chicagoan see Louise deKoven Bowen, *Baymeath* (n.p., 1934), and *Growing up with a City* (New York, 1926), and Edward Wagenknecht, *Chicago*, "Centers of Civilization Series" (Norman, Okla., 1964). The most understanding and entertaining account of the Chicago context of Jane Addams' activities is Francis Hackett, "Hull House—A Souvenir," *Survey*, LIV (June 1, 1925), 275–80. See also Edith Abbott's memoirs which were most helpful for the period 1908–21, in *Social Service Review*, XXIV (September–December, 1950), 374–94, 493–518, and her "Grace Abbott and Hull House" and "Hull House of Jane Addams," *ibid.*, XXVI (September, 1952), 334–8. Other articles that are especially revealing of the Chicago situation are Bertha Damaris Knobbe, "When Jane Addams Was Young, Some Incidents in the Early Life of the First Citizen of Chicago and the Founder of Hull House That Have Hitherto Been Unpublished," *Woman's World* (Chicago) XXXI (January, 1915), 7–8. Henry B. Fuller, "The Upward Movement in Chicago," *Atlantic Monthly*, LXXX (October, 1897), 534–47 is the best example of mugwump reform in Chicago. Three memoirs contain valuable information on the Chicago situation: Graham Taylor, *Pioneering on Social Frontiers* (Chicago, 1930); Louis P. Lochner, *Always the Unexpected, A Book of Reminiscences* (New York, 1956); and Robert Morss Lovett, *All Our Years, the Autobiography of Robert Morss Lovett* (New York, 1958). Finally I should like to credit Charles A. and Mary R. Beard, who in *The American Spirit, a Study of the Idea of Civilization in the United States* (New York, 1942), developed so forcefully a theme which has been my concern in this study.

CHAPTER II: ROCKFORD FEMALE SEMINARY—AND AFTER

For an introduction to the Illnois of Jane Addams' youth see Ray Ginger, *Altgeld's America, the Lincoln Ideal versus Changing Realities* (New York 1958). Tangential, but occasionally useful for my study, were Dixon Ryan Fox (ed.), *Sources of Culture in the Middle West, Backgrounds Versus Frontier* (New York & London, 1934), and John D. Davies, *Phrenology, Fad and Science, a 19th Century American Crusade* (New Haven, 1955).

The standard work on women's education is Thomas Woody, *A History of Women's Education in the United States* (2 vols.; New York & Lancaster, Penn., 1929). Professor Woody's book is an encyclopedia of information which he managed to subdue. He emphasized the importance of physical education. Mary Caroline Crawford, *The College Girl in America* (Boston, 1904), is useful for its description of college customs and its emphasis on the special value of the college woman "to the world as an exponent of culture. The future of American culture depends on the women." This same emphasis is extended in suggestive ways by Louise Schutz Boas, *Woman's Education Begins, the Rise of Women's*

Colleges (Norton, Mass., 1935), and Marion Talbot, *The Education of Women* (Chicago, 1910). Mrs. Talbot, who was dean of women at the University of Chicago, also wrote, with Lois Kimball Mathews Rosenberry, *The History of the American Association of University Women, 1881–1931* (Boston & New York, 1931), which is a valuable study of how college women regarded themselves. Anna Peck Sill patterned Rockford Seminary on Mary Lyon's Mount Holyoke. There are two good studies of the Massachusetts model. Sara D. (Locke) Stowe, *History of Mount Holyoke Seminary, South Hadley, Massachusetts during its First Half Century, 1837–1887* (Springfield, Mass., 1887), is a wonderfully dated description of the earnest life of duty and piety at the seminary. Arthur C. Cole, *A Hundred Years of Mount Holyoke College, the Evolution of an Educational Ideal* (New Haven, 1940), is a more modern and sober treatment. Mabel Newcomer, *A Century of Higher Education for American Women* (New York, 1959), was not useful for my purposes.

More especially on Rockford, Edward Dwight Eaton, *Historical Sketches of Beloit College* (New York, 1928), describes the sponsorship of Rockford and Beloit by transplanted New England Congregationalists and Presbyterians. Donald G. Tewksbury, *The Founding of American Colleges and Universities before the Civil War with Particular Reference to the Religious Influences Bearing Upon the College Movement* (Teachers College, Columbia University, "Contributions to Education," No. 543; New York, 1932), describes the supporting role of the Society for the Promotion of Collegiate and Theological Education in the West. Royal Brunson Way, *The Rock River Valley, Its History, Traditions, Legends and Charms . . .* (3 vols.; Chicago, 1926), is full of detail about the early days at the seminary. The centennial study commissioned by Rockford College, *Profiles of the Principals of Rockford Seminary and Presidents of Rockford College, 1847–1947* (Rockford, 1947), is an uneven series of essays. Sally Lou Coburn's essay on "Anna Peck Sill, 1852–1884," is adequate, but a more racy account is in the memorial booklet, *Memorials of Anna Peck Sill, First Principal of Rockford Female Seminary 1847–1889* (Rockford, 1889). Two books helped me understand the religious enthusiasm at Rockford: Timothy L. Smith, *Revivalism and Social Reform in Nineteenth Century America* (New York & Nashville, 1957), and Whitney R. Cross, *The Burned Over District, the Social and Intellectual History of Enthusiastic Religion in Western New York, 1800–1850* (Ithaca, 1950). The Cross study was especially relevant since Miss Sill grew up and "found her salvation" in the area and during the years about which he wrote.

Other aspects of Rockford can be appreciated through Dorothy S. Ainsworth, *The History of Physical Education in Colleges for Women, as Illustrated by Barnard, Bryn Mawr, Elmira, Goucher, Mills, Mount Holyoke, Radcliffe, Rockford, Smith, Vassar, Wellesley, and Wells* (New York, 1930), and Vida D. Scudder, *Social Ideals in English Letters* (New York & Boston [1896] 1910). Miss Scudder was almost exactly Miss Addams' contemporary. Miss Scudder's career at Smith and then Oxford and her founding of a college settlement in New York City in 1889 make her book important in understanding what literary ideals the humanitarians found in the standard English authors. I found insight on Mazzini, William Morris, and Ralph Waldo Emerson in a book by Jane Addams' friend, Henry Demarest Lloyd, *Mazzini and Other Essays* (New York, 1910). In addition to Miss Scudder's work I have consulted Frederick William Roe, *The Social Philosophy of Carlyle and Ruskin* (New York, 1921); James L. Halliday, *Mr. Carlyle My Patient, a Psychosomatic Biography* (New York, 1950); John A. Hobson, *John Ruskin, Social Reformer* (Boston, 1898); John Henry Raleigh, *Matthew Arnold and American Culture* ("University of California Publications, English Studies," No. 17; Berkeley & Los Angeles, 1957), and William Robbins, *The Ethical*

Idealism of Matthew Arnold, a Study of the Nature and Sources of His Moral and Religious Ideas (London, 1959). An awkwardly written, but important, synthesis of the thought of these men is Raymond Williams, *Culture and Society, 1780–1950* (Garden City [1958] 1960).

The literature on the settlement movement is extensive. For the American side of this story the standard works are Robert A. Woods and Albert J. Kennedy, *Handbook of Settlements* (New York, 1911), and their *The Settlement Horizon, a National Estimate* (New York, 1922). The first two chapters of the latter work describe briefly the English background. For a fuller understanding, I read Arnold Toynbee's *Industrial Revolution* (Boston [1884] 1956), the collection of lecture fragments so affected Toynbee's university friends. For a nice description of this personal impact see G. N. Clark, *The Idea of the Industrial Revolution* (Glasgow, 1953). Two of Toynbee's friends produced moving memoirs of their association with him. F. C. Montague, *Arnold Toynbee* ("Johns Hopkins University Studies in Historical and Political Science," VII; Baltimore, 1889), pp. 1–70, and Alfred Milner, *Arnold Toynbee, a Reminiscence* (London, 1895). A fine study of the intellectual background of these men is Melvin Richter, *The Politics of Conscience, T. H. Green and His Age* (Cambridge, Mass., 1964).

On the founding and early years of Toynbee Hall see Samuel Lane Loomis, *Modern Cities* (New York, 1889); Werner Picht's disenchanted *Toynbee Hall and the English Settlement Movement* (London, 1914); the authorized and useful J. A. R. Pimlott, *Toynbee Hall, Fifty Years of Social Progress, 1884–1934* (London, 1935). I have also used Will Reason (ed.), *University and Social Settlements* (London, 1898). Two articles particularly reveal the motives of many of the men who lived in English settlements. Samuel A. Barnett, "The Universities and the Poor," *Nineteenth Century*, LXXXIV (February, 1884), 255–61, reveals Barnett mulling over plans for what he later directed as Toynbee Hall. Edward Cummings, "University Settlements," *Quarterly Journal of Economics*, VI (April, 1892), 257–79, gives an unvarnished and forthright picture of the achievements and failings of settlements, especially Toynbee Hall. Canon and Mrs. Samuel A. Barnett write of their hopes in their *Practicable Socialism* (London, 1888), and their *Towards Social Reform* (London, 1909). Dame Henrietta Octavia Barnett wrote an awkward biography of her husband, *Canon Barnett, His Life, Work, and Friends* (London, 1918), filled with dubious recollections, partisan argument, and unnumbered letters and excerpts from his papers. In addition to Dame Henrietta's work I read Beatrice Webb's *My Apprenticeship* (London [1926] 1950), and William Thomson Hill's *Octavia Hill, Pioneer of the National Trust and Housing Reformer* (London, 1960). Both books enriched my understanding of the kind of people drawn to activities centered in Toynbee Hall.

CHAPTER III: HULL HOUSE—THE FIRST DECADE

There are several books that explained the English settlement movement to Americans. Loomis' volume, *Modern Cities*, has already been cited. Stanton Coit, who had lived at Toynbee Hall, wrote *Neighborhood Guilds: an Instrument for Social Reform* (London, 1891). Robert A. Woods, also a resident at Toynbee Hall, returned to Boston in 1891 and described the whole London charitable picture in *English Social Movements* (New York, 1891). Jane Addams frequently referred those who asked for background information to Woods' book.

The American pioneers in settlement work gathered at Plymouth, Mass., in the summer of 1892, and seven speeches delivered there were published as *Philanthropy and Social Progress* (New York, 1893). A revealing speech delivered there, not included in the volume, is V. D. Scudder, "The Place of University Settlements, II,"

Andover Review, XVIII (1892), 339–50. Another good explanation of the settlement impulse is in the series of papers read at the National Conference of Charities and Correction and printed in its *Proceedings* (1896). Julia Lathrop, Florence Kelley, Mary E. McDowell, and Graham Taylor have essays there. C. R. Henderson, *Social Settlements* (New York, 1899), is a good general statement, far better in explaining the motives and hope of the founders than Arthur C. Holden, *The Settlement Idea, a Vision of Social Justice* (New York, 1922).

Part of the vitality of the settlement approach was its dissatisfaction with organized charitable effort at the end of the nineteenth century. Robert H. Bremner, *From the Depths, the Discovery of Poverty in the United States* (New York, 1956), is an excellent account of how philanthropy was organized and the various tensions within this organization. This is also the theme of his more general *American Philanthropy* ("Chicago History of American Civilization"; Chicago, 1960). A valuable source work on these matters is Amos G. Warner, *American Charities, a Study in Philanthropy and Economics* (New York, 1894), a book that Jane Addams occasionally cited in her writings. Two studies of more conservative philanthropies are C. Howard Hopkins, *History of the Y.M.C.A. in North America* (New York, 1951), and Frank Dekker Watson, *The Charity Organization Movement in the United States, a Study of American Philanthropy* (New York, 1922). The most interesting settlement men and women became suspicious of the various city charity organization societies. The grounds for their suspicions are commented upon in Marvin E. Gettleman, "Charity and Social Classes in the United States, 1874–1900," *American Journal of Economics and Sociology,* XXII (1963), 313–29, 417–26. Evidence that the suspicion was mutual is found in Mary E. Richmond's pithy "Discussion of 'Settlement Work,'" *Charities Review,* IV (June, 1895), 462–3.

There is no good history of the development of social work. Two memoirs are basic, but neither pretends to be a systematic account: Graham Taylor, *Pioneering on Social Frontiers* (Chicago, 1930), and Edward T. Devine, *When Social Work Was Young* (New York, 1939). On a more specialized topic see Reinhold Niebuhr, *The Contribution of Religion to Social Work* (New York, 1932). Frank J. Bruno, *Trends in Social Work, 1874–1956* (New York, 1957), is an account based solely on the published proceedings of the National Conference of Charities and Correction, later the National Conference of Social Work, and presently the National Conference on Social Welfare. In addition to desultory reading in these proceedings, I have read the settlement periodical *The Commons* (April, 1896–October, 1905). It was published in Chicago by Graham Taylor who had ambitions to make his settlement's paper the national spokesman for the settlement movement. *The Commons* contains much local news as well as important national settlement news. I have not read the complete files of its successors. I have collected and used all available issues of the irregular Hull House *Bulletin,* 1896–1905/1906, and its successor the *Hull House Yearbook,* 1906/1907.

Since various religious motives were a crucial part of the settlement movement, it is fortunate that there are adequate studies of late nineteenth-century religion in America. Charles H. Hopkins, *Rise of the Social Gospel in American Protestantism, 1865–1915* (New Haven, 1940), is the standard work. A somewhat later treatment is Henry F. May, *Protestant Churches and Industrial America* (New York, 1949). See also Abel Aaron, *The Urban Impact on American Protestantism, 1865–1900* (Cambridge, Mass., 1943). More suggestive for my purposes were James Dombrowski, *Early Days of Christian Socialism in America* (New York, 1936). For an expression of these ideas coming directly out of the Chicago context see Shailer Mathews, "The Significance of the Church to the Social Movement," *American Journal of Sociology,* IV (1898–9), 603–20. Ellen Gates Starr retained her early piety and was converted to the Roman Catholic Church in 1920. On Miss Starr see Eleanor Grace Clark, "Ellen Gates Starr, O.S.B., 1859–1940, Life of the Co-foundress of Hull House," *Commonweal*, XXXI (March 15, 1940), 444–7. I am indebted to Jill Conway for suggesting that there was light on the kind of high-powered relationships which some of these women had with each other in K. A. McKenzie, *Edith Simcox and George Eliot* (Oxford, 1961). I asked Dr. Alice Hamilton whether there were erotic elements in these relationships. She told me that my question measured the distance between her generation and my own. Women of her generation would never have imagined female homosexuality as a basis for this kind of friendship, she said, and there was none of it in the settlement movement.

There are materials available to reconstruct the early history of Hull House, but they are scattered. The most helpful articles were some early newspaper stories: Eva Bright, "Work of Two Women," unidentified newspaper clipping in S. Alice Haldeman's Scrapbook in the Ellen Gates Starr Papers. See also Miss Mora Mants, "Two Women's Work," Chicago *Tribune*, May 19, 1890, p. 1, col. 7; "Pictures for the Poor," Chicago *Inter-Ocean*, June 21, 1891, p. 7, col. 6; and "Hull House Kitchen," *ibid.*, August 24, 1893, p. 8, col. 3. Two magazine articles before the settlement opened are revealing: Lelia G. Bedell, "A Chicago Toynbee Hall," *Woman's Journal*, XX (May 25, 1889), 162, was written by the woman who later came to talk to neighborhood women about physiology and hygiene; and Mary H. Porter, "A Home on Halstead Street," *Advance*, XXIII (July 11, 1889), 500.

The following articles were especially valuable in discovering the spirit of the early years at Hull House: Agnes Sinclair Holbrook, "Hull House," *Wellesley Magazine*, II (January 20, 1894), 171–80; W. D. Johnson, "The New Social Movement: Hull House," *Brown Magazine*, VI (November, 1894), 53–9; M. B. Powell, "Hull House," *Godey's Magazine*, CXXXII (May, 1896), 466–71; Dorthea Moore, "A Day at Hull House," *American Journal of Sociology*, II (March, 1897), 629–42; Florence Kelley, "Description and Work of Hull House," *New England Magazine*, XVIII (July, 1898), 550–66; Alzina P. Stevens, "Life in a Social Settlement—Hull House, Chicago," *Self-Culture Magazine*, IX (March, 1899), 42–51; A. B. Pond, "The Settlement House," *Brick Builder*, XI (July, August, September, 1902), 140–5, 160–4, 178–85; Charlotte Teller, "Miss Jane Addams, of Hull House, Chicago," *Everybody's*, VIII (February, 1903), 169–71; Edith A. Brown, "Jane Addams and Her Work," *Pilgrim*, VIII (January, 1904), 3–5; Anne Forsyth, "What Jane Addams Has Done for Chicago, a Fight for the Betterment of a Great City," *Delineator*, LXX (October, 1907), 493–7; and Nicholas Kelley, "Early Days at Hull House," *Social Service Review*, XXVIII (December, 1954), 424–9.

The most colorful entry into Chicago history in the 1890's is through William T. Strad's scarlet narrative *If Christ Came to Chicago, a Plea for the Union of All Who Love in the Service of All Who Suffer* (Chicago, 1894). The academic entry is through Charles Edward Merriam, *Chicago, a More Intimate View of Urban Politics* (New York, 1929). The most powerful women's organization has been described in Henriette Greenbaum Frank and Amalie Hofer Jerome (comps.), *Annals of the Chicago Woman's Club for the First Forty Years of Its Organization, 1876–1916* (Chicago, 1916). R. S. Baker perceptively described attempts by those at Hull House to deal with their corrupt alderman in his "Hull House and the Ward Boss," *Outlook*, LVIII (March 26, 1898), 769–71. The women at the settlement doubtless wrote "The Aldermanic Campaign," *Hull House Bulletin*, III (April–May, 1898), 4. The ultimate withdrawal of the alderman is recorded in "'Johnny' Powers Turns His Back on Chicago," Chicago *Record-Herald*, May

5, 1901), p. 41. Modern accounts of the campaigns against Powers are Sidney I. Roberts, "The Municipal Voters' League and Chicago's Boodlers," *Journal of the Illinois State Historical Society*, LIII (Summer, 1960), 117–48; Allen F. Davis, "Jane Addams *vs.* the Ward Boss," *ibid.*, LIII (Autumn, 1960), 247–65; and Anne Firor Scott, "Saint Jane and the Ward Boss," *American Heritage*, XII (December, 1960), 12–17, 94–9.

On immigrants in America see the first chapter, "The Influence of Immigration on American History," in Arthur Meier Schlesinger, *New Viewpoints in American History* (New York, 1922), and the book by one of Schlesinger's graduate students which develops some of his suggestions, Marcus Lee Hansen's *The Immigrant in American History*, ed., Arthur M. Schlesinger (Cambridge, Mass., 1948). Oscar Handlin has written an often moving story of immigrant adjustment to American life in *The Uprooted, the Epic Story of the Great Migrations that Made the American People* (New York, 1951). For a critique of this work, based on close study of the Italians in Chicago, and especially in the Hull House neighborhood, see Rudolph J. Vecoli, "*Contadini* in Chicago: A critique of *The Uprooted*," *Journal of American History*, LI (December, 1964), 404–17. Of considerable interest is Oscar and Mary Handlin's essay, "The United States," in *The Positive Contribution by Immigrants*, which is the third volume of UNESCO, "Population and Culture" (Paris, 1955). John Higham's fine book *Strangers in the Land, Patterns of American Nativism, 1860–1925* (New Brunswick, 1955), has been most helpful in estimating how the settlement workers differed from other Americans in their ideas about immigrants. Higham took "Another Look at Nativism," in the *Catholic Historical Review*, XLIV (1958), 147–58, and tried to relate status rivalries in American life to nativism. A helpful book on this topic and our movement for immigrant restriction, although limited to New England, is Barbara Miller Solomon, *Ancestors and Immigrants, a Changing New England Tradition* (Cambridge, Mass., 1956). Maldwyn A. Jones, *American Immigration*, "Chicago History of American Civilization" (Chicago, 1960), is a brief, scattered account.

CHAPTER IV: EDUCATIONAL THOUGHT

The books I found most helpful for a general understanding of educational thought were Lawrence A. Cremin, *The Transformation of the School, Progressivism in American Education, 1876–1957* (New York, 1961), and Merle Curti, *Social Ideals of American Educators*, Part X of A.H.A. Commission of the Social Studies in the School Report (New York, 1935). Cremin's book is nicely organized, clearly and cleverly written. His article, "The Revolution in American Secondary Education, 1893–1918," *Teacher's College Record*, LVI (March, 1955), 295–308, was also helpful. Cremin's work may be compared with John L. Childs, *American Pragmatism and Education, an Interpretation and Criticism* (New York, 1956). I also read Nancy Portia Potishman, "Jane Addams and Education" (unpublished Master's thesis, Columbia University, 1961), which was especially helpful for its bibliography.

Since John Dewey and Jane Addams were close associates, I sampled the trackless literature on Dewey and progressive education. I read John Dewey, *School and Society* (Chicago [1899] 1959), and *The Child and the Curriculum* (Chicago [1902] 1959). Dewey's interesting "The School as a Social Center," in National Education Association, *Journal of Proceedings and Addresses* (1902), pp. 373–83, reflects most clearly his experiences at Hull House. This theme is treated systematically in Chapter VIII, "The School as a Social Settlement," in John and Evelyn Dewey's *Schools of Tomorrow* (New York, 1915). John Dewey, *Democracy and Education, an Introduction to the Philosophy of Education* (New York [1916]

1961), makes explicit the hopes and aims of his educational philosophy. On Dewey see Paul Arthur Schilpp (ed.), *The Philosophy of John Dewey* (New York [1939] 1951); Oscar Handlin, *John Dewey's Challenge to Education, Historical Perspectives on the Cultural Context* (New York, 1959); and Max Eastman's essay on Dewey in his *Heroes I Have Known, Twelve Who Lived Great Lives* (New York, 1942). Dewey's early experiments are reported at great length in Katherine Camp Mayhew and Anna Camp Edwards, *The Dewey School, the Laboratory School of the University of Chicago, 1896–1903* (New York & London, 1936). Also valuable on the Chicago background were Robert L. McCaul, " Dewey's Chicago," *School Review*, LXVII (Summer, 1959), 258–80, and Robert Eugene Tostberg, "Educational Ferment in Chicago, 1883–1904" (unpublished Master's thesis, University of Wisconsin, 1960). Since Francis Wayland Parker's progressive educational experiments preceded Dewey's and since Tostberg says Parker " spoke frequently " at Hull House (p. 95), I also consulted Francis W. Parker's " An Account of the Work of the Cook County and Chicago Normal School from 1883 to 1889," *Elementary School Teacher and Course of Study*, II (June, 1902), 752–80, and Dewey's appreciation of Parker in his *Characters and Events: Popular Essays in Social and Political Philosophy*, I (New York, 1929), 95–99. On another important woman in this situation see John T. McManus, *Ella Flagg Young* (Chicago, 1916).

Important for Parker, Dewey, and Jane Addams was the kindergarten movement, and the educational philosophy of Froebel that underlay it. Two books in 1908 illustrated the connection between kindergartens and other aspects of progressive educational thought. Nina C. Vandewalker, *The Kindergarden in American Education* (New York, 1908), and Susan E. Blow, *Educational Issues in the Kindergarden*, Vol. 58 in " International Education Service," ed., William Torrey Harris (New York, 1908). *The Kindergarten Magazine* was published in Chicago and was filled with information on the local situation. Among the most helpful articles were two unsigned articles: " Evolution of the Kindergarten Idea in Chicago, Mrs. Alice H. Putnam and the Froebel Association," *Kindergarten Magazine*, V (June, 1893), 729–733, and " The Chicago Free Kindergarten Association," *ibid.*, 734–738. See also Nina C. Vandewalker, " The Kindergarten in the Chicago School System," *ibid.*, IX (May, 1897), 679–686, and Mary Jean Miller, " Account of the Chicago Kindergarten Club," *ibid.*, X (November, 1897), 203. Another article of interest, because it reports on James Addams' visit to Dr. Montessori's school in Rome, was Bertha Payne Newell's chapter on Alice H. Putnam in *Pioneers of the Kindergarten in America* (New York & London, 1924).

Besides Parker and Dewey, Jane Addams assimilated the kind of evolutionary theory associated with G. Stanley Hall. See his " The Contents of Children's Minds on Entering School," *Princeton Review*, II (May, 1883), 249–72; his " The Ideal School as Based on Child Study," *Forum*, XXXII (1901–2), 24–39; and of course his big work, *Adolescence, Its Psychology, and Its Relations to Physiology, Anthropology, Sociology, Sex, Crime, Religion and Education* (2 vols.; New York & London [1904] 1920). His study entitled *Youth, Its Education, Regimen, and Hygiene* (New York & London, 1907), is a summary of the practical and pedagogical conclusions of *Adolescence*. For a review of the literature of child study in Illinois from 1880–95 see Sara E. Wiltse, " A Preliminary Sketch of the History of Child Study in America," *Pedagogical Summary*, III (1891), (189)–212.

In *Youth*, Hall insists that " we really retain only the knowledge we apply (p. 33), and devotes two chapters to industrial education and manual training. Dewey formulated the idea in different words but industrial education was an important reform of early progressive educators. I read through the *Bulletin* of the National Society for the Promotion of Industrial Education for the years 1907–18.

On this organization, see Robert Ripley Clough, "The National Society for the Promotion of Industrial Education, Case Study of a Reform Organization, 1906–1914" (unpublished Master's thesis, University of Wisconsin, 1957). The standard work is Charles Alpheus Bennett, *History of Manual and Industrial Education, 1870–1917* (Peoria, 1937). The most important American advocate of manual training was C. M. Woodward. For his arguments in favor, see *Manual Training in Education* (London, 1890). A later argument which tries to show what new demands have been forced on public schools by rapid economic and industrial changes is Frank Tracy Carlton, *Education and Industrial Evolution* (New York, 1908). Katherine Elizabeth Dopp in *The Place of Industries in Elementary Education* (Chicago, 1905), argues for industrial education at the beginning levels of public education. M. W. Murray tries to illuminate the confusion in terminology in his "The Relation of Manual Training to Industrial Education," in National Education Association, *Journal of Proceedings and Addresses* (1908), pp. 786–92.

On the relation of social settlements to these educational movements, see Morris I. Berger, "The Settlement, the Immigrant, and the Public School, a Study of the Influence of the Settlement Movement and New Migration upon Public Education, 1890–1924" (unpublished Ph.D. dissertation, Columbia University, 1956). Adult education in the settlements is adequately described in Gaynell Hawkins, *Educational Experiments in Social Settlements* (New York, 1937). For various expressions of settlement pressure on the schools see Chapter V, "The Child," in Robert Hunter, *Poverty* (New York, 1904); Graham Taylor, "The Public School as a Social Center," *The Commons*, VI (December, 1901), 16–7; M. K. Simkovitch, "The Settlement and the Public School," *ibid.*, VIII (May, 1903), 10–2; and her "The Public School, Its Neighborhood Use as a Recreational and Social Center," *ibid.*, LX (September, 1904), 406–17. These attitudes are expressed systematically in Eleanor Tournoff Gluech, *Community Use of Schools* (Baltimore, 1927).

Information on the school board troubles is difficult to find. I read the printed report of the Chicago Board of Education which shed practically no light on the disputes. The minutes may contain more information, but I have not tried to locate and read them. Louis F. Post, one of the school board members who was purged and later won reinstatement through the courts, edited *The Public*, a single-tax journal. I read Volumes VIII, IX, and X, finding a good deal of information on the issues and actors, even if from a biased point of view. Chicago newspapers, notably the *Tribune*, were parties to legal actions brought by the school board, and their reports were exuberantly inaccurate. I have not been able to consult a file of the Chicago Teachers Federation *Bulletin* which might contain additional information on these matters. George S. Counts, *School and Society in Chicago* (New York, 1928), deals cursorily with events before 1920. Allen F. Davis, "Raymond Robbins: the Settlement Worker as Municipal Reformer," *Social Service Review*, XXXIII (June, 1959), 131–41, deals briefly with Robbins' part in the matter.

CHAPTER V: URBAN RECREATION

Two books persuaded me that play was a topic worth investigating and might shed light on other aspects of Jane Addams' thought. Johan Huizinga, *Homo Ludens, a Study of the Play Element in Culture* (Boston, 1955), first published in 1944, is a brilliant attempt to derive civilization from play forms. Roger Caillois, *Man, Play, and Games* (Glencoe, 1961), attempts to broaden the categories that Huizinga employed and to organize the vast variety of games into a simple typology.

There are several standard surveys of recreation and physical education in America, including Wilbur P. Brown and Elmer D. Mitchell, *The Theory of*

Organized Play, Its Nature and Significance (New York, 1923); and E. A. Rice, *History of Physical Education* (New York [1958] 1926). Both have been kept up to date by more recent editions which incorporate the substance of these editions. Martin H. and Esther S. Neumeyer, *Leisure and Recreation, a Study of Leisure and Recreation in Their Sociological Aspects* (New York, 1936), contains a helpful review of theories of play from the point of view of social psychologists in the late 1920's and early 1930's. Charles K. Brightbill, *Man and Leisure, a Philosophy of Recreation* (Englewood Cliffs, N.J., 1961), is a textbook with much insight.

I discovered that the more specialized literature on play reveals a great deal about general movements in American thought. A wider spectrum of intellectuals than I had supposed analyzed and described play. The most helpful treatment of play for this study was in William James, *Principles of Psychology* (n.p. [1890] 1950). Karl Groos, *The Play of Animals* (New York, 1898), developed James's description of the play instinct. His more sophisticated *The Play of Man* (New York, 1901), argued that "play makes it possible to dispense to a certain degree with specialized hereditary mechanism by fixing and increasing acquired adaptations" (p. 395). In addition to James and his followers, G. Stanley Hall published a widely accepted interpretation of play. For his most systematic treatment see his *Adolescence*, I, 202–36. Luther Gulick, a pioneer in developing the athletic emphasis in the Y.M.C.A., worked in Springfield, Mass., and contributed to Hall's researches in nearby Worcester. See Luther Gulick, "Psychological, Pedagogical, and Religious Aspects of Group Games," *Pedagogical Seminary*, II (March, 1899), 135–51; and his, "Interest in Relation to Muscular Exercise," *American Physical Education Review*, VII (June, 1902), 57–65; and a collection of his essay fragments published posthumously, *A Philosophy of Play* (New York, 1920). One of Hall's students, who directed the city playgrounds in Pittsburgh, gave a full exposition to Hall's position; see George Ellsworth Johnson, *Education by Play and Games* (Boston, 1907). W. I. Thomas, who was on the faculty of the University of Chicago, treated play in "The Gaming Instinct," *American Journal of Sociology*, VI (1900–1), 750–63, as a psychic reaction (p. 751), the objects of which differed through history. The most complete treatment of the play instinct is in Edwin Asbury Kirkpatrick, *Fundamentals of Child Study* (New York, 1903).

For a more pragmatic emphasis see John Dewey, "Play," and "Play and Education," in Paul Monroe (ed.), *Cyclopedia of Education* (New York, 1913), IV, 725–7. For a definition tinged with Anglo-Saxon, Aryan racial inheritance see Henry S. Curtis, *Education Through Play* (New York, 1915), or E. D. Mitchell, "Racial Traits in Athletics," *American Physical Education Review* (March–May, 1922). Joseph Lee, a Boston mugwump reformer especially interested in playgrounds, managed to combine almost all of these ideas in his enthusiastic and unsystematic *Play in Education* (New York, 1915).

More recent authors have analyzed play in Freudian terms. See Erik H. Erikson, "Studies in the Interpretation of Play, Clinical Observation of Play Disruption in Young Children," *Genetic Psychology Monographs*, XXII (1940), 557–671; Lawrence K. Frank, "Play in Personality Development," *American Journal of Orthopsychiatry*, XXV (1955), 576–90; and the most interesting Franz Alexander, "A Contribution to the Theory of Play," *Psychoanalytic Quarterly*, XXVII (1958), 175–93.

In addition to these diverse treatments of play, a number of men have used a theory of play to try to prove certain convictions they believed to have been true. Prince Kropotkin, *Ethics, Origin and Development*, trans., Louis S. Friedland and Joseph R. Peroshinkoff (New York, 1924), interpreted play as a part of the social instinct toward mutual aid and mutual sympathy in which he rooted progress, justice, and morality. Kropotkin's picture hung in Miss Addams' Hull House office along with those of Tolstoy, Lincoln, Henry George, Savonarola, Altgeld,

Mazzini, George Eliot, and John Addams, according to Charlotte Teller, " Miss Jane Addams, of Hull House, Chicago," *Everybody's*, VIII (February, 1903), 169–71. Josiah Royce interpreted play as loyalty, a word which denoted for him an ideal morality. See Royce's *Race Questions, Provincialism and Other American Problems* (New York, 1908), and his *Philosophy of Loyalty* (New York, 1908). Many people made a similar identification to Howard S. Brancher, "Play and Social Progress," *Annals*, XXXV (1910), 325–33. One member of the Playground Association of America, G. E. Johnson, even wrote of "Play as a Moral Equivalent of War," *American Physical Education Review*, XVI (May, 1910), 291–301. Historians who have pointed to the conservation movement as a continuity of progressive thought in the twentieth century might consider John Collier's "Leisure Time, the Last Problem of Conservation," published in the Progressive year in *Playground*, VI (June, 1912), 93–106. A modern account, which is filled with suggestions about the roles of sport and leisure in American society is Renel Denney, *The Astonished Muse* (Chicago, 1957).

On the playground movement there are two useful books: Henry S. Curtis, *The Play Movement and Its Significance* (New York, 1917); and Clarence E. Rainwater, *The Play Movement in the United States, a Study of Community Recreation* (Chicago, 1922). There are also several useful chapters in Joseph Lee, *Constructive and Preventive Philanthropy* (New York, 1902). On the different but related topic of school playgrounds and wider use of school plants see H. S. Curtis, "Vacation Schools, Playgrounds and Settlements," in U.S. Bureau of Education, *Report of the Commissioner* (1903), I, 2–38; Edward J. Ward (ed.), *The Social Center* (New York, 1913); and appropriate sections of Charles E. Doell and Gerald B. Fitzgerald, *Brief History of Parks and Recreation in the United States* (Chicago, 1954). There is a large periodical literature on this subject, among the most helpful are Mary Josephine Mayes, "Our Public Schools as Social Centers," *Review of Reviews*, XLIV (1911), 201–8; and David Blaustein, "The Schoolhouse Recreation Center as an Attempt to Aid Immigrants in Adjusting Themselves to American Conditions," *Playground*, VI (Democracy, 1912), 329–34.

I read the early *Proceedings* and *Yearbooks* of the Playground Association of America and the first six volumes of the Association's magazine, *Playground*. On the founding of the Association, see H. S. Curtis, "How It Began," *Recreation*, XXV (May, 1931), 71, 106; and Chapter VI of Ethel Josephine Dorgan, *Luther Halsey Gulick* (Teachers' College, Columbia University, Contributions to Education No. 635; New York, 1935).

On recreation developments in Chicago see Chapter II, "The History of Public Recreation in Chicago," *Chicago Recreation Survey* (Chicago, 1937); and Elizabeth Halsey, *Development of Public Recreation in Metropolitan Chicago* (Chicago, 1940). I used several other sources to gain an understanding of the special Chicago concern for playgrounds: Charles Zeublin, "Municipal Playgrounds in Chicago," *American Journal of Sociology*, IV (1898–9), 145–58; E. B. DeGroot, "Recent Playground Development in Chicago," *American Physical Education Review*, XIII (1908), 426–67; and Graham Romeyn Taylor, "Recreation Development in Chicago Parks," *Annals*, XXV (1910), 304–23. For a note on the more aristocratic movement in New York see Walter Vrooman, "Parks and Playgrounds for Children," *Century*, XLIII (December, 1891), 317–8.

CHAPTER VI: CLIMAX AND DISSATISFACTIONS: THE PROGRESSIVE CAMPAIGN OF 1912

The two best studies of feminism are Ernest R. Groves, *The American Woman, the Feminine Side of a Masculine Civilization* (New York, 1937); and Eric John Dingwald, *The American Woman* (New York, 1956), the latter equipped with a helpful bibliography.

Women who have written about their changing role have concentrated on the contest to win the suffrage. Thus we have a wealth of studies of this particular effort. Elizabeth Cady Stanton, Susan B. Anthony *et al.* (eds.), *History of Woman Suffrage* (Rochester & New York, 1881–1922), is the standard work which others have mined for information. Abbie Graham, *Ladies in Revolt* (New York, 1934), contains nothing original. Two studies adopt a larger focus and attempt to relate the changing economic and social situation to women's claims for the vote. Inez Haynes Irwin, *Angels and Amazons* (Garden City, 1933), is a lively account which toward the end tends to become merely a listing of names. Eleanor Flexner, *Century of Struggle, the Woman's Rights Movement in the United States* (Cambridge, Mass., 1959), like the Irwin volume, concentrates on the suffrage struggle and fails to illuminate how other forces were promoting more important changes in women's role in American life.

More specialized studies that helped me understand the earnestness of this topic to contemporaries of Miss Addams included Lester F. Ward, " Our Better Halves," *Forum*, VI (November, 1888), 266–75; and his *Psychic Factors in Civilization* (Boston [1892] 1906), in the latter of which Ward asserts that " from the standpoint of nature, and according to the normal processes of evolution, the female is the principal sex and constitutes the main trunk of development . . ." (p. 87). Otis Tufton Mason, *Woman's Share in Primitive Culture* (New York, 1894), emphasizes woman's predominance in the prehistory of civilization. William I. Thomas, in his *Sex and Society, Studies in the Social Psychology of Sex* (Boston, 1907), gave a full and suggestive statement of some of the insights in Thorstein Veblen's picture of the American woman in his brilliant *Theory of the Leisure Class, an Economic Study of Institutions* (New York, 1899). Mason, Thomas, and Veblen were all colleagues at the University of Chicago. Another Chicagoan, Lloyd Dell, who taught a class in English literature at Hull House in 1909 and 1910, has an interesting chapter contrasting the militant Emmeline Pankhurst with Jane Addams' passion for conciliation in his *Women As World Builders, Studies in Modern Feminism* (Chicago, 1913). Jessie Taft, *The Woman Movement from the Point of View of Social Consciousness* (Chicago, 1915), shows how Jane Addams' ideas were drawn on and related by associates and friends. Her contemporary, Ida M. Tarbell, perceptively analyzed the changing social demands on her generation in *The Business of Being a Woman* (New York, 1919). A long time Hull House resident wrote the report on women for President Hoover's Research Committee on Recent Social Trends. Sophonisba P. Breckenridge, *Women in the Twentieth Century, A Study of Their Political, Social and Economic Activities* (New York, 1933), is written by a member of the second generation in the settlement movement, but is clearly informed by the attitudes of the pioneering generation. The best bibliography of feminism, although weighted toward women as military figures, is in Mary R. Beard, *Woman as a Force in History, a Study in Traditions and Realities* (New York, 1946).

One of the most important areas in which Americans were prepared for the social justice demand of the Progressive party was municipal reform. In the cities, especially Midwestern cities, Americans gained experience with socialism. On the development of these services and the defense of them in the name of social democracy refer to the previously cited Lincoln Steffens' *Autobiography*; Brand Whitlock, *Forty Years of It*; and to Russel B. Nye, *Midwestern Progressive Politics* (East Lansing, Mich., 1959). In addition Tom L. Johnson, *My Story* is revealing on Cleveland. On Toledo, and the really remarkable mayor there, see Brand Whitlock, " ' Golden Rule ' Jones," *World's Work*, VIII (September, 1904), 5308–11, and Ernest Crosby, " Golden Rule Jones, the Late Mayor of Toledo," *Craftsman*, VII (February, March, 1905), 530–47, 679–88. Charles Zueblin, a professor of sociology at the University of Chicago by way of settlement work summarized these developments in *American Municipal Progress* (New York, 1916). For a thorough treatment of various experiments in public ownership see Frank Parsons, *The City for the People, or the Municipalization of the City Government and of Local Franchises* (Philadelphia, n.d.). Richard T. Ely's little *The Coming City* (New York, 1902), is an easy introduction to many of these movements. Delos F. Wilcox, *The American City, a Problem in Democracy* (New York, 1905), covers the whole range of municipal reforms. Frederick C. Howe, *The City the Hope of Democracy* (New York, 1906), argued persuasively for a rebirth of democracy, which he believed demanded " co-operative effort to relieve the costs which city life entails. We already see this manifest in many forms, in our school libraries, parks, playgrounds, kindergartens . . ." (p. 7). Approaching the problem from this background, I am not persuaded that Morton and Lucia White, in *The Intellectual Versus the City, from Thomas Jefferson to Frank Lloyd Wright* (Cambridge, Mass., 1962), have described American attitudes toward the city in their full complexity. They have certainly misread and garbled Jane Addams' attitude.

The year 1912 was one of great excitement. Fifty years later the accounts of the Progressive amalgam exude enthusiasm and earnestness. Richard Hofstadter remarks in his *Age of Reform, from Bryan to F.D.R.*, that " the Progressive mind was characteristically a journalistic mind . . ." (p. 185). Certainly the journalists at the Progressive convention produced some extraordinary material. William Allen White wrote glowing reports for papers served by George Mathew Adams. Even the Chicago *Tribune* relented from its usual practice of depicting Miss Addams as a sentimental but dangerous fool. Periodicals also printed glowing articles: Herbert Knox Smith, " The Progressive Party," *Yale Review*, n.s., II (October, 1912), 18–32; Chester H. Rowell, " The Building of the Progressive Platform," *California Outlook*, XIII (August 17, 1912), 5–6; William Menkel, " The Progressives at Chicago," *Review of Reviews*, XLVI (September, 1912), 310–7; and the useful Richard Harding Davis, " The Men at Armageddon," *Colliers*, XLIX (August 24, 1912). Not all reports were favorable of course. An anonymous editor for *The Argonaut* (San Francisco), LXXI (August 31, 1912), 131, wrote: " Miss Jane Addams, sitting with closed eyes, rapt and ecstatic, at the Chicago convention must have been a sight in which the pathetic and the absurd struggled for mastery. Human faith and enthusiasm are edifying spectacles, even when they degenerate, as they usually do, into credulity and emotionalism, and credulity and emotionalism may be described as Miss Addams' long suit if we may be allowed the use of so worldly an expression. . . . We can only marvel at the faith that is still able to invest a political platform, and a particularly raw and sordid one, with all the sanctities of a divine revelation. Even Mr. Roosevelt must have smiled at the sight of Miss Addams with the bait—all of it—in her mouth. It was undeniably good fishing." For an accurate, if partisan, account see William Jennings Bryan, *A Tale of Two Conventions, Being an Account of the Republican and Democratic National Conventions of June 1912, with an Outline of the Progressive National Convention of August of the Same Year* (New York, 1912).

These emotional assessments should be tempered with Amos R. E. Pinchot, *History of the Progressive Party, 1912–1916*, ed., Helene Maxwell Hooker (New York, 1958); and Harold L. Ickes, " Who Killed the Progressive Party? " *American Historical Review*, XLVI (January, 1941), 306–37. Allen F. Davis has captured some of the excitement in his " Social Workers and the Progressive Party," *American Historical Review*, LXIX (April, 1964), 671–88. Victor Rosewater, *Back Stage in 1912, The Inside Story of the Split Republican Convention* (Philadelphia, 1932);

and Frank K. Kelly, *The Fight for the White House, The Story of 1912* (New York, 1961), contain little of interest. Donald R. Richberg, *Tents of the Mighty* (New York, 1930), is a disillusioned account of the whole Progressive attempt. Claude G. Bowers, *Beveridge and the Progressive Era* (Cambridge, Mass., 1932), is particularly good on the 1912 conventions and the Progressive campaign. Oscar King Davis, *Released for Publication, Some Inside Political History of Theodore Roosevelt and His Times, 1898–1918* (Boston, 1925), is a most useful and dependable source for much of the maneuvering close to Roosevelt.

Since the Progressive party was so much a personal gathering around Roosevelt, I read Henry F. Pringle's critical *Theodore Roosevelt, a Biography* (New York [1931] 1956); and John Morton Blum's brilliant, short *The Republican Roosevelt* (Cambridge, Mass., 1954). I have depended on George E. Mowry's most useful account, *Theodore Roosevelt and the Progressive Movement*, already cited. Roosevelt's major campaign addresses are in *Social Justice and Popular Rule, Essays, Addresses and Public Statements Relating to the Progressive Movement, 1910–1916*, Vol. XIX of his *Works* (New York, 1925). These can be compared with Wilson's campaign speeches in John Wills Davidson (ed.), *Crossroads to Freedom* (New Haven, 1956). Elting E. Morison and others have selected and edited the *Letters of Theodore Roosevelt* (Cambridge, Mass., 1951–4) in volumes seven and eight of which I have done occasional, rewarding reading.

For statistical studies of the election see Edgar E. Robinson, "Distribution of the Presidential Vote of 1912," *American Journal of Sociology*, XX (July, 1914), 18–30; his *The Presidential Vote, 1896–1932* (Stanford, n.d. [ca. 1934]); and Charles Hickman Titus, *Voting Behavior in the United States, a Statistical Survey* ("U.C.L.A. Publications in Social Science," No. 5; Berkeley, 1935). For various explanations of these voting patterns, see Angus Campbell, Gerald Gerin, and Warren E. Miller, *The Voter Decides* (Evanston, 1954), and Wilfred E. Binkley, *American Political Parties* (New York, 1958).

CHAPTER VII: NEUTRALITY

Merle Curti, *Peace or War, the American Struggle, 1636–1936* (New York, 1936), is particularly good in describing the high hopes of men and women in the American peace movement in the opening years of the twentieth century. The third and fourth volumes of Arthur S. Link's *Wilson* narrate the President's attempts to maintain American neutrality in 1915 and 1916 and explain his lack of response to the proposals originated by the pacifists whom Jane Addams led. Ernest R. May, *The World War and American Isolation, 1914–1917* (Cambridge, Mass., 1959), is a compelling book in the way it illuminates how and why German, English, and American leaders made their decisions. The sixth volume of Ray Stannard Baker, *Woodrow Wilson, Life and Letters* (Garden City, 1927–37), remains valuable as a short account beside Link's exhaustive treatment. The *War Memoirs of Robert Lansing, Secretary of State* (Indianapolis & New York, 1935), give his side of the dispute over preparedness. Daniel M. Smith, *Robert Lansing and American Neutrality, 1914–1917* ("University of California Publication in History," Vol. 59; Berkeley & Los Angeles, 1958), has depended on Lansing's own defense of his actions. I have also read large parts of Charles Seymour (ed.), *The Intimate Papers of Colonel House* (Boston & New York, 1928). Alice Hamilton wrote a wonderful review of Colonel House's diary in "Colonel House and Jane Addams," *New Republic*, XLVII (May 26, 1926), 9–11, in which she maintains that the ladies' hopes for a neutral conference were less naïve than House "who held himself powerful enough, single-handed, to break down secret treaties and dictate a just peace to a war-mad world." Lawrence W. Martin, *Peace Without Victory*,

Woodrow Wilson and the British Liberals (New Haven, 1958), describes Wilson's debt to various Europeans. By concentrating on Wilson, Martin failed to describe the other Americans who championed these liberal peace ideals. I found Martin's bibliographic essay particularly helpful. English liberals summarized their peace hopes in Charles R. Buxton (ed.), *Towards a Lasting Settlement* (London, 1915). Included in this volume was A. Maude Royden's "War and the Woman's Movement." The American response to these essays can be found in Randolph S. Bourne (ed.), *Towards an Enduring Peace, a Symposium of Peace Proposals and Programs, 1914–1916* (New York, n.d. [1916]). For a similar later statement see Emily Green Balch's *Approaches to the Great Settlement* (New York, 1918), which is mainly a collection of documents, especially Socialist and labor protests and suggestions.

I also read through files of two periodicals for this period of neutrality: *The Seven Arts* for 1916–7, and *The New Republic*, 1914–7. Charles Forcey, *The Crossroads of Liberalism, Croly, Weyl, Lippmann and the Progressive Era, 1900–1925*, cited above, is most relevant here. See also for a few insights into the workings of *The New Republic*, Norman Angell, *After All, the Autobiography of Norman Angell* (London, 1951).

I have depended heavily on Marie Louse Degen, *The History of the Woman's Peace Party* ("Johns Hopkins University Studies in Historical and Political Science," Vol. LVII; Baltimore, 1939). It is a full and measured account, not careful of accuracy, and full of exaggeration, but nevertheless of considerable value as a document. The New York (State) Legislature, Joint Committee Investigating Seditious Activities, *Revolutionary Radicalism—Its History, Purpose and Tactics, with an Exposition and Discussion of the Steps Being Taken to Curb It* (4 vols.; Albany, 1920), is the report of the Lusk Committee, which raided an office in New York City and published many of the letters they seized in this report.

On the special neutral strategy of a mediation conference see Walter I. Trattner, "Julia Grace Wales and the Wisconsin Plan for Peace," *Wisconsin Magazine of History*, XLIV (Spring, 1961), 203–13. Although opposed to the women's plans editorially, the New York *Times* covered The Hague congress fully and described their activities accurately and in detail. For especially relevant material see an interview of Jane Addams by Edward Marshall, "War's Debasement of Women," New York *Times Magazine*, May 2, 1915, pp. 3–4, and another interview reported in the *Times* of May 14, 1915, in which Miss Addams commented on the *Lusitania* by urging her country "to be the one great nation to keep clear of the war. When this terrible conflict is over all Europe, indeed, all the world, will look to America to act as a balance in the readjustment of the relations of the nations." See also a perceptive interview by Edward Marshall, "Jane Addams Points the Way to Peace," New York *Times Magazine*, July 11, 1915, pp. 4–5. The Woman's Peace party position is defended briefly against Theodore Roosevelt's labels of "base and silly" by Gertrude M. Pinchot in a letter to the editor of the New York *Times*, December 22, 1915, p. 8, col. 6. The best reports of The Hague congress and Jane Addams' subsequent trip presenting the congress resolutions are Mary Chamberlain, "The Women at The Hague," *Survey*, XXXIV (June 5, 1915), 219–22; and Alice Hamilton, "At the War Capitols, Miss Addams' Journey," *ibid.*, XXXIV (August 7, 1915), 417–22, 433–6.

The best account of the Ford peace ship is Louis P. Lochner, *America's Don Quixote, Henry Ford's Attempt to Save Europe* (London, 1924); the American edition is titled *Henry Ford—America's Don Quixote* (New York, 1925). Lochner's fair-minded treatment supplements Robert Morss Lovett, "Apostles of World Unity, IV Jane Addams," *World Unity Magazine*, I (January, 1928), 261–6, in which Lovett, a long-time friend of Miss Addams, writes that the Ford venture

" may have been a gesture so futile as to be ridiculous—still it was a movement of generous faith at a time when more responsible politicians were afraid to act. No one suffered by it except the participants. In any case, the peacemakers at Versailles have no license to cast their stones at the peacemakers of The Hague and Stockholm " (p. 264).

CHAPTER VIII: THE WAR YEARS AND AFTER

The suspension of activities by many of the established peace societies after America's declaration of war is told in Edson Leon Whitney, *The American Peace Society, a Centennial History* (Washington, 1928); and in Ruhl J. Bartlett, *The League to Enforce Peace* (Chapel Hill, 1944). The latter study also describes how that organization was seduced into supporting the Lodge amendments to the League Covenant. Emerson Hough, *The Web, the Authorized History of the American Protective League* (Chicago, 1919), is a boastful account of another kind of organization that flourished during the months when America was at war. The collapse of an organized peace effort and the intensification of demands for national unity represented by the American Protective League provide a background to Arno J. Mayer, *Political Origins of the New Diplomacy, 1917–1918* (New Haven, 1959), which describes Wilson changing war aims after February, 1917. Randolph Bourne, *Untimely Papers*, ed. James Oppenheim (New York, 1918), is a moving collection of the essays Bourne wrote in 1917–8, bitterly prophesying the kind of failure and collapse that the exertions and demands of the war spirit would produce in America and in Europe. Bourne argued that the consequences of America's entry into the war clearly contradicted the reasons President Wilson advanced for entering the war. A speedy end of the war by negotiation, before Germany was exhausted and her morale destroyed, was most likely to nurture democratic impulses. " A Germany forced to be democratic under the tutelage of a watchful and victorious Entente would indeed be a constant menace to the peace of Europe " (p. 84). For another characteristic reaction to the war and the months immediately after see Walter Weyl, *Tired Radicals and Other Papers* (New York, 1921). H. C. Peterson and Gilbert C. Fite, *Opponents of War, 1917–1918* (Madison, 1957), is a useful account of radical and pacifist activity during the war. For helpful examples of the changing climate of opinion toward pacifists see Vida D. Scudder, " The Doubting Pacifist," *Yale Review*, VI (July, 1917), 738–51; and *The Tattler*, " Notes from the Capitol, Jane Addams," *The Nation*, CII (February 3, 1916), 134, which reported that " Miss Addams is still, except for a certain surface hardening, due to contact with the larger world outside, the same vivid and interesting personality as in her comparative youth (in the Progressive campaign). What she has lost in the intensity of her appeal appears to have been sacrificed in an endeavor to do too much in too many alien and untried fields, with its incidental diffusion of her native force."

Ida Clyde Clarke, *American Women and the World War* (New York & London, 1918), describes the Committee on Women's Defense Work of the Council of National Defense, through which most American women were organized for war work. The chapter on Illinois includes many Hull House workers and supporters, and especially praises their Americanization drive, without mentioning Jane Addams. Donald Johnson, *Challenge to American Freedoms, World War I and the Rise of the American Civil Liberties Union* (Lexington, Ky., 1963), is a straightforward account of the Union's origins in the group of social workers and friends who first met at the Henry Street Settlement in 1914. Jane Addams' attitude toward war work is described in an enlightening interview with the editor of the Boston *Herald*, June 14, 1926, p. 16, col. 3.

A good history of relief efforts in Europe is Frank M. Surface and Raymond L. Bland, *American Food in the World War and Reconstruction Period, Operations of the Organizations Under the Directions of Herbert Hoover, 1914 to 1924* (Stanford, 1931). From the armistice until a formal peace treaty was signed the U.S. Congress refused any food to be sent to former enemies; the Quakers moved into Germany, however. See Mary Hoxie Jones, *Swords into Ploughshares, an Account of the American Friends' Service Committee, 1917–1937* (New York, 1937). These efforts have also been nicely summarized in Merle Curti, *American Philanthropy Abroad, a History* (New Brunswick, 1963).

CHAPTER IX: PACIFISM

Two periodical articles suggest new ways to understand the confusion of the 1920's, a confusion that has been reflected in studies of the decade: Henry F. May, "Shifting Perspectives on the 1920's," *Mississippi Valley Historical Review,* XLIII (1956–7), 405–27; and Arthur S. Link, "What Happened to the Progressive Movement in the 1920's?" *American Historical Review,* LXIV (1959), 833–51.

The traumatic opening of the decade is best recorded in the concise but unexciting *Red Scare, a Study in National Hysteria, 1919–1920* (Minneapolis, 1955), by Robert K. Murray. Stanley Coben, *A. Mitchell Palmer, Politician* (New York & London, 1963), deals with the scare and the raids, and it apportions blame heavily on Palmer and also on J. Edgar Hoover. Norman Hapgood (ed.), *Professional Patriots, an Exposure of the Personalities, Methods and Objectives Involved in the Organized Effort to Exploit Patriotic Impulses in these United States During and After the Late War* (New York, 1927), discusses the relations between various organizations and the connections of these groups with the military, big business, organized labor, and education.

There is no good historical treatment of pacifism, although subject indexes abound with references to all sorts of materials. I have not attempted a complete survey of this large field. Sir Alfred Zimmern, *The American Road to Peace* (New York, 1953), is a useful narrative, although it does not deal very perceptively with pacifism. John Kendall Nelson, "A Descriptive Study of American Pacifist Thought in the Inter-War Period, 1919–1941" (unpublished Master's essay, University of North Carolina at Chapel Hill, 1956), is a survey of *The World Tomorrow, The Christian Century,* and *The New Republic.* Charles S. Macfarland, *Pioneers for Peace through Religion, Based on the Records of the Church Peace Union (Founded by Andrew Carnegie), 1914–1945* (New York, 1946), was not very helpful. Jessie Wallace Hughan, *Three Decades of War Resistance, The War Resisters' League* (New York, 1942), is more useful as an encyclopedia of organizations and names. Lyman Bessie Burbank, "Internationalism in American Thought, 1919–1929" (unpublished Ph.D. thesis, New York University, 1950), includes a clear-sighted and perceptive critique of many peace organizations in the 1920's. Burbank's bibliography led me to items I would otherwise have missed. I have also read two other dissertations. Noel Franciscan, "Pacifism as a Social Movement" (unpublished Ph.D. thesis, Duke University, 1952), establishes several useful distinctions. Carroll Spurgeon Fragins, "Critiques of Pacifism by Some American and British Philosophers since 1914" (unpublished Ph.D. thesis, Northwestern University, 1954), was of little aid in this study.

The best insights into the range of pacifism in the 1920's and early 1930's are in the pacifist magazine *The World Tomorrow,* and in Devere Allen's discursive and disorganized *The Fight for Peace* (New York, 1930). The essays, especially Reinhold Niebuhr's "The Use of Force," in Devere Allen (ed.), *Pacifism in the Modern World* (Garden City, 1929), are also valuable because they indicate the wide spectrum of pacifism between the wars. Allen's voluminous papers were deposited at Swarthmore too late to be of use in my study.

On the outlawing of war, see John E. Stoner's dissertation, *S. O. Levinson and the Pact of Paris, a Study in the Technique of Influence* (Chicago, 1942); and the more cynical Robert H. Ferrell, *Peace in Their Time, the Origins of the Kellogg-Briand Pact* (New Haven, 1952), with its good bibliography.

Three studies had more direct relevance to this study. In 1945 Jane Addams' *Peace and Bread in Time of War* was republished with an introductory essay by John Dewey in which he distinguished between two methods and attitudes toward peace. Dewey contrasted the traditional political-legal attitude with its emphasis on force with the method Miss Addams had described in her 1922 book, methods formed to care for human needs. Herbert W. Schneider invited a number of prominent philosophers to comment on this distinction and on Jane Addams' denigration of the political-legal methods, in "Discussion of the Theory of International Relations," *Journal of Philosophy*, XLII (August 30, 1945), 477–97. David A. Swope has written a useful study in his "The Women's International League for Peace and Freedom, United States Section, 1919–1941" (unpublished Honors' thesis, Harvard University, 1963). The League's Washington lobbyist has left some lively memoirs which concentrate on her remarkable career after 1925: Dorothy Detzer, *Appointment on the Hill* (New York, 1948).

Martin David Dubin, "The Development of the Concept of Collective Security in the American Peace Movement, 1899–1917" (unpublished Ph.D. thesis, Indiana University, 1960), describes the growing consensus in the peace movement of the need for a world court with sanctions. His study emphasizes the radical nature of the Women's International League for Peace and Freedom's rejection of all force.

Especially important for understanding Jane Addams' pacifism is Alymer Maude's eyewitness account of "A Talk with Jane Addams and Count Tolstoy," *Humane Review*, III (October, 1902), 203–18. One of Jane Addams' fellow Chicagoans was also influenced by Tolstoy's theory of nonresistance. Clarence Darrow, *Resist Not Evil* (Chicago, 1903), although slanted toward the problem of judicial punishment, describes certain alternatives to force. William James, "The Moral Equivalent of War," was first delivered in altered form at the 1904 Universal Peace Congress which Jane Addams attended. On Gandhi, see Roman Roland, "Mahatma Gandhi," *Century Magazine*, CVII (December, 1923, January, February, 1924), 163–81, 389–405, 590–604, for a popular treatment; and Gandhi's own *An Autobiography, the Story of My Experiments with Truth* (Boston, 1957), which first appeared serially in English in the magazine *Young India* during 1928 and 1929.

Personal descriptions of Miss Addams' pacifism are not numerous. An early statement is Ella W. Peattie, "Women of the Hour, No. 1, Jane Addams," *Harper's Bazaar*, XXXVIII (October, 1904), 1004–8, and the very perceptive Dorothy Detzer, "Memories of Jane Addams," *Fellowship*, IV (September, 1938), 4–5.

For a good description of the last years which Jane Addams lived at Hull House see "Hull House in 1932" in Edmund Wilson, *The American Earthquake, a Documentary of the Twenties and Thirties* (Garden City, 1958), pp. 447–64.

INDEX

A

Abbott, Edith, quoted, 136
Abbott, Grace, 125n
Adams, Herbert Baxter, 42n
Addams, Alice (Mrs. Haldeman), 39, 61
Addams, Anna Haldeman, 28, 29, 36, 37, 42: quoted, 35; in Europe, 40–41
Addams, Jane: historical estimate, 17–26, 214–16
Addams, John Huy, 27–29, 39, 42, 43
Addams, Mary, 28
Aged, the, 124, 126, 133, 152, 213
Agriculture, 27, 107: food and, 83, 178; Addams on farm life, 113
Altgeld, John Peter, 67
American Association for Labor Legislation, 126
American Association of University Women, 55
American Civil Liberties Union, 149n
American Commission on Conditions in Ireland, 187
American Committee for Relief in Ireland, 187n
American Economic Association, 128
American Friends Service Committee, 185, 186
American Journal of Sociology, 66, 67–68
American Legion, 193–94
American Protective League, 174
American Relief for Russian Women and Children, 187n
American Sociological Association, 68n
American Sociological Society, 128
American Union Against Militarism, 149n, 169n
American Welfare Association for German Children, 187n
Anarchists, 55–56, 173, 193n
Andover House, Boston, 23, 51n
Angell, Norman, 156, 159n

Anti-Oorlog Rad, 151
Aristotle, 107, 113
Armenia, 187
Armour Mission, 53–54, 86
Arnold, Matthew, 38, 39, 40, 44: on culture, 81, 91, 109n
" Art and Labor " (Starr), 66
Arts, the, 87, 124, 138: culture and, 24, 25, 65, 82, 83, 92, 93; Ellen Starr and, 43, 52, 66, 96-97; Toynbee Hall and, 44, 48, 49, 50; play and, 108, 109, 111, 117, 118–19
Asquith, Herbert, Earl of, 156
Association of Collegiate Alumnae, 55
Assyria, 209
Austria, 156, 157, 187

B

Baker, Ray Stannard, quoted, 76
Balch, Emily G., 157, 163
Balliol College, 45
Baltimore, Md., 41–42, 56
Baltimore Conference on Charities, 42n
Bannister, Zilpah Grant, 29n
Barnett, Henrietta Octavia, 44–45, 46
Barnett, Samuel A., 45, 50: quoted, 44, 47–48, 49
Beard, Charles, quoted, 25
Beard, Mary, quoted, 25
Beecher, Catherine E., 28
" Belated Industry, A " (Addams), 68n
Belgium, 151, 156, 157
Beloit College, 29, 32, 33n
Benedict XV, Pope, 156n
Berger, Victor, 174
Berlin, Germany, 153, 156, 158
Berne, Switzerland, 156n
Berry, E. A., cited, 43n
Bethmann Hollweg, Theobald von, 156, 168n
Binford, Jessie, quoted, 113
Board of National Popular Education, 29n
Bohemian-Americans, 55, 66